Colm Ó Caodháin
An Irish singer and his world

Colm Ó Caodháin

An Irish singer and his world

Ríonach uí Ógáin

CORK UNIVERSITY PRESS

First published in 2021 by
Cork University Press
Boole Library
University College Cork
Cork T12 ND89
Ireland

Library of Congress Control Number: 2020945045

Distribution in the USA Longleaf Services, Chapel Hill, NC, USA.

British Library Cataloguing in Publication Data
A CIP catalogue record for this book is available the British Library.

ISBN: 9781782054313

Printed by BZ Graf in Poland

Design and typesetting by Alison Burns at Studio 10 Design, Cork

Cover painting: Stiofán Ó Caodháin
Photograph: Nick Bradshaw

www.corkuniversitypress.com

CONTENTS

Acknowledgements

I would like to acknowledge the assistance and support of the following institutions and bodies in whose care are the Colm Ó Caodháin recordings, manuscripts and other relevant material: the British Broadcasting Corporation, Cnuasach Bhéaloideas Éireann UCD, the Irish Traditional Music Archive, Raidió Teilifís Éireann, Smithsonian, UCD Archives.

I am very grateful to Cork University Press, and to Maria O'Donovan in particular, for ongoing, meaningful support.

Many people have assisted with the publication in numerous ways and a special word of thanks to: John Barrett, Harry Bradshaw, Peter Browne, Nicholas Carolan, Margaret Cloherty, Marian Deasy, Kelly Fitzgerald, Seán Guairim, Ailsa Holland, Tommy Keane, the late Liam Mac Con Iomaire, Jackie Mac Donncha, Conchúr Mag Eachain, Nicky McAuliffe, Peter McCanney, Frances McGee, Linda McGee, Seán McKiernan, Máire Ní Chaoimh, Róisín Nic Dhonncha, Máire Ní Fhlatharta, Dónall Ó Braonáin, Mary and Tomás Ó Caodháin, Stiofán Ó Caodháin, the late Máirtín Ó Caodháin, Anne O'Connor, Pádraig Ó Héalaí, Simon O'Leary, Maitiú Ó Murchú, J.J. O'Shea, Jean-Michel Picard, Laura Ryan, Tom Sherlock, Lisa Shields, Máire Uí Chonaire.

Facing page: Colm Ó Caodháin and his daughter Máire, 1945. COURTESY NFC
See full image on page 7.

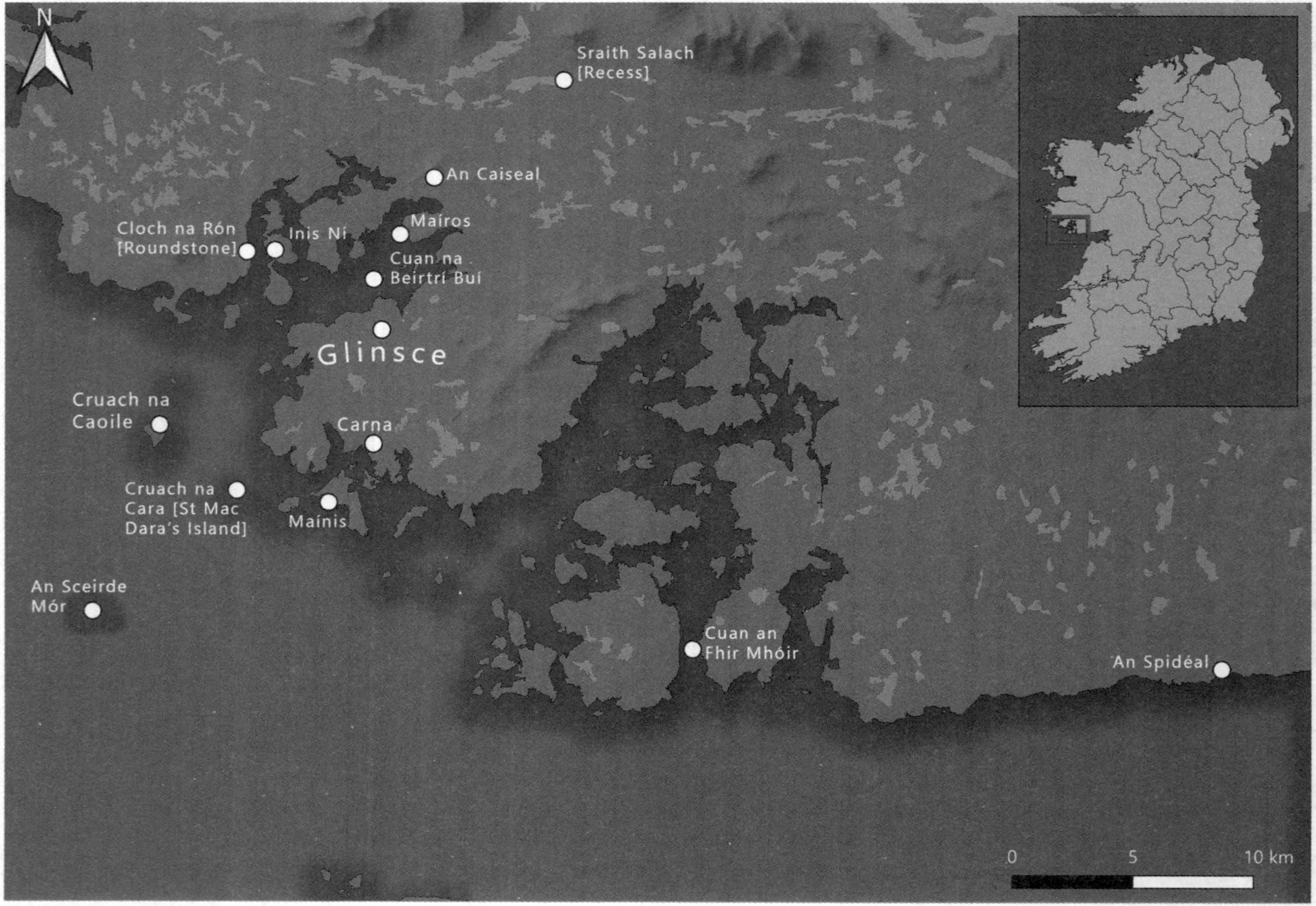
N
Sraith Salach
[Recess]
An Caiseal
Cloch na Rón
[Roundstone]
Inis Ní
Mairos
Cuan na
Beirtrí Buí
Glinsce
Cruach na
Caoile
Carna
Cruach na
Cara [St Mac
Dara's Island]
Maínis
An Sceirde
Mór
Cuan an
Fhir Mhóir
An Spidéal
0
5
10 km

INTRODUCTION

Colm and His World

Colm Ó Caodháin[1] was both ordinary and extraordinary. He was a singer, storyteller, musician, lilter, whistler and dancer but, above all, he had a zest for life, for living and for fun. Colm was from Glinsce, a coastal townland west of the village of Carna in Conamara, County Galway, where he spent most of his life. The area was, and still is, renowned for its singing and storytelling traditions. Joe Heaney (Seosamh Ó hÉanaí), who was a relation of Colm, Seán Choilm Mac Donncha, Seán Jeaic Mac Donncha and Johnny Joe Pheaitsín (Seán'ac Dhonncha) are among those who come to mind in relation to singing. Storytellers Pádraigín Mhacaí (Mac Con Iomaire), Pádraig Veailín Ó Nia and Cóilín Ó Cualáin feature, especially in the narrative tradition. Men in particular are prominent, but women featured too. Meaigí Nic Dhonncha of Fínis island and Máire Nic Dhonncha (Máire Williamín) of An Aird Mhóir, Cill Chiaráin, County Galway, are among those recorded in the National Folklore Collection (NFC).[2]

Colm's native townland of Glinsce is in the barony of Ballinahinch, an area renowned for its physical beauty. Although Glinsce is officially included in the Gaeltacht or Irish-speaking district, Irish is not very widely spoken there today. The demise of Irish had already started in the early to mid-1940s, by which time English was prevalent. Although Glinsce was not among the poorest areas of Conamara at the end of the nineteenth and beginning of the twentieth centuries, it was sufficiently impoverished to merit the attention of the project known as *Lady Dudley's Scheme for the Establishment of District Nurses in the Poorest Parts of Ireland* and nurses were sent to the area in an attempt to remedy the situation.[3] The first report of this scheme, covering the period April 1903 to April 1904, stated that three parishes in the area, including the parish of Maíros, had a population of 2,367 between them, with a valuation of £1.2.0 *per capita,* in contrast to three nearby parishes, known as 'Ceantar na nOileán' [The Island District], which had a population of 3,621 and a valuation of 8/= *per capita*. The descriptions published in connection with Lady Dudley's Scheme, which relate to the time when Colm was ten years of age, indicate that there was a good deal of hardship in the area including hunger and illness.

These elements contributed significantly to emigration from Glinsce and the surrounding area: between 1851 and 1891 the population had declined from 172 to 75 inhabitants.[4] At this time, towards the end of the nineteenth century, fishing and kelp-burning were the most common occupations for local people.[5] We read too that by 1892, the local farming prospects were far from good. Cattle and sheep were small in stature and described as shrunken and difficult to fatten. Food and other supplies were brought to the nearby harbours of Carna, Cill Chiaráin and An Caiseal. One of the remarkable traits of the community, according to the early anthropologist and ethnographer Charles Browne, was their independence as regards food, clothing and fuel. In relation to social life and interaction, song and story, music and dance took centre stage side by side with the material poverty. This was noted by Browne, who observed:

> Whatever its poverty in other respects, and probably on account of that very poverty and backwardness, this district is rich in its folklore. Legends, traditions, old songs etc. are to be heard at the winter fireside and many old customs are kept up which have died out elsewhere.[6]

This tradition was part and parcel of the heritage of the Ó Caodháin family. It was Colm's embodiment of this tradition that drew a number of collectors to him to seek out and collect his lore. Colm was proud of his family and could trace his ancestors for generations, at least in the male line on his father's side. Colm informed the collector Séamus Ennis (1919–82)[7] that his name was Colm Mháirtín Thomáis Phádraig Ó Caodháin – Pádraig being his great grandfather's name.[8] He said his father used to bring flour by boat from Galway to the village of Roundstone, and often encountered very bad weather on his travels. Frequently, he was forced to spend the night sheltering in Galway Bay. He often walked home from Cill Chiaráin, a distance of about ten miles.[9] He also ferried turf, in a twelve-ton boat, to County Clare and to Kinvara and the Aran Islands in County Galway. Much of his work was of a heavy, physical nature. Maintenance of boats, sails and fishing equipment, in addition to making lobster pots and fishing gear, were demanding jobs, while the building and maintenance of houses was another arduous task that took its toll. Fuel came from the nearby bog, and the associated work was not only physically demanding, but created additional seasonal pressure for the Conamara fisherman *cum* farmer.

Colm was born on 15 June 1893. He was known as Colm Mháirtín Thomáis and also nicknamed 'Colm an Bhlácaigh', because Tomás, his grandfather, looked like a man whose surname was 'Blácach' and was known as 'An Blácach'.[10] His father was known as 'Caodháin *bádóir*' or 'boatman'. His mother was Máire Nic Con Iomaire from Inis Ní, near Roundstone, County Galway. Colm was the eldest of nine children and was reared in a home full of music and singing. He was very interested in both and enjoyed company and fun. As we find in Chapters 1 and 3 of this publication, he often described how much he enjoyed visiting neighbouring houses with his father and how he picked up songs and stories from the older people.[11]

Colm acquired most of his songs, and the accompanying enthusiasm for them, from his grandfather and grandmother on his father's side. Colm's grandfather, Tomás Ó Caodháin, was a well-established and locally highly regarded singer.[12] Colm said that as a young fellow he was constantly in his father's company and that they were always singing and lilting and his father would advise and correct him if he made any mistakes.[13] His father, he said, wouldn't care if there were a thousand people listening to him, he would still put him right if he noticed a mistake in a song.[14] His father's advice to him was that he should start a song by singing gently and that he could then raise it gradually so that there would be no danger of his voice breaking.[15] Colm said that at that stage of his life, he loved songs and music but that later on he almost began to forget them as he became involved in making his own way in the world, raising and supporting his own family.

Colm's father had his own favourite songs – songs like *'Éirigh i Do Shuí a Bhean an Leanna!'* ['Rise up Woman of the Alehouse!']; this he said was the best song one could sing in company.[16] Colm too had his favourite songs. One of these was a well-known love song, *'Taobh Thiar de Chlaí na Teorann'* ['Behind the Boundary Wall'], a song which, Séamus Ennis informs us, Colm's great-grandmother also sang. Whenever this song was being sung in the house or anywhere else, Colm's uncle would start to cry, and so the song developed a special significance for the Ó Caodháin family. Colm believed they had a very good version of it. He also had favourite airs to the songs.[17] One of these was the air to *'Ceaite na gCuach'* ['Ceaite of the Curls'].[18]

Colm spent little time at school but, nevertheless, he said that he managed to learn a certain amount of English.[19] In 1939, he married Bairbre Ní Cheannabháin from An Aird Mhóir, Cill Chiaráin in County Galway and they had five children – two daughters (Máire and Bairbre) and three sons (Máirtín, Tomás and Cóilín). He was in his mid-forties when he married, which was not uncommon at the time, but he was of the opinion that he had left it very late.[20]

Fig. 1: Bairbre, Colm's wife, Colm and their child, Máire, in Glinsce *c.* 1942.
COURTESY THE Ó CAODHÁIN FAMILY

Over a period of forty years Colm shared his songs and stories with local people and with folklore collectors who visited. He had been noted as a fine storyteller as early as 1937, when Mairéad Ní Chathasaigh from An Aird Thoir, Carna, County Galway, collected a version of an international folktale from him, a story entitled 'Tadhg Mac Craith' or 'Thady McGrath'.[21] Mairéad, a part-time collector with the

Fig. 2: Colm, his mother Máire, his wife Bairbre Ní Cheannabháin and the children, Bairbre, Cóilín and Máire, *c.* 1945. COURTESY NFC

Irish Folklore Commission (IFC), who lived a few miles from Glinsce, wrote down this tale from Colm which he said he had heard from his father twenty years earlier.[22]

The collector who spent by far the most time with Colm was Séamus Ennis, who worked for lengthy periods in Conamara between 1942 and 1946. Colm was his main contributor or informant. The Ó Caodháin household at the time consisted of Colm, his wife and children and Máire, his mother. Séamus Ennis was struck by Colm's stature and appearance on their first encounter in 1943. He wrote that Colm generally dressed in Conamara tweed and had a special suit for Sundays.[23]

Colm was the eldest in his family and was particularly close to his father, who taught him how to fish and to farm and generally make his way in life. However, after some years, the fishing in Conamara failed and he emigrated to Scotland, where his brother and other relatives had already gone in search of work. It appears that he found work in Glasgow, although he did not spend a significant amount of time there.[24] During his lifetime, Colm was part of vernacular traditional music and song in the part of County Galway known as Iorras Aithneach.[25]

Later, most likely in the 1930s, the Land Commission bought a substantial portion of the Ó Caodháins' holding. The family left their old house and Colm built a new one. It was the first house he had ever built.[26] It appears there was some discussion with the Land Commission engineer who came to visit, in relation to the layout and construction of the new home. The Land Commission communicated to Colm that if he were to sell one part of his holding they would offer him part of another holding. Colm, however, designed his own plan, and when the engineer called back, Colm drew the new plan on the road and told the engineer that he wanted the house to be built towards the sun, as the sun would go around the house. This was one of the points on which the engineer disagreed with Colm, but when the engineer finally agreed and Colm built the house according to his own plan, the house was never damp.[27]

It is not difficult to see Colm as the exemplar contributor to the early days of folklore collecting in Ireland, as he possessed many of the traits that allow us to understand vernacular culture. He was also a gifted craftsman and he made, for example, a plane from the iron wheel of a donkey cart, while he also fashioned other tools to make his own furniture.[28] In later years, he had a bicycle with rubber pedals and when they became worn, he made his own timber pedals.[29]

When Séamus Ennis, a native of north County Dublin, was appointed full-time collector of music and song for the commission in 1942, he spent a considerable amount of time collecting in Conamara, especially in Iorras Aithneach, on the island of Fínis, in Carna, Aill na Brón, and Maínis island. The very first reference to Colm Ó Caodháin in Ennis' diary appears on 20 August 1942, when Colm was recommended to Ennis as a singer.[30] Their first meeting did not occur until 25 May 1943, with Ennis recording in his diary that he was given a warm welcome and experienced a great night. Colm sang, lilted and danced.[31]

Fig. 3: Séamus Ennis taking notes from Colm Ó Caodháin, Glinsce, Carna, County Galway, 1945, while his daughter Máire looks on. COURTESY NFC

The collector recognised immediately the richness of the source he had encountered, noting in his diary that Colm had a great deal of material. Progress in exhausting the repertoire was slow, however, because he had so much to contribute on every topic. It was easy to work with him and, although he was a slow speaker, Ennis did not wish to hurry him.[32]

Colm was a man of music and song and his skills in these areas were praised by Ennis.[33] He was able to assist Ennis and other collectors, who had only pen and paper when they began collecting from him. The songs required particular patience from Colm, as Ennis had to collect music and text and then marry the two while also including intricacies and ornamentation. Colm would correct him as Ennis sang the song for him, in order to ensure it had been written as Colm wished. Colm wanted the material to be precisely and truthfully documented. If he was not certain of something, he would qualify it by saying '*le leisce bréag a dhéanamh*' ['for fear of telling a lie'], or '*ní maith liom a rá … le faitíos nach mbeadh sé ceart*' ['I don't like to say it … for fear it might not be right']. By the same token, a comment such as '*tá mé cinnte de sin* anyways' ['I'm sure of that anyway'] communicated Colm's conviction for accuracy.[34]

During Ennis' time with the commission another IFC collector visited Colm to record his stories and other lore. Liam Mac Coisdeala (1906–96), a former teacher, began collecting for the commission in August 1935. He spent a number of years collecting in the Carna district and recorded the longest folktale ever collected in Ireland, '*Eochair Mac Rí in Éirinn*', from storyteller Éamonn de Búrca (1866–1942), from Aill na Brón in the Carna area. In early summer 1944 Séamus Ó Duilearga (1899–1980), honorary director of the commission, visited Séamus Ennis in Conamara. On his way back to Dublin, he called to see Liam Mac Coisdeala who lived in Newcastle, in Galway city. Ó Duilearga explained to Liam that Ennis had met Colm and was gathering a vast store of music and song from him, and suggested that Liam should also visit Glinsce and record some of Colm's tales and lore.[35] Consequently, Mac Coisdeala began making Ediphone[36] recordings of Colm in September 1944. Liam wrote that he sourced a box of cylinders from Seán Ó Súilleabháin and then travelled with the Ediphone machine by bus to Carna.[37] When he arrived at Colm's house in Glinsce, Colm welcomed him warmly. It transpired that Colm had already encountered Liam a few years previously when Liam was visiting Éamonn de Búrca in hospital in Galway and Colm had been present.[38] Colm explained that his repertoire consisted largely of songs, and that the townland of Glinsce was not known for storytelling, though he did recount for Liam a version of '*Conchúr an Dá Chaora*' ['Conchúr of the Two Sheep'] and the collector was greatly impressed.[39] Over the course of this first week of September 1944 it transpired that Colm had a large repertoire of tales, religious lore and much else. Mac Coisdeala drew on *A Handbook of Irish*

Folklore,[40] the guidebook for field collectors compiled by Seán Ó Súilleabháin, and he mentioned items in it to Colm. In all, Liam filled twenty-four Ediphone cylinders during that week, and in January 1946 he returned and collected additional material.[41] As Séamus Ennis and Liam stayed in the same lodging house on at least one occasion, they doubtless discussed their collecting work, and certainly Liam lent Ennis the Ediphone machine to make sound recordings of Colm and others.

Colm derived great pleasure from his own repertoire. He entered the Carna Feis[42] in June 1944 and was quite successful there. In a letter to Seán Ó Súilleabháin, archivist with the commission, Séamus Ennis said that they had a great day at the *feis*, where there were competitions in storytelling, music, dancing and athletics, adding that, despite bad judges, Colm won a number of prizes.[43] He was glad that he himself had nothing to do with the judging. Colm won three prizes at the *feis* – one for an old poem, another for lilting and a third for singing. Ennis wrote that Colm would probably enter the Oireachtas, the largest national annual event of this kind, but apparently this never came to pass.

Although long periods of time might have elapsed since Colm had sung a particular song, he was almost always able to remember the words and if he happened to forget some of them from time to time, he was sure to recall them at a later stage.[44] This occurred with the song in English called 'It's Happened of Late', which the older people in Glinsce sang when he was a boy. From his first attempt to recall this song, Colm gradually remembered it over the space of two nights and a day.[45] Ennis said of his singing voice that it could sometimes be a little rough and high-pitched, but that when they were together quietly at the end of an evening and everyone else asleep in bed, the singer's voice would be very melodious and smooth.[46]

Unusually for an informant, Colm communicated his thoughts about the work of collecting and about the pleasure he gained from the experience. Although these accounts are in Ennis' handwriting, Colm's personality comes across very strongly, in particular when he refers to the Ediphone, which made its appearance in 1944 on this particular collecting scene.[47] The Ediphone was of great assistance, as the collector was no longer solely dependent on pen and paper;

the recording could be transcribed at a later stage and he was able to relisten to it as required. Initially, Colm was rather doubtful about the new machine and indeed a little afraid of it. He dubbed it '*an seanfhear*' ['the old man'] because, he maintained, it distorted what he had sung or spoken into it and the recordings sounded as if they had been made by an old man. He said that when he listened back he couldn't recognise his own voice and that it sounded as if the machine needed to take a drink.[48]

By 1947, the Irish Folklore Commission had acquired a disc-cutting machine in order to record material. Colm first encountered this newer form of technology when he saw a large vehicle approaching, but thought it was part of a turf-cutting expedition. Then he recognised Séamus Ennis in the car and he went to meet the visitors. Ennis introduced him to his colleague and said they had come to record Colm. Ennis brought a box into the house and laid it on the table, Colm commenting that it was not at all the same as the Ediphone machine and noting that it was an enormous item.[49] Ennis took out a large chest from the car, along with what Colm called a *súgán* or straw rope which was one of the wires connecting the Presto recording machine to the recording deck which remained in the car. Ennis then fetched yet another *súgán* from the car and placed it on the table and tied the first *súgán* to the box. Colm recorded some items and was highly pleased with the quality when it was played back to him.[50]

Colm introduced a number of people whom he held in high regard to Séamus Ennis, which facilitated the collector in his work. Most of these individuals lived in the Glinsce area and were friends or relatives of Colm's. As an example of such an introduction and of a day's collecting, Ennis instances Friday, 9 June 1944, when he and a local man, Colm Ó Domhnaill, paid a visit to Saint Colmcille's holy well in Leitreach Ard, Carna. When they heard a familiar shout they realised that Colm Ó Caodháin was about and they joined him. Colm and Séamus went to Maíros and had a drink there and then on to Colm's brother's house, with Ennis describing how Colm created a jovial atmosphere.[51] On another occasion Séamus was in the area of An Caiseal, near Glinsce, intending to do some collecting in Inis Ní. The Ó Caodháin family, he notes, was of help, with Colm's sister, in particular, of great assistance.[52] In 1945, Colm brought Séamus from Glinsce to Inis Ní in his sailing boat and introduced him to local people and especially singers in the area.[53]

Colm was called upon to help Séamus with his work in other ways as well. In May 1945, Sune Dahlberg, a Swedish diplomat, visited Ireland and met with Séamus Ó Duilearga, who recommended that he visit the west of Ireland. Ennis introduced Dahlberg to Colm and they went on a sailing trip around the harbour. Colm spoke in English to the Swedish guest and told him as they headed out in the boat, 'I'll give you a couple-o'-jaggle-about-over-an'-across.' This was like double Dutch to the Swede, although he managed to understand Colm's intention well enough because of his lively and rhythmic way of communicating. Colm sang songs and told stories for Sune and Séamus on the trip[54] and Ennis wrote down a song from Colm so that the visitor could see how they worked together.

It is clear that from the outset, Colm and Ennis had an exceptionally good working relationship. In describing working with Colm, Ennis gives expression to the highest praise accorded to any of his informants.[55]

As they became better acquainted, additional dimensions to the relationship became evident, not least their love of music and the fact that both were musicians, which made for a type of cross-fertilisation between collector and informant. Colm gave Séamus Ennis tunes, songs and lore that Ennis later included in his repertoire, among them a slip jig called 'Dusty Miller'. It seems that Colm called this tune 'Titse Miller' and when Ennis heard him play it, probably on the melodeon, he recognised it as one his own father had played.[56] Ennis noticed, however, that as Colm played it, the tune had a particular rhythm, which neither he nor his father had previously encountered. Colm also knew a special dance which went with this tune.[57]

Much of Colm's extended family lived close by or in neighbouring townlands. Neansaí, his sister, was married to Josie Ó Clochartaigh and they lived in An Caiseal, twelve kilometres from Glinsce. Colm was a regular visitor to their home and often stayed overnight. Sometimes when visiting he told bawdy stories; he would put the smaller children outside the room before he began, letting them back in again when he'd finished.

Fig. 4: Colm and his youngest sister, Neansaí, in her house, 1970.
COURTESY MARGARET CLOHERTY

Colm and Josie smoked pipes and Colm would put his pipe on the mantelpiece before going to bed. Josie brought his pipe to his bedroom, which Colm thought was not a good idea. There was an accordion in Neansaí's house and Colm played it, his last tune before retiring at night being 'St Patrick's Day in the Morning'. He always sang a song before going to bed.[58]

Colm's sense of humour was noted by Ennis, who wrote, for example, that one night he went to Glinsce and that Colm's brother was there with another man and that they started having some fun. Colm told Séamus to put aside his books and that they would make it a night of mischief. They spent the night playing games and tricks that the old people used to play and Ennis collected these also.[59]

Colm had an extraordinarily wide range of material. His ease of conversation, his interests and his knowledge motivated Ennis to transcribe Colm's account of his life. The account fills thirty pages of manuscript material. It comprises the first chapter of this book and was chosen as it is a first-hand account of how Colm saw his own life. Here we are witness to his daily work, which is an example also of the lifestyle of many fishermen, farmers and builders in the area at the time. Colm described his work throughout the year. At one point, for example, he ranged through his routine from January to May 1944, including tilling, seafaring, scallop-fishing, decorating the house, building walls, making querns for grinding corn and much else. The friendship between Colm and Ennis comes to the fore again and again in the Ennis diaries.[60] Largely founded on the mutual respect and fondness which the two men had for each other from the outset, the friendship is all the more remarkable when we consider Colm was well into his forties while Séamus was in his early to mid-twenties when they met. Colm may perhaps have regarded Ennis as akin to a son. Ennis' diary entry for 26 May 1943 indicates that on his second collecting visit to Colm, progress had already been made on both the social and professional levels.[61] Colm Ó Caodháin and Séamus Ennis often discussed matters other than music and dance, as it was not possible to isolate Colm's daily routine from his interaction and work with collectors. However, these discussions do not appear to have been unduly intrusive.[62]

Certainly, the sense of humour and fun which they shared helped in the development of their friendship. On one occasion, Ennis was in Colm's house collecting material and a rooster was nearby. The noise made by the rooster was making the collecting work very difficult, so the two men decided to calm the rooster by giving it bread soaked in *poitín*.[63] Rather than calming the rooster, however, this had the opposite effect and the rooster reacted by flapping its wings, making more noise and causing a furore. Bairbre, Colm's wife, was coming home and as she approached the house she heard the commotion. She asked the two men what had happened to the rooster and eventually they confessed. A sack was then put over the rooster's head and it was put in an outhouse. The rooster fell unconscious and they thought it had died, but after two days it recovered.[64]

Informant and collector spent many a night together, singing and playing music. Colm contributed to Ennis' enthusiasm for making a trip west, with the collector referring to Colm as '*Colm Ó Caodháin as Glinsce, m'fhear ceoil féin*'[65] ['Colm Ó Caodháin from Glinsce, my

Fig. 5: Colm Ó Caodháin's *púcán*. Drawn by Simon Coleman, 1959. COURTESY NFC

own music man']. Colm was at ease with the collecting process and welcomed opportunities to share his rich language and repertoire of storytelling and song. In the realm of music and song, Colm employed a special vocabulary. He used the Irish word *criotán*,[66] for example, saying it meant 'choked sometimes', describing a trait he had inherited from his father. Colm maintained that people with this characteristic in their singing were the best singers.[67] His comments underline the recognition of technique in terms of aesthetics within the community and his appreciation of these aesthetics.

Seafaring, fishing and boats were central to Colm's life, just as they were to the life of the community. Colm's routine for fishing was described by Ennis, underlining the immediacy of the engagement with the sea. Often, informant and collector would bring buttermilk and potatoes on fishing trips and would roast mackerel straight from the sea on a turf fire in the boat.[68] Colm's yearly cycle of sowing and planting, reaping and harvesting, is highlighted in Ennis' diary.

Ennis also lent a helping hand, planting cabbages or mangels or assisting with butter churning.[69] He was regarded as part of the Ó Caodháin family during his periods in the west. We are also witness to Colm's work as he went scallop-fishing with a dredge. He mentioned that his mother would never wake anyone up who was going to sea – probably for fear she might be sending someone out to drown.[70] On one occasion Ennis arrived in Glinsce for some collecting, to discover Colm down at the harbour, covered in black tar, a result of tarring the small canvas boat or curach as he prepared for the scallop-fishing season. Colm's brother Pádraig was also there.[71] When they returned to the house Colm greeted everyone, as was his custom whenever he went into his own house. Potatoes and tea were prepared and consumed, following which they drew their chairs up to the fire, cut tobacco and filled and lit their pipes. There was a sense of competition between Pádraig and Colm in the course of the evening as versions of songs were compared and discussed.[72] Perhaps this competition reflected a keenness for accuracy they had inherited from their father.

In addition to the songs, advice and guidance about singing that he received from his father, Colm doubtless also acquired the practical skills of boat maintenance and sailmaking from him. He spoke more of his father than his mother, but she does feature also and was centre stage in Colm's life. She had a rich, idiomatic spoken Irish, and on one occasion welcomed Séamus Ennis to the house in Glinsce with '*Nár ba liachtaí sop ar an teach ná fáilte romhat!*', indicating that her welcome for him was greater than the number of wisps of straw on a thatched roof. She was often witness to collectors visiting Colm, with Séamus Ennis describing a typical scenario: while Ennis wrote from Colm, Colm's mother rocked Colm's baby in the cradle by the fire, crooning as she did so.[73]

According to Colm's daughter Máire, he always wanted to have his work finished at six o'clock in the evening. He would come home then and put his feet up and sing if he were so inclined. And then other things would occur: five, six or seven men, perhaps, would come in to the house on winter evenings. It was like a family gathering. They would talk about what the poets composed long ago and would discuss different versions of songs. Most of these visitors were younger than Colm Ó Caodháin. Some of them fished alongside him. He and the neighbours were very close.[74] It appears that the public houses in Carna at that time did not welcome singing, so Colm, Ennis and others would travel by boat to Roundstone, and this group also included Séamus Ó Duilearga when he visited.[75]

Colm shared how he came to have the songs and how the arrival of Séamus Ennis reaffirmed and revitalised the songs which he had almost forgotten for him. He described how, when he saw how well he and Ennis were getting along, he would always try to have new songs ready for him. But with the passing of time, Colm wanted Ennis to continue visiting and in order to achieve this, he held back some of the songs for Ennis' next visit.[76]

Ennis realised this, writing that Colm was always commenting to him about the number of songs he had left to offer. At one point, Colm suggested that Ennis buy a house in Carna to spend time there while the collecting work was in progress.[77] Colm's loneliness following Ennis' collecting trips was described by the collector, as was his own sadness: Ennis once wrote in his diary that Colm was close to tears.[78]

Colm always welcomed Ennis heartily, as was the case in May 1944 when Ennis arrived to find Colm digging in the field in front of the house, in the rain, wearing old clothes and looking bedraggled. Colm was anxious to talk to Ennis and bring him up to date on all the work he had done planting and seafaring since Ennis' previous visit.[79] Ennis believed that Colm would be at ease in any company,[80] but noted that he would not tell vulgar or crude stories in the presence of women; such stories were most likely told late at night in male company when the women had gone to bed. This is not only a reflection of Colm's personality but was also the custom at the time.[81] Colm had many types of songs. He was especially proud of some and liked others for different reasons. '*Port na Giobóige*' ['The Unfortunate Widow's Tune'] is particularly associated with him. This was the first piece Colm sang for Séamus Ennis. '*Port na Giobóige*' was a piece of nonsense the old people used to sing and recite for fun with accompanying gestures when they had drunk some *poitín*. Before singing it, Colm was at pains to describe its background and context.[82] The composition itself is very lively and funny and in the sound recording one can sense his good humour and his enjoyment of it. Colm described the social situation in relation to singing this and other songs. He had songs in Irish and in English. He also had snatches of songs in English which travelled to Glinsce with local young men who had gone to east Galway, most likely for seasonal work, when Colm was a young man. In the case of two songs, 'Hughie O'Hara' and 'Mister Dooley', Ennis thought they were similar to music-hall songs and not worthy of great consideration, but that the accompanying airs were of interest.[83] Colm sang 'Captain Wedderburn's Courtship', a Child ballad,[84] while another song in English he clearly enjoyed was 'Soldier, Soldier, Will You Marry Me Now?'[85] He admitted however to having some difficulty with a macaronic version of the song '*An Cailín Fearúil Fionn*' ['The Assured Fairhaired Girl'], perhaps because he had to change back and forth from Irish to English when singing it.[86]

Colm's fluency in, and mastery of, English comes across in the sound recordings of his singing, his compositions and his conversations.[87] Séamus Ennis appears to have thought that Colm might not have been all that familiar with English. When in February 1944 Colm received calico from the commission to make a sail, he sent a letter of thanks in English to Séamus Ennis, telling him how happy he was to have received the gift. Ennis sent this communication from Colm to the commission, in which he requested that the letter and envelope should be kept safely. Ennis believed that Colm dictated the letter in Irish and someone translated it for him.[88] Nonetheless, Ennis interviewed him in English in 1954 for the BBC.[89] Colm, however, would sometimes ask for help in filling out application forms of one kind or another or in writing official letters in English.

Colm believed that the background to a song was important and invariably told all that he knew about the song – its author, date and so on – before singing it. The subject matter of many of the songs is doubly important because of its close connection to people to whom it refers, or to those whose lives were exemplified in the songs. Colm's brother Pádraig, who lived in Dubhithir, near Carna, once told of how his father, on a visit to Galway city, began singing '*Máire Ní Mhongáin*' in a public house. This is a lament by Máire Ní Mhongáin, many of whose children had emigrated. The person serving behind the bar happened to be a son of Máire Ní Mhongáin and he bent his head and started to cry. When the song was finished he took hold of Pádraig's father's hand and shook it and poured a large jug of whiskey.[90]

A song could often be the trigger for discussion and debate. When Séamus Ennis was collecting '*Amhrán Tom Neansa*' ['Tom Neansa's Song'], a song about sailing, from Colm, the collector described how the discussion included descriptions of sailing in Galway Bay and on the County Clare coast, in addition to Colm's detailed knowledge of waves, currents and hidden rocks in these seas.[91]

Colm sang late into the night, sometimes until two in the morning. He composed songs in both Irish and English, among them two humorous examples from 1944 in praise of the Ediphone machine.[92] He also composed a song about Séamus Ennis coming to record him with this machine, of how the collector arrived at his house one night wanting to fill the machine with '*nótaí ceoil*' ['notes of music']. Among Colm's other compositions was a song about a rooster and some hens he saw laying waste a corner of a field he had just planted; it was a comic song and he sang it for the collector.[93]

One of the traits shared by Ó Caodháin and Ennis was their talent for composition. Colm composed a song about Ennis[94] and Ennis composed a song entitled '*Colm Ó Caodháin as Glinsce*' ['Colm Ó Caodháin from Glinsce'], which gave Colm a great deal of pleasure.[95] Ennis described, in the form of an *aisling* or vision poem, how he met a beautiful woman. She recognised Ennis but when he called her a '*stáidbhean*' ['beautiful woman'], she replied that she was, in fact, Colm Ó Caodháin from Glinsce, who was wearing a kind of skirt because his trousers had been torn!

Sometimes Colm liked to add a verse of his own composition to a well-known song. He did this with a lighthearted song called '*Gugannaí Gú*' and also with a song called '*Mé Féin is Tú* Féin' ['Myself and Yourself'].[96] On another occasion he made up a title for a tune he knew and used this title at a later stage in order to help him recall the melody. The tune was called '*Ruidín Beag a D'imigh Uaim*' ['A Little Thing I Lost']. The collector appended a note to his transcription of it explaining that Colm couldn't remember the tune first time round but when it came to mind he had made up a title for it, putting words to the first verse which would remind him when Ennis came the next time. So Colm had no difficulty recalling it on Ennis' next visit.[97]

Colm loved stories and lore of all kinds. He had a vast store of riddles, proverbs, curses, blessings and other items. His language was clever, precise and full of wit. He loved the rhythm of speech and of music and the sound of words flowing. He had children's rhymes and other verses which might not have a very well-defined tune, but which were, as he described them himself, 'nonsense which was half music and half humming'.[98] Colm also played the melodeon, he could lilt and he danced. He was a fund of information on many topics. In a reply to a questionnaire on the Famine which the commission circulated, Ennis wrote over fifty pages from him.[99] Colm's warm personality and vast repertoire were also remarked upon by other collectors. For example, in September 1944 the collector Liam Mac Coisdeala visited Colm and wrote how pleased he was with his visit to Glinsce and his regret he could not spend more time there. Liam and Colm got to like each other very much; Liam had recorded over fifty pieces from him in the course of the week and said he wished he could have had a month in his company.[100]

Colm was eager to have his store of material documented and recorded and enjoyed the collectors' visits as he shared his repertoire with them. In 1945, Séamus Ennis wrote, with a note of sadness, that he believed he had harvested most of Colm's repertoire of songs and music. And yet, whenever he returned, Colm, without fail, had new material for him.[101]

As Colm's fame as a singer began to spread, many more people came to collect from him. Both transport and methods of recording were constantly improving, and a number of disc recordings of Colm were made. Disc recordings were a complicated affair and it is most likely that Caoimhín Ó Danachair of the commission joined Séamus Ennis on a visit to Colm in 1947 and, using the commission's mobile recording unit, recorded material from him on disc.

Séamus Ó Duilearga also visited Colm and came away most impressed. Proinnsias de Búrca collected stories and lore from him in the late 1950s amounting to some 130 pages. In 1958, de Búrca wrote to Ó Duilearga stating that he was of the opinion that Colm had already given all of his material to Séamus Ennis and to Liam

Mac Coisdeala.[102] Ciarán Bairéad (1905–76), a full-time collector who worked for the most part in County Galway, collected from Colm in the late 1960s and early '70s. Each of these individuals used different methods of collecting and each of them acquired different varieties of lore, as well as different versions of tales and song. Nor were they the only people to seek Colm out. In 1947, Séamus Ennis, then working for Radio Éireann, which he had joined on leaving the commission, visited Colm[103] and was responsible for introducing the American collector Alan Lomax to him. Subsequently, Ennis, while working for the BBC, recorded him again.[104] In 1974, in the course of producing a documentary programme for RTÉ about Séamus Ennis, Éamon de Buitléar had the foresight to bring Ennis on a visit to Colm, then in his eighties.[105]

Although a wealth of material was collected from Colm, little of it has become available outside of the archive. In addition to the *Columbia World Library of Folk and Primitive Music,*[106] in or around 1955 the Cultural Relations Committee of the Department of External Affairs[107] compiled a selection of music and song from Ireland which had been collected for the BBC. It was called '*Tiachóg Ceoil as Éirinn*', which means a collection of folk songs and melodies from Ireland. Brian George of the BBC selected the archive material which was edited by Séamus Ennis, who also wrote the notes. The two discs in this compilation were intended for use in Irish embassies abroad, and were never published. The recordings contain a version of '*Bean Pháidín*' from Colm and also '*Port na Giobóige*'. Colm's singing features on the record entitled 'Child Ballads Vol. 2' in the series 'Folksongs of Britain' published by Topic Records in 1961; here the recording of Ó Caodháin was made by Alan Lomax and Séamus Ennis. The song featured is part *of* '*A Pheige na gCarad*' or 'Our Goodman' (Child ballad no. 274). He can be heard singing his version of '*Johnny Seoighe*' on the CD *Amhráin ar an Sean-Nós,*[108] while he lilts the tune 'The Mountain Top' on the CD *Ireland: Musics of the world*.[109] In summer 2019, a 1970s recording of the song '*Bríd Thomás Mhurchadha*' was published on a CD entitled *Tabhair Mo Ghrá go Conamara* [Bring My Love to Conamara] which presents recordings of a compilation of singers.[110]

This publication contains thirty-three audio items recorded from Colm, which represents an edited selection of a much larger body of material that includes manuscript, sound and music transcriptions. In all this, songs are to the fore. Colm's song repertoire also included well-known love songs such as *'Caisleán Uí Néill'* ['*Ó Néill*'s Castle'] and *'Dónall Óg'* ['Young Dónall'] as well as lighter songs such as *'Bean Pháidín'* ['Páidín's Wife'] and *'Dú-in Dú'* [nonsense vocables]. He also had songs of close relevance to his own district, such as *'Bád an Chaisil'* ['The Boat from An Caiseal'] and *'Céad Míle Slán Leat a Leitir Ard'* ['A Hundred Thousand Farewells to You, Leitir Ard']. Some slightly bawdy songs were taken down from him as well, although these appear to have been collected in manuscript form only. This is a song type that has not been well documented in the Irish-language song tradition,[111] for a number of possible reasons: it might happen that some people were reluctant to sing these songs for the collector or that a collector was reluctant to ask for such items, but Colm and Ennis knew each other well enough not to be influenced by such considerations. The chief characteristic of Colm Ó Caodháin's songs and singing, however, is the sense of sheer enjoyment and infectious fun that is conveyed; in one recording, he bursts out laughing at the end of a song.

The imagination plays a central role in songs and lore and the oral tradition is best experienced in the living performance. That said, we are fortunate that we can experience some of Colm's repertoire through sound recordings and manuscript material which offer us considerable insights.

Colm Ó Caodháin enjoyed good health and, even with advancing years, he is remembered as walking without a stick.[112] He died on 31 January 1975 and is buried in the cemetery at Maíros, near Glinsce. In some ways, Colm Ó Caodháin was a very ordinary man, a fisherman and a small farmer in Glinsce, typical of the Conamara he lived in, and it might be said that he did not change the course of the world. He experienced the normal joys and sorrows of life and dealt with these as he encountered them. In other ways, he was extraordinary, extremely talented with an exceptional zest for life and for fun. It is certainly true that, because of his generous nature, he has provided us with an intimate and profound insight into the life and repertoire of a Conamara singer in the 1940s and has left a body of material which, as an inheritance, is difficult to surpass.

Colm Ó Caodháin is an example of a man of songs who was a musician, storyteller and dancer, and who understood the importance of his repertoire and shared it with great generosity. We are fortunate indeed that he was visited by a number of collectors and that the friendship between him and Séamus Ennis blossomed in such a remarkable fashion. Due to Colm's generosity and regard for his own traditions, we are the wiser, not only of the Glinsce music tradition but of a great deal more besides. We have received a considerable insight into life in rural west County Galway in the middle of the twentieth century. It is both a privilege and an enriching experience for us to encounter Colm and his world.

CHAPTER 1

'In My Youth and Prime'[1]

The Irish Folklore Commission, founded in 1935, focused primarily on aspects of oral tradition other than music and song, and the late 1930s and early 1940s were arguably the 'golden years' of collecting in Ireland, when a number of full-time collectors worked in the field. Séamus Ó Duilearga, director of the commission, was considerably influenced by the approach to folklore studies in northern European countries. This approach emphasised the importance of recording the collecting situation and its milieu. As a result, in its fieldwork the Irish Folklore Commission stressed the importance of documenting context. This emphasis on contextualisation was underlined in advice given to Ó Duilearga by Carl von Sydow, the Swedish scholar who stressed the importance of collectors familiarising themselves with the tradition-bearers' lives at close quarters.[2]

The collecting of music is a long-established tradition in Ireland and the subject was approached with vigour from the beginning of the eighteenth century.[3] When Séamus Ennis began working for the commission in 1942 he was familiar with the work undertaken previously.

Colm's account of his life was collected and transcribed by Séamus Ennis in 1945, two years after their first meeting. Ennis wrote in his diary entry for Wednesday, 1 August 1945, 'I recorded an account of his life from him on the Ediphone.'[4] It must have taken more than an hour to make the recordings on Ediphone cylinders. Ennis mentions wax cylinders 'one', 'two', 'three' and 'four', indicating that he used four cylinders in total. The Ediphone was a dictating aid to collectors and their use meant that once the recording was made, the transcription could be undertaken. Once the transcription was completed, collectors posted the transcribed material and a box of cylinders back to the offices of the Irish Folklore Commission in Dublin, where the cylinders were shaved and prepared for re-use for further recording by collectors. It took several hours to make the handwritten transcription of Colm's account from the cylinders. The amount of time Ennis spent on this underlines his recognition of Colm's importance.

We can imagine the endless exchanges between Colm Ó Caodháin and Séamus Ennis about music, song, stories and life in Glinsce. The following account is reproduced here as Colm told it to Séamus.[5]

The transcription gives a sense of Colm's life experiences, as well as the importance of song and story for him and for his generation. In the translation process, the emphasis is on conveying something of Colm's style and power of expression in Irish, which does not always find an equivalent in modern colloquial speech in English.

TUAIRISC CHOILM AR A SHAOL

(Eiteán 1) Fear mise a tháinig suas in éindí le m'athair i nGlinsce ó bhí mé mo pháistín bheag, lag, tá tuairim is deich mbliana is dá fhichead ó shin ann nó go dtáinig sé san iomarbhá go raibh mé féin in ann mo ghnaithe féin a dhéanamh. Agus b'fhada liom ná a bhfaca tú riamh san am sin go dtagadh an geimhreadh. Ar an ngeimhreadh i gcónaí (bhíodh muid ag faire) go dtagadh sé le go dtéadh muid amach chuile oíche ag déanamh spraoi go dtí na seandaoine seo, mar ní raibh aon áilneacht sa domhan ach iad ag gabháil fhoinn agus ag inseacht seanchais go mbeadh sé in am codlata san oíche. Is ar ndóigh, mo léan géar! Níor linn ab fhaillí é – rud ar bith bhí siad sin a rá, ní bhíodh muide dhá ligean thar a gcluasa féin gan é phiocadh suas chomh maith is d'fhéad muid é. Ach bhí mise ag obair liom mar sin.

Ansin fuair m'athair báidín dá chuid féin, is bhínn féin is é féin amach ar an bhfarraige ag iascach in éineacht agus, ní as ucht mise dhá rá é go deimhin, ba mhaith uaidh é dhéanamh. Ní raibh fear ar bith dá bhfaca mé san áit seo a raibh cloigeann air chomh meabhrach agus bhí air le haghaidh chuile shórt ealaíon sa domhan a d'fhéadfadh fear a dhéanamh faoi chúrsaí bád is chuile shórt.

Tá siad ag tabhairt leasainm ormsa anois – tugann siad 'Colm an Bhlácaigh' orm. Is é an t-údar a bhí leis sin, bhí m'athair mór, sean-Tomás, bhí sé an-mhór ann féin, an-leitheadach. Agus san am sin, an bhfuil a fhios agat, ní bhíodh na daoiní chomh tugtha suas agus tá siad anois agus dá bhfeictaí culaith mhaith éadaigh ort, ná hata ná rudaí áirthid ar bith mar sin, ná bróga maithe, déanfaí iontas – an uaisle bhí ag plé leat. Ach fébrí[6] *cé bhfuair m'athair mór é, níor stop sé is níor mhór-chónaigh sé ariamh, go bhfuair sé carabhat. Agus chonaiceas ag gabháil anuas an garraí ar maidin é, is níor airigh an tseanmhuintir ag gabháil amach chun an aifrinn ar maidin é agus nuair a bhí an tseanlady amuigh sa doras, dúirt sí go raibh fear mór ag gabháil anuas an garraí agus 'Seas amach,' a deir sí lena fear, 'go bhfeice tú cén fear é féin.'*

'Diabhal,' ar sé, 'a chonaic mé ariamh ach an Blácach!'

Ach nuair a tháinig sé seo isteach, bhí a fhios cé bhí ann agus ón lá sin go dtí an lá seo, tá 'An Blácach' ag leanúint suas linne. Bhíodh sé ag cur – ?[7] *– feirge i dtosach ar na seandaoine é thabhairt orthu, ag ceapadh go mba 'shlur' é bhí dhá chaitheamh orthu, go mba masla é, ach leigeadar as sin.*

Bhíodh mise is m'athair ag obair in éineacht, ag gabháil amach go Sceirde ag iascach, go Carraig an Míle, go Cruach na Caoile, Cruach na Cara, Carraig Chabhalta, Carraig Muiribhe, Béal Chuain an Dúin, Bolg Mór is Bolg Beag – chuile áit siar ansin ag marú mangach is dhá dtabhairt abhaile. Ansin, nuair a fuair seisean bás, go ndéana Dia trócaire air, bhí mise mé féin is báidín againn péin agus bhínn ag iarraidh bheith ag déanamh an ealaín chéanna.

Tá mise in ann a ghabháil an fhad siar leis an gcéad Chaodhánach acu – Conchúr Ó Caodháin. A gcuala sibh caint riamh ar Nóra Ní Chonchúir Bháin ar dearnadh an t-amhrán di? Is iomú duine nach bhfuil a fhios aige cén Conchúr é sin. Ach tá mise ag inseacht daoibse cén Conchúr é féin – gurb é Conchúr Ó Caodháin é bhí i nGlinsce; agus is é an t-ainm a bhí ar a mhac, Tomás Ó Caodháin; agus is é an t-ainm a bhí ar mhac Thomáis Uí Chaodháin, Pádraig Ó Caodháin; agus is é an t-ainm a bhí ar mhac Phádraig Uí Chaodháin, arís ar ais Tomás Ó Caodháin. Tugtaí Sean-Tomás ar an gcéad Tomás mar gheall ar Thomás óg a thíocht agus ba shin é m'athair mórsa – Tomás óg; agus m'athair Máirtín Ó Caodháin agus mé féin Colm Ó Caodháin; agus tá leaidín beag agam féin anois a bhfuil Cóilín Ó Caodháin air agus tá sé amuigh sa ngarraí anseo anois.

Well, nuair a tháinig m'athairse suas in inmhe ansin, a bheith in ann a ghabháil, ag saothrú cion fir, chuaigh sé in éindí lena uncail ag bádóireacht móna go Contae an Chláir agus go hÁrainn agus bhídís ag cur móna soir go Contae an Chláir, chuig dream daoine a bhí ann a dtugaidís na Ceatharnaís orthu agus bhíodar féin agus iad féin an-bhuíoch dá chéile. Ansin, nuair a bhí sé achar fada ag bádóireacht na móna in éindí leis an uncail, creidim gur cheap sé go raibh sé ag gabháil ag déanamh páighe níos fearr dhó féin mar gheall air go raibh na gasúir le tóigeáil aige is an mhuirín lag air, a ghabháil go baile Chloch na Rón go dtí Tomás Ó Griallais. Bhí bád páirteach ag Tomás Ó Griallais agus ag Joe Clochartaigh a bhí i Roundstone (ceannaí siopa bhí ann, agus ní raibh fear ar bith san áit seo bhí ina fhear chomh tréan leis in airgead lena linn; agus ba mhaith an fear é le bheith ag obair ina bhád). Agus bhí m'athair in éindí leis ina bhád ariamh chúns bhí sé in ann, nó gur chrap an aois chomh mór é is go mb'éigin dó fanacht sa mbaile.

Taispeánadh ón Mhaighdean Mhuire

An t-uncail seo, Máirtín Ó Caodháin, a raibh sé ag bádóireacht in éindí leis chun tosaigh, ag bádóireacht na móna. Bhí bád le cur amach as an gcaladh acub agus le seoladh go Contae an Chláir le lucht móna. Agus ar maidin, dúirt an seanfhear 'Muise,' deir sé, 'ní maith liom a ghabháil chun seoil inniu. Ba mhaith liom a ghabháil go Carna inniu,' a deir sé, 'agus faoisidin a dhéanamh don Mhaighdean Mhuire. Amáireach lá le Muire – faoisidin a dhéanamh don Mhaighdean Mhuire is a ghabháil chun comaoineach amáireach.'

'Ó, well,' a deir a bhean leis, 'fág do bhád istigh sa gcaladh agus téirigh agus déan é sin.'

D'fhága sé an bád istigh sa gcaladh agus chuaigh sé chun faoisidine san oíche agus chun comaoineach lá arna mháireach. Agus nuair a tháinig sé abhaile, sheoladar leis an lucht móna agus bhí báid go leor seolta soir romhthub. Bhí go maith. Nuair a bhíodar soir i lár Chaoláire na Gaillimhe, tháinig an oíche orthub agus dhubhaigh sé suas ina cheo is ina shalachar san oíche agus bhí an oíche chomh dubh le tóin an phota agus ní bheadh a dfhios agat cé dtabharfá d'aghaidh.

'Tabhair anuas an dorú atá faoin deic,' a deir an seanfhear leis, 'agus tomhais cén doimhne tá faoin mbád anois – bhfuil mórán uisce fúithi?' nuair a bhí scathamh maith den oíche caite.

Thug sé anuas an dorú agus chaith sé amach an luaidhe go tóin poill agus thomhais sé é agus ocht bhfeá domhain a bhí an áit. Faoi cheann scathamh eile, dúirt sé leis é thriáil arís agus thriáil sé aríst agus ocht bhfeá a bhí sé. Agus faoi cheann scathamh eile, dúirt sé: 'Triáil aríst é,' deir sé, agus ocht bhfeá bhí sé.

'Níl a fhios agam,' a deir an seanfhear, 'cén áit i gCaoláire na Gaillimhe a bhféadfá bheith anois ach i mBéal an Spidéil, mar níl aon áit eile i gCaoláire na Gaillimhe atá in ann an domhain sin a sheasamh chomh mar a chéile ach Béal an Spidéil.'

Bhíodar ag seoladh isteach gur cuireadh ar thrí feá iad. Bhíodar ag seoladh isteach gur cuireadh ar fheá go leith iad agus ní raibh mórán uisce le spáráilt an t-am sin acub. Agus chuala m'athair-sa nuair a chuaigh sé suas chun tosaigh ag leigean na seolta cinn faoin mbád, chuala sé an flaipínteacht a bhí an t-uisce a dhéanamh ar na halltrachaí ann. Agus nuair a bhíodar ag gabháil timpeall amach – faitíos orthu go raibh an bád le bheith briste faoin gcarraig – las an solas ar chéibh an Spidéil! Ní raibh aon áit anoir, ó Ghaillimh anoir, a cheap siadsan nach bhfeicfeá – bhainfeá marc di leis an solas a bhí uirthi – ag ceann na céibheach. Agus ní raibh sé de thriáil aige na seolta cinn a bhaint ar chor ar bith chun tosaigh – bhíodar istigh i mbéal na céibheach – ach an seol mór, chaith sé dhe é agus bhí sé ag púitseáil leis na seolta cinn ar bhealach eicínt mar ní raibh mórán triála acu. Bhí sé an-ghorráisceach orthu, an spota; agus tháinig isteach insa gcéibh agus bhí aon bhád amháin istigh sa gcéibh agus iad ina gcodladh agus dhúisigh sé iad.

'Á,' a deir an seanfhear, 'siod é bád Bheairtlí Chaonaigh a bhí chun tosaigh orainn agus is é an chaoi ndeachaigh sé amach agus las sé teine ar an gcéibh ag déanamh comhartha dhúinn.' Ach cén sórt bád a bheadh ann ach bád as Maínis!

'A dtáinig aon bhád anseo ó thit an oíche?' a deir an seanfhear le fear Mhaínse.

'Níor tháinig,' a deir sé, 'níl aon bhád ann ach muide.'

'An bhfaca sibh solas ar bith?'

'Ní fhaca, mar tá muid théis bheith ina gcodladh.'

Chuaigh an seanfhear is m'athair amach ar chéibh an Spidéil. Céibh mhór fhada í agus tá an-chuimse airde inti. Agus chuadar ón áit íochtair go dtí an áit uachtair, na staighrí, gach uile áit faoin domhan, thóraíodar abhus agus thall, féachaint an bhfaighdís cosúlacht le teine nó le rud ar bith agus ní raibh sin le feiceáil ann. Well, chomh cinnte is tá mise ag inseacht daoibhse an méid seo, gurb í an Mhaighdean Mhuire a las an solas sin an oíche sin ag tabhairt solas dó sin le thíocht isteach chun na céibheach.

Taispeánadh eile

Well, an taispeánadh sin a fuair sé an oíche sin, ba mhór an ceann é. Sheoladar as an mBeirtreach Buí, 'trip' eile le lucht móna ag gabháil soir agus ní rabhadar amach ach ag Oileán Lachan, áit atá amach ó Mhaínis, nuair a chuaigh m'athair suas ag leigean na seoltaí faoin mbád go ngabhfadh sé timpeall. Tháinig an fear roimhe ar an dic – ach ní fhaca sé an fear; chuir sé a dhá láimh isteach ar a chliabhrach agus bhrúigh sé siar ar ais é; agus leig m'athair na seolta fúithi mar sin féin, agus nuair a chuaigh sé siar: 'Ní oibreoidh mise an bád seo níos faide dhuitse inniu,' a deir m'athair leis an uncail.'Céard tá tú ag iarraidh orm a dhéanamh?' deir an t-uncail.'Tá mé ag iarraidh ort í a chasadh ar ais,' a deir sé, 'san áit a d'fhág tú.'Is éard a bhí san uncail fear an-tostach, an-chiallmhar, agus níor chuir aon fhear ariamh aon chomhairle air nach ndéanfadh sé.

'"Alright" a mhic ó,' deir sé, 'ní ghabhfaidh mise taobh thiar dhíot féin air.'

Chasadar ar ais í agus nuair a bhíodar ag tíocht anoir ag áit a dtugann siad Bealach na Srathrach air, chonaiceadar chucub aniar báid Roundstone, a bhí ag gabháil go Gaillimh. Chonaiceadar 'stripáilte' ina gcuid crainnte iad, gan falach agus na seolta tugthaí amach ar an bhfarraige uathu agus éadan ag tíocht ar an stoirm i bhfad níos airde ná cnoc – ag freagairt dóbsan.

'Á! a chladhaire fir!' a deir an seanfhear le m'athair, 'féach an mbeifeá ag baint di na seolta agus dhá gcumhdach, dhá gceangal!'

Chuaigh m'athair suas agus thosaigh sé ag baint di na seolta, agus ní raibh aon áit acu le maireachtáil ansin, cheap siad, ach Cuan na hAirde, soir in áit a dtugann siad 'Faoi Tigh Shiobháin' air. Idir Maínis agus An Aird Thoir atá sé. Agus nuair a tháinig an 'squall' agus bhuail sé an bád, bhí na seolta crapaithe ag m'athair uilig dhi, ach an búm agus an geafail agus nár mhór an gála é, chomh mór agus bhuail sé na sparraí, an bháid, gan 'stitch', ar bith éadaigh; chuir sé uisce ar trí no ceathair d'fhóidreachaí den mhaolóig a bhí os cionn bord uirthi; chuir sé chomh hard sin é; agus an fheamainn a bhí caite os cionn na (Eiteán 11 ar lean) móna – chaithidís feamainn an t-am sin i gcónaí os cionn na móna le haghaidh nach mbeadh cosa na ndaoine ag pléascadh na móna, agus ag ceapadh go rabhadar ag déanamh roinnt sábháilt ó bháisteach ar an mhóin ag an am céanna – ach chuala mé m'athair ag rá, bhí an fheamainn ar an maolóig os cionn na móna leis an fhad seo achair de bharr báisteach agus droch-aimsire, agus bhí sí chomh fliuch le feamainn a bhainfeá sa gcladach. Agus ina dhiaidh sin féin, nuair a bhuail an gála an bád, ní raibh aon bhlas meáchan ag an ngála ag tabhairt na feamainne fliuch leis ach oiread agus dá mba páipéar dóite é! Agus chuadar suas go ndeachadar suas chun Tigh Shiobháine agus chuadar chun ancaire ann. Agus bhí na báid eile, cuid acub tháinig siad ann agus cuireadh cuid acu le fána. Agus nár mhór an taispeánadh é sin a fuaireadar, freisin, an t-am sin! Dhá dtéidís chun cinn an lá sin – marach an taispeánadh fuair m'athair ag Oileán Lachan – dhá dtéidís chun cinn, ní feicfí aon amharc ar cheachtar acu go deo.

Well, nuair a tháinig mise suas ansin in éindí le m'athair – ba mé an chéad duine den 'fhamily' agus bhí ochtar againn ann. Ach nuair a fuair siadsan in ann roinnt rudaí dhéanamh iad féin, chuaigh mise ansin ag iarraidh bheith ag saothrú, ar nós mar bhíodh m'athair, ag tabhairt airgid chun an tí freisin, ag cúnamh do m'athair le haghaidh an chuid eile acub a thóigeáil. Agus is é an chéad áit a ndeachaigh mé ag saothrú, go Baile Chloch na Rón, ag iascach ronnachaí. Agus bhí muid ag déanamh neart airgid de réir mar d'fhághadh muid an aimsir. Bhí mé oíche amháin amuigh agus bhí chúig phunta dhéag le fáilt agam de bharr na hoíche agus go deimhin tá mé a rá leat go raibh sé maidin Dé Domhnaigh nuair a bhí na heangachaí glanta againn; agus is breá an lear a d'ól mé féin i Roundstone an lá sin. Tháinig m'athair siar go dtí mé Dé Domhnaigh agus thóg sé mé agus thug mé suas m'athair i dteach an ósta is chuaigh muid isteach gur ól muid a ndóthain agus go raibh muid ag gabháil fhoinn is ag déanamh spraoi.

Agus chuaigh mé as sin, nuair a tháinig an fómhar go Gaillimh ag iascach scadán mar ba é an dlí, an dtuigeann tú, bád ar bith bheadh amuigh ar na ronnachaí, nuair a thiocfadh an fómhar ghabhfadh sí go Gaillimh freisin ar shéasúr na scadán.

Bhí mise ag iascach i mBaile Chloch na Rón anois an oíche seo agus chuaigh muid amach chun na farraige. Oíche chailm a bhí inti agus ní raibh blas gaoithe ann. Is chuir muid a gcuid eangachaí agus deireadh na hoíche bhíodh fear faire a dhúiseodh suas tú, san am ceart le éirí le tosaí ag tarraingt do chuid líonta isteach. Agus dhúisigh an fear muid, dúirt sé linn éirí go raibh an oiread fíogaí – (scríob ar an eiteán do fhocal nó dhó anseo) – a bháid, agus go mba mhór an seó é. Fíogaí – sin – is éard a thugann siad orthu sin – an Béarla – 'dogfish'. Shocraigh muid suas sinn féin, chuir muid orainn a gcuid éadaigh gur thosaigh muid ag tarraingt a gcuid líonta agus go deimhin bhí cuid mhaith acub iontub freisin. Ach nuair a bhí muid ag seoladh isteach, dúirt an fear a bhí ag cinnireacht an bháid liom péin, dúirt sé liom a ghabháil ag gabháil an bháid, go ngabhfadh sé féin a chodladh. Chuaigh mé féin ag gabháil an bháid agus d'fhan leaid eile suas in éindí liom, mar nuair a bheifeá ag ragairne na hoíche fada ní bheifeá in ann a bheith siúráilte an dtitfeá i do chodladh nó nacha mbeadh gan fear faire bheith in éindí leat; mar ba rud an-chontúirteach daoine a bheith ina gcodladh agus bád – dhá dtitfeadh gach uile dhuine ina gcodladh inti, ba rud an-dona ar an bhfarraige é, i measc maidhm agus tanaí. Ach bhí mé féin ag gabháil an bháid agus nuair a bhí mé ag tíocht isteach ag Sceirdí, bhreathnaigh mé síos insa gcábán agus chonaic mé an fear a bhí fanta suas in éindí liom ag brath ar titim ina chodladh.

'Ó, a dhiabhail!' a dúirt mise, 'éirigh suas as sin is fainic an dtitfeá i do chodladh, faitíos go dtiocfadh aon néal ormsa anseo! Cuir síos "tincan" tae agus an teine!'

Ach thosaigh sé ag réiteach an tae, féibrí scéal é, agus le linn na cainte chuala mé an t-urchar taobh amuigh dhíom. Ach níor leag mé blas suntais air sin, mar is minic a chloiseadh muid rath-'bounce' mór torainn amuigh sa bhfarraige, agus tháinig mé isteach.

Nuair a bhí muid ag gabháil isteach ag Cruach na Caoile tháinig fear an bháid aníos nuair a bhí an tae réidh.

'Tá tú fada go leor ansin anois,' a deir sé liomsa, 'is téigh féin a chodladh scathamh.'

Ar ndóigh b'fhada liomsa go bhfuair mé an seans le gabháil a chodladh, is chuaigh mé a chodladh. Agus nuair a caitheadh amach an t-ancaire ar ród Chloch na Rón aisti, bhí torann breá ag an slabhra, ach má bhí féin níor dhúisigh sé Colm! Bhí Colm bodhar air!

Ach nuair a bhí mé scathamh maith i mo chodladh, tháinig ceann den chriú amach i mbáidín chugam agus thosaigh sé do mo dhúiseacht agus dúirt sé: 'Éirigh suas as sin a chladhaire! Tá Tommany báite!' Well! Ba an rud is mífhortúnaí rinne aon fhear ariamh le fear a bheadh ina chodladh, drochscéala fhógairt air agus é ina chodladh, mar is rud an-dona é. Agus mar gheall go raibh an codladh orm péin is gur fhógair sé an drochscéala, chaith mé scathamh fada agus ní raibh a fhios agam beirthe ná beo céard a bhí mé a dhéanamh liom péin. Ach mar sin féin, chuaigh mé os cionn dic agus bhreathnaigh mé isteach ar an gcéibh agus ní fhaca mé mórán slua daoine riamh ba tréine ná chonaic mé istigh ar an gcéabh. Is é an t-údar a bhí leis an slua daoine bheith ar an gcéabh, bád fada tháinig isteach ann, Agus dúirt ceann de na hiascairí a bhí amuich i mbáidín beag go bfaca sé féin an bád seo a tíocht suas le taobh an bháid seo a báthadh – bád Tommany Thomáis Hughie as an Aird Thoir- gur báthadh é féin agus a bheirt mhac agus a chuid daoine muinteartha, go mba slán gach áit dá gcloisfear é!

Tháinig an bád seo suas lena dtaobh, a dúirt an fear seo a chonaic as an mbád eile í, agus cheap sé gurb éard a chaith sé isteach, mar bheadh baraille beag a raibh 'ammunition' ann isteach inti, ach creidim nach maith a bhí sé cinnte céard é féin. Ach féibrí cén scéal é nó nach scéal é, báthadh an bád; agus phléasc an bád ó chéile. Agus i ndiaidh aimsir an chogaidh mhóir a bhí ann roimh an gcogadh seo, agus bhí gach uile dhuine ag ceapadh ansin go mba é an German a tháinig agus rinne é sin – más é nó marab é. Ach bhí fear an 'lighthouse' ar an Oileán Iathrach (Árainn) ag rá go bhfaca sé féin an 'crowd' daoine uilig ag gabháil amach i gcloigeann an bháid, agus an bád ag pléascadh agus ag gabháil go tóin an phoill.

Ach féibrí scéal é, bhuail an oiread droch-mhisneach muide an t-am sin, mar gheall ar an gcontúirt a d'éirigh, agus na báid uilig, agus nach ndeachaigh aon bhád amach níos mó. Ach nuair a caitheadh chuile shórt, agus chuadar amach arís ag tóraíocht, ní raibh aon ronnach ann. Féibrí cén fáth é, ní raibh aon ronnachaí ann agus níor dearnadh aon iascach ariamh ó shin orthu agus briseadh suas na báid agus thiteadar sna crompáin gan aon bhlas a dhéanamh. Níl aon ronnachaí ó shin ann, agus níl fhios agam cén fáth é, ach d'fhéadfadh sé gur mar gheall ar an éagnach mór contráilte a dhéanamh é; mar chloisinn seandaoine ag rá fadó, ní raibh cuan ar bith insa domhan a raibh an scadán ag tíocht fadó ann ná Cuan na Beirtrí Buí, agus bhíodh na seandaoine ag déanamh a gcuid eangachaí iad féin, bíodh a fhios agat, agus ag tóigeáil an-chuimse éisc agus scadáin.

Ach breac an-'tenderáilte' an scadán, mar bhí bean i Leitir a hArd[8] *fadó agus bhí sí le pósadh, cheap sí – cheap a fear go bpósfadh sé í, agus dúirt sé léi thíocht go Baile Chloch na Rón agus go bposfaidís ann – go raibh airgead le fáil aige ann. Agus ní dhearna sé ach an bhean a thabhairt leis i mbáidín agus is é an t-ainm a bhí ar an mbean Bríd Bairéad. Agus os cionn Inis Srathair in áit eicínt i bpoll domhain a bhí ann, bháigh sé an bhean. Agus nuair a tháinig sé i dtír go Roundstone, é féin agus an fear a bhí in éindí leis, nár mhaith meabhrach an bhean, bean ósta bhí ann, nuair a chuadar isteach ag ól deoch ann, dúirt sí: 'Sin fear a bhfuil murdar déanta aige, go cinnte,' a deir an bhean istigh. Creidim gur aithnigh sí ar a chosúlacht é.*

Ach le linn an lae sin, ó d'imigh an lá sin agus ó tharla sé, níl scadán ariamh le fáilt an bealach seo; b'fhéidir go dtóigfeá leathchéad amantaí, scór amantaí agus seacht n-uaire gan ceann ar bith. Agus is éard a bhí na sean-daoine a rá gur mar gheall ar an éagnach contráilte a déanadh, an cuan a bheith fágthaí ag an iasc an t-am sin.

Go hAlbain

Nuair a buaileadh suas an iascach ansin, ní raibh aon tsásamh agam péin go dtéinn go hAlbain, mar bhí go leor de na daoine muinteartha gaibhte go hAlbain agus ní raibh i gceist acub ach Albain. Agus chuaigh mé go hAlbain. Bhí mo dhearthháir thall freisin agus bhí an-fháilte romham ansin. Ghabhfainn amach ar an tsráid tráthnóna théis an tsuipéir agus gach uile fhear do mo thabhairt féin isteach ag tabhairt – gach uile fhear is a dheoch féin aige do Cholm. Agus m'anam go bhfuil mé ag rá leat go raibh mé in ann slám maith dhíob ól freisin, cuir i gcás go raibh an pórtar an-tsaor ag gabháil.

Bhí go maith. 'Is olc an áit a dtáinig tú anois!' a dúirt cuid acu, 'níl stróc ariamh le déanamh anseo!'

Bhí cúpla 'sean-navvy' ina seasamh ann, is dúradar ná raibh aon jab in áit ar bith anois in Albain ach jab a bhí thiar i gCloigeann Dóran. 'Ach má tá féin,' a dúradar, 'níl aon fhear in ann é sin a sheasamh; tá sé ró-throm'.

Feicim go leor daoine a tíocht ann agus barúil acu dhób féin. Is oibríonn cuid acu uair a chloig ann, is cuide dhíob leathuair; is cuide dhíobh nach bhfuil in ann stróc ar bith a dhéanamh ann, is tá siad a leigean orthub féin. Nuair a chuaigh mé féin isteach go dtí mo 'landlady' san oíche, d'fhiafraigh mé dhi, 'Cén sort áite é Cloigeann Dóran?'

'Ó, a dhiabhail!' a deir sí, 'fan glan ar Chloigeann Dóran,' a deir sí. 'Ná bíodh tada le déanamh agat leis! Tá sé sin uafásach.'

'M'anam,' a deirimse, 'nach bhfuil aon jab eile le fáil is tá mé ag ceapadh – dúisigh thusa mé ag a sé a chlog ar maidin go dtriálfaidh mé féin cén sórt áite é Cloigeann Dóran.'

(Eiteán III). Ní dhearna mé féin ach a ghabháil ar an traen ar maidin agus mo thraen a thabhairt liom go Cloigeann Dóran agus a thíocht ansin mé féin agus naonúr eile. Agus tháinig muid anuas agus bhí an lá roinnt fuar agus bhí sé ag déanamh sórt claidhreachas beag báistí. Ach má bhí féin,

ní raibh hata ná caipín ar aon fhear dhá raibh ag obair anseo agus chonaic muid a ngail uile ag imeacht astu freisin mar sin féin de bharr allais, agus dúradar féin le chéile nach tada gan tada an áit seo!

Ach sheas mé féin suas le taobh 'bothy' beag a bhí ann – sin é an t-ainm a thugaidís ar an áit a mbíodh a ndinnéar is an teine bheag istigh acu. Sheas mé suas lena thaobh agus bhí droch chulaith éadaigh curtha agam orm péin, seanbhróga a raibh 'concrete' orthu – 'cement' – agus seanéadach dona, mar ní thaispeánfadh sé don mhuintir thall go mba fear oibre thú ghá mbeifeá ag gabháil le do chulaith Domhnaigh ag iarraidh obair. Is éard a d'fhiafróidís díot – is éard a d'fhiafródh an 'gaffer' díot ab é a chuid oibre féin a bhí tú iarraidh, dá bhfeiceadh sé ag tíocht thú le culaith mhaith éadaigh. Ach chonaic sé mé féin, gléasta suas le haghaidh na hoibre agus d'fhiafraigh sé dhíom a raibh mé ag iarraidh oibre agus dúirt mé gurb' ea. 'Well, más ea,' deir sé, 'tá áit agam dhuitse ach níl aon áit agam d'fhear ar bith eile.' Shílfeá go mb'fhearr liom péin ná bhfaca mé ariamh dhá 'startálfaí' ceann eicínt de na fir in éindigh liom, le go mbeadh muid féin i gcomhluadar le chéile píosa den lá, ach níor 'startáil'; ach d'oibrigh mé féin liom.

Tá mé dhá rá leat, má d'oibrigh féin, go mba crua an obair é. Ag obair le gual a bhí muid, ag tarraingt guail amach as waiginí traenach i dtosach agus dhá chur síos i málaí agus dhá chur ar charr mór. Agus bhí capall mór ansin ann le haghaidh é sin a tharraingt síos ar chéibheannaí adhmaid; agus trí fichid mála a ghabhadh ar gach uile charr acub sin agus dhá tharraingt síos ag bád pléisiúir le haghaidh bheith a gabháil ag rith anoir an [tayaster?] le daoine móra. Agus ba 'shiftannaí' a bhí ann, agus ba éard é an 'shift' trí bhád a réiteach agus bheadh sé déag airgead le fáil agat.

Ach san oíche, nuair a bhí an lá caite agam péin, ní raibh agam ach ag cur mo mhéarachaí suas ag breith ar mo léine ag iarraidh bheith ag tarraingt mo léine aníos as na poill a bhí curtha isteach ins na guaillí agus bhí an fhuil le feiceáil agam amach thrí na guaillí. Ach dúirt mé go mba chuma liom. Ní raibh tada trom ná te agam an t-am sin, bhí mé go láidir gan dabht. Ach tháinig mé abhaile is bhí mé ag gabháil suas thrí na staighrí ag teach mo lóistín – bhí go leor 'flightannaí' staighrí le 'climbáil' agam, tuairim is chomh maith le ceathair nó cúig de stórtha – agus ba mheasa dhom é ná an chuid eile uilig, ag iarraidh bheith gabháil ó staighre go staighre. Ach bhí mé chomh tuirseach sna cosa is go mb'éigin dom ar deireadh bheith ag breith ar íochtar an treabhsair ag iarraidh bheith ag crochadh na gcos ag gabháil suas na staighrí.

Is mar sin féin, nuair a tháinig mé isteach, 'Well, creidim gur le haghaidh do bháis a tháinig tú aniar anseo,' a deir an 'landlady', ar sise, 'féibrí scéal é!' Ach bhí go maith, bhí mé ag obair liom ansin, ag obair liom ansin nó go raibh an jab ar thoba bheith thart. Leis an scéal a ghiorrú, nuair a tháinig bád isteach deireanach sa lá agus dúirt an Johnston seo go dteastódh gual a chur inti sin agus dúirt na 'seannavvies' seo – bhíodar 'well up', níos faide ann ná mise: ní raibh mise ag rá tada – dhá bhfaighdís 'shift' aisti – ba éard é an 'shift' trí bháid – ach mara bhfaighdís 'shift' aisti seo, nach ndéanfaidís é. Agus dúirt sé nach bhfaigheadh.

'Well,' a deir sé, 'níl súil agam a bheith briste lib, féibrí scéal é; téigí ag obair mar ní sheasfaidh an jab ach trí lá eile.'

'Mura bhfuil,' deirimse, 'go bhfóire Dia orm!' – chuimhnigh mé i mo chroí gur fear mé féin a bhí ar bóthar ag tóraíocht jab eile.

Ach nuair a chuaigh mé soir go Dumbarton, san oíche agus 'mheeteáil' mé mo chuid leaids féin, d'fhiafraigh mé dhíob a raibh aon 'chance' in áit ar bith le feiceáil agus dúirt fear muintearach liom go raibh sé istigh in 'yard' Barney, seans; go raibh fear ag gabháil ag imeacht amáireach amach as an obair agus go mbeadh áit ansin agam go cinnte.

Chuaigh mé isteach lá arna mháireach is níor bhac mé leis na trí lá thíos. Chuaigh mé isteach agus fear as Donegal, Barney Boyle, a bhí ann agus go deimhin fear gnaíúil! agus d'fhiafraigh mé féin an mbeadh aon 'chance' ar 'start' agus dúirt sé go raibh.

'Tearaigh isteach amáireach,' a deir sé, 'má tá leabharthaí agat.'

Chuaigh mé féin isteach amáireach is bhí mé ag obair ann is diabhal mórán achair a bhí mé ag obair in éindigh leis nuair a bhí 'an-value' aige orm péin agus fear eile as Donegal, fear a dtugaidís Paddy Harkin air. Ach bhí muid ag obair linn is é an chaoi raibh sé againn ar deireadh, go raibh 'trustaithe' déanta aige seo dhínn, uilig; d'airigh sé go raibh muid ag déanamh ár gcuid oibre go dúthrachtach, mar ba mhaith linn rud ar bith dhéanfadh muid cuma bheith air. (Tú féin atá ag gabháil go maith dhuit féin agus tú i do chara dhuit féin.) Ach is é an chaoi ar caitheadh an scéal ar deireadh, níor thaitnigh liom an pháighe a bhí ann – ag rith ar airgead a bhí mé – is ní dhearna mé ach a ghabháil go Clydebank, go dtí jab eile i gClydebank, an áit a raibh páirtnéar agam, fear a bhí ag tolladh plátaí le haghaidh soitheach. Agus cheap sé amach – briseadh an tseachtain roimhe sin é féin agus a chuid fear agus cheap sé amach go mba iad na fir – leag sé an milleán ar na fir – go mba iad na fir ba ciontaí agus fuair sé an 'squad' nuaidh seo. Ach leis an scéal a ghiorrú, féibrí scéala é, chuaigh muid leis agus ní raibh muid oibrithe ach aon lá amháin, nuair a fuair muid an bóthar freisin. Ní raibh an fear in ann na gnoithe dhéanamh, an fear a bhí ag cinnireacht an deis tolladh – is é ainm a thugann siad ar an deis i mBéarla 'punch'. Ach fuair muid 'an mála' tráthnóna agus tháinig muid ar ais aríst agus níor leig an faitíos dhom péin inseacht do mo 'landlady' céard a bhí éirithe dhom, mar bhí a fhios agam – bhí mé ag ceapadh go maródh sí mé. Ach faoi cheann scathaimh b'éigin dom é inseacht!

Ach ocht déag a fuair muid de bharr an lae agus bhí mé amuigh ar an mbóthar ansin lá arna mháireach gan fios agam céard a dhéanfainn. Ach d'fhair mé na daoine bhí ag tíocht amach as 'yard' Mhic Mullen go bhfeicinn a mbeadh aon 'chance', mar bhí daoine muinteartha dhom ann. Agus fear a dtugaidís 'Seán na Corann' air, fear fearúil a bhí ann, d'fhiafraigh mé dhe an mbeadh aon 'phower' aige 'start' fháilt dom agus dúirt sé go ndéanfadh sé a dhícheall. D'ól mé féin is é féin na hocht déag, féibrí scéal é – is gearr a bhí muid dhá dhéanamh! – agus chuaigh muid isteach ag tóraíocht an jab, is ní raibh aon bhlas ar deireadh agam ach 'giorria nó dos raithní'. Bhuail mé liom amach is chuaigh mé isteach in mo jab féin, mar bhí mé dallta is ba chuma liom fuits. Is bhí mé gabháil thrí na daoine mar bhí deich gcéad fear ann, is ní leagfaí aon tsuntas ort ag gabháil thrí na daoine ann. Ach ní leigfeadh an náire dhom a thíocht i láthar m'fhear féin, cheap mé, mar gheall ar gurbh é an chaoi raibh sé ag íoc amach daoiní as an jab – bhí an jab ionann is a bheith réidh.

Mar sin féin, féibrí cén chaoi bhfaca sé mé, chonaic sé mé, is tháinig sé go dtí mé is d'fhiafraigh sé dhíom céard a tharla dhom. 'Á,' deirimse, 'tharla an mí-ádh dhom. Thóig mé mo chuid leabhra is mo chuid airgid anseo an lá cheana go dtéinn abhaile. An áit ar hiarradh abhaile mé is casadh na daoine muinteartha dhom ar an tsráid is chuaigh muid ar an ól agus an t-airgead a thabharfadh mise abhaile, is é an chaoi ar ól mé an t-airgead sin. Agus tá mé anois i mo bhromachán bliana, gan Murchadh gan Mánas, is mé go dona agus bhí mé ariamh.'

'Á, a Chaodháin,' a deir sé, 'bhí mise ag cur do thuairisc go maith, mar bhí mé ag caitheamh i do dhiaidh! Agus fuair mé tuairisc mhaith cé ndeachaigh tú. Ach cén fáth ná raibh sé de mhisneach agat a thíocht isteach go dtí mé lá arna mháireach?'

'Á, muise, go raibh míle maith agat,' a dúirt mé féin.

'Well, tearaigh isteach ar maidin,' a deir sé, 'féibrí scéal é. Tá an oiread

seo fear curtha chun bóthair agamsa,' deir sé, 'ó shin, ach ina dhiaidh sin féin,' a deir sé, 'chúns bheidheas mé beo is go bhfanfaidh tusa liom, beidh jab agat. Tá mise ag gabháil ag oscailt jab anois,' a deir sé, 'i nGlasgow nuair a bheidheas an jab seo réidh agam agus ná bac thusa le baile, ná le plean ar bith, agus fan in éindigh liom, agus beidh jab le do shaoil agat.'

Well, bhí go maith. Bhí mé an-bhuíoch de agus bhí muid ag obair in éineacht go bhfuair mé scéal as an mbaile a ghabháil soir le haghaidh an earraigh – a thíocht le haghaidh an earraigh. Agus dúirt mé le mo dheartháir a thíocht, is mé féin fhágáil thall. Agus dúirt sé liom má bhí aird ar an mbaile agam, a ghabháil abhaile. Ach féibrí scéal é, creidim go raibh sé in ndán dom é dhéanamh. Tháinig mé abhaile agus chuir mé an t-earrach. Agus céard a thiocfadh le linn an t-am sin go díreach ach an 'coal strike', 'strike' an ghuail a bhí ann ins an am sin, agus ní raibh aon phiocadh suas ar an áit níos mó.

Ach féibrí scéal é, nuair a fuair mé an chéad seans aríst, chuaigh mé anonn, agus an obair a bhí déanta ag an 'gcoal strike' – bhí chuile áit curtha thrína chéile aige. Agus bhí mé scathamh fada thall ag tóraíocht aon jab agus ní raibh aon jab le fáil Ach tháinig mé abhaile aríst agus tá mé ag obair liom ar na garrantaí anois agus ag déanamh lá iascach amach ar an bhfarraige agus ag baint mo chuid féir agus ag cur mo chuid fataí. Agus corr-uair, castar Séamus Ennis liom agus bíonn sé (?).[9] *Agus ní as ucht mé féin dhá rá é, agus fainic an sílfidh sibh gur gaisce ar bith tá mé dhéanamh as mar gheall ar go bhfuil sé i láthair! Ach ní hea! Fear mise insíos amach an fhírinne féibrí cén scéal é. Diabhal a miste liom beo cé bheidheas ag éisteacht liom! Is é an fear é is éasca fhoghlaim a chonaic mé fós ariamh. Thriáil mé go leor daoine óga agus is maith an scathamh chaith mé ag fógairt orthu 'déan seo agus déan siúd' is b'fhéidir gur in aimhréidh insna rópaí … ach siod é an buachaill nach bhfuil ag gabháil anonn ná anall air is go bhfuil na gnoithe déanta ar an bpointe aige!*

Well ansin. Talamh seo Ghlinsce, bhfuil a fhios agat, chuile dhuine agus a gharraí féin aige; agus bhí an talamh gan roinnt gan riar air. B'fhéidir go mbeadh garraí abhus agus garraí thall agat. Ach tháinig an Congested Board ansin agus roinn siad an talamh agus thug siad a chuid féin do gach duine dhe. Agus ina dhiaidh sin féin, ní dhearna sé sin an malrait ba chóiriúla. Bhí an fear mór, bhí sé mór i gcónaí; bhí rud eicínt in araí agus anuas ar an bhfear bocht ná raibh sé ag fáilt a cheart.

Ach féibrí scéal é, bhí 'engineer' ón Land Commission, tháinig sé anuas, fear a dtugaidís O'Grady air, agus ba éard é sin seanfhear mánla, meabhrach, deas, a thabharfadh a cheart féin do chách. Cailleadh é ó shin le pian chroí, go ndéana Dia trócaire air! Ach d'fhiafraigh sé dhíomsa dhá n-imínn as an seanteach a raibh muid ann, ag ceapadh go raibh mé ró-ghar do theorainn fear eile, go dtabharfadh sé 'an-ghrant' dhom as teach a dhéanamh. Agus d'fhiafraigh mé dhe cén 'grant', is dúirt sé go dtabharfadh sé seacht scóir punt dom; agus d'insigh mé do m'athair é san oíche.

'Á,' deir m'athair, 'is bocht an rud duitse', deir sé, 'is a bhfuil d'anró faighte agat ag réabadh cloch ó thainig sé de rath ionat, is anois díreach go bhfuil tú réidh leothu, thú ghabháil ina gcionn aríst!'

D'insigh mé d'O'Grady lá arna mháireach é.

'Well,' a deir O'Grady, 'tabharfaidh mé ocht scóir dhuit.'

Is nuair a d'insigh mé do m'athair é, 'Bydad, is mór an t-airgead é,' deir sé. 'Is fearr duit a ghabháil chun cinn leis, mar tá muid fada go leor sa tsean-áit seo, féibrí scéal é.' Agus chuaigh mé chun cinn leis agus rinne mé an teach seo mé féin.

Fear mé nach bhfuil aon scoil ná Béarla foghlamtha aige, agus bhí mé in ann an teach a dhéanamh, míle buíochas le Dia! agus nuair a bhí mé dhá dhéanamh, nuair a bhí an teach déanta agam (níor chuir mé aon tslinn (Eiteán IV) suas ariamh), ach thosaigh mé ag oibriú an chloiginn agus ag cuimhneamh sa gcloigeann céard ba cheart dom a dhéanamh. San oíche nuair nach mbíodh tada eile do mo bhadráil, tharraingínn anuas mo chuid 'cardboard' chugam agus d'fhaighinn mo shiosúr agus thosaínn ag tarraingt amach geanntrachaí agus dhá ngearradh agus dhá gcur suas; ach míle buíochas le Dia! chonaic mé ar an bpointe cén plean leis an slinn a chur suas agus chuir mé suas an tslinn agus rinne mé an teach.

D'oibrigh mé liom a déanamh tíobhaí ansin. D'oibrigh mé suas faoi Bhun na gCnoc, suas ag Sraith Salach, Seanadh Chaola is Maínis, is Inis Ní, An Caiseal, ag déanamh liom tíobhaí nó go raibh formhór na dtíobhaí déanta agus nach bhfuil níos mó acu le déanamh. Ach tá mé titithe siar in aois chomh mór is creidim á mblaoití féin orm a déanamh teach, nach bhféadfainn freastal air mar gheall ar a bhfuil le déanamh sa mbaile agam. Leig mé ró-fhada mé féin gan pósadh agus ní bheidh na gasúr in ann aon chúnamh thabhairt dom go mbeidh mé féin ag imeacht i mo chrotaí! (gáirí ag Colm anseo).

Tá áit anseo, Mám Éan, a d'fhága Naomh Pádraig ann. Nuair a bhí sé ag beannú na hÉireann, d'fhága sé thuas i mbéal Mhám Éan tobar breá agus d'fhága sé an leaba – pictiúir na leaba – gearrtha isteach mar bheadh leaba téatair ann, gearrtha isteach i dtaoibh na haille. Agus daoine bhíos ag iarraidh leigheas, codlaíonn siad istigh sa leaba san oíche agus ar maidin lá arna mháireach, nuair a bhíonns an lá ag éirí, ba geall le lucht bóthair agus casúir an torann a chloisfeá acu sin ag 'hammeráil' ar an leaba sin ag baint píosaí den leaba is dhá dtabhairt abhaile le haghaidh leighieas. Ach bhíodar ag 'hammeráil' ar an leaba is is é an scéal é, go bhfuil an leaba fíorbhriste anois. Ach bhí mé féin ann, mar níl aon spóirt mar bhí nach mbínn ag iarraidh ghabháil ann, ná áit ar bith den tsórt; agus bhíodh neart poitín ann agus gabháil fhoinn ann insan oíche. Ach bhí mé féin ag gabháil fhoinn, péibrí scéal é, go maidin agus ar maidin, thréis mo thurais a thabhairt, bhí mé gabháil fhoinn romham anuas agus mo mháthair in éindí liom. Ach shiúil dhá bhean as Iorras Mhór – dhá bhean óga, bhreá, dheas – anuas i mo dhiaidh féin is tháinig duine acu gach aon taobh díom agus chuireadar lámh faoi mo mhuineál. Agus dúradar liom go raibh mé ag gabháil in éindí leob féin! Ar ndóigh, mo léan géar! Níor leob ab fhaillí é. Bhailigh mise leob agus níor stop mé is níor mhórchónaigh mé go ndeachaigh mé isteach ar an traen ag Srath Salach in éindí leob; go ndeachaigh mé as sin go ndeachaigh mé go Baile na hInse; is gur shiúil mé anuas ó Bhaile na hInse go ndeachaigh mé isteach go hInis Ní, agus go dtáinig mé i mo churachaín canbháis aniar aníos tráthnóna agus mé trom tuirseach. Ach tá mé ag rá leat nár admhaigh mé dhób sa mbaile go raibh mé tuirseach, mar ní bheadh mórán truaighe dhom!

Tá daoine go leor anois ag caint ar sheanchas agus ar amhráin agus tá gach uile dhuine ag rá gur aige féin atá an ceart agus tá cuid acu ag rá nach acu atá an ceart; ach tá mise cinnte den rud atá mé féin ag rá. Níor chuala mise ariamh in áit ar bith insa bpobal seo, agus chuala mé m'athair dhá rá agus chuala mé chuile dhuine de na seandaoine ag rá go mba é fear Ghlinsce riamh an fear a … go mba leis an cáca, nuair a bhídís réidh le chéile. Ba leis an cáca. Níor tháinig sé ar áit ar bith riamh, duine in áit ar bith, ná raibh fear Ghlinsce in ann dó le amhráin, le spraoi agus le greann – Na Caodháin. ('Caodháin Bádóir' a thugaidís ar m'athair-sa mar gheall ar go mbíodh sé ina bhádóir.) Bhínnse ansin leigthí amach ar phiocadh suas amhráin agus bhínn ag gábháil fhoinn agus m'athair do mo threorú; agus ní leigeadh sé mórán achair mé dhá mbeadh aon 'mhistake' déanta sa gcúis, go bhfógraíodh sé orm. Dheamhan a miste leis dhá mbeadh míle fear ag éisteacht leis, ach dhá bhfeiceadh sé in aimhréidh san amhrán mise – is minic a bhínnse dallta agus mé ag rá amhrán agus d'fhógraíodh seisean go raibh mé ag gabháil contráilte ansin. Mar nuair a bheidheas go leor óil déanta agat agus tú ag gabháil fhoinn, tá sé an-éasca agat faillí dhéanamh.

Bhí fear eile de cholceathair dhó ansin, anseo a dtugaidís Pádraig na Corann mar ainm air. Is é an fáth Pádraig na Corann a thabhairt air mar gheall ar go mbíodh sé istigh ina chónaí ar Chora, a mbíodh an taoille ag gabháil thimpeall air. Agus bhí fear eile i nGlinsce lena ais a dtugaidís Tomás Ó Uaithnín air; agus bhí fear eile ann, athair m'athar, Tomás Ó Caodháin. Well, ní raibh sé le fáil abhus ná thall aon fhear ab fhearr ná Tomás Ó Caodháin ag gabháil fhoinn. Bhídís ag ceapadh amach go mb'fhearr mac Uí Uaithnín ag gabháil fhoinn agus d'abraíodh cuide de na seandaoiní 'Th'anam ón diabhal! cén chaoi ndéarfá go mb'fhearr mac Uí Uaithnín?' Ar ndóigh, níor ól mise aon deoch ariamh ar mhac Uí Uaithnín. Ach ní raibh mé mar sin le mac Uí Chaodháin; d'ól mé deoch air! agus dhá dheoch!

Well, bhí mo mháthair mhór ansin ar an mbealach chéanna. Bhí an oiread seanchais aici is ná raibh aon ríochan leis. Is ea, leasmháthair do m'athair [é seo i bhfreagra ar cheist uaimse] agus dhá mbeadh a fhios agamsa go dtiocfadh sé san iomarbhá choidhchin go dteastódh uaim péin an chaint seo a dhéanamh, bheadh míle agam thar mar tá. Ní raibh agam ach cuid acu. Leig mé i ndearmad iad – cheap mé nach dteastóidís uaim. Ach dhá mbeadh aon mheabhair agamsa go gcasfaí Séamus Ennis orm (nó an seanfhear seo [an Ediphone] is go mbeinn ag cur cainteannaí isteach ina bholg – le píce!), tá mé ag inseacht duit go mbeadh seanchas agamsa le cuir ann freisin! Ní fhaca mé aon bhlas in m'óige ach málaí faochan, seanchipín agus sean-úllaí!

Bhí fear sa mbaile seo cheana a dtugaidís Peaitsín Mháirtín Shéamuis air agus ní raibh aon chinneadh leis le fonn (Fág sin! – lena mhac óg a bhí ag cur isteach air) – fear de chlainne Chonraoi. (Gabhfaidh sibh mo leithscéal faoin méid sin an áit a raibh an gasúr seo agus píce féir aige ag brath ar mé tholladh!) Chaith Peaitsín Mháirtín Shéamuis seo go leor dá shaoil thall i Meiriceá i gcruth agus go raibh an oiread fonn aige agus gur thaitnigh sé chomh mór le muintir Mheiriceá agus go raibh fear an 'bhand' dhá iarraidh le haghaidh – ag freagairt an 'bhand' i gcaitheamh an lae. Ach tháinig sé go hÉirinn agus bochtaíodh anuas ar bhealach eicínt, an diabhal bocht! go raibh sé ag imeacht ó theach go teach ar deireadh. Ach bhí sé i dteach de chol-ceathair de m'athair an oíche seo, agus mar gheall ar na hamhráin mhaithe bheith aige, agus go raibh a fhios ag na 'lads' go raibh – agus bhí slaghdán agus slócht ar mo dhuine bocht – tháinig na 'lads' isteach. Agus bhí a fhios acu ná raibh sé in ann aon amhrán a rá, ach ag baint amhrán gan bhuíochas dhe, is céard a rinneadar – le 'Amhrán Tom Neansa' ach thosaigh ag rá ceathrú dhe, agus is é an ceathrú dúradar i dtosach, an ceathrú bhí amuigh ina lár. Agus an ceathrú dheireanach chuireadar ina thosach é.

'Muise, Dia sin dhá réiteach, a mhuirnín!' a deir sé, nuair a chonaic sé an bhail a bhí dhá chur ar an amhrán breá. Ach nuair a bhíodar scathamh fada ag plé leis 'Á! dúnaí bhur mbéal!' a deir sé, 'níl sib in ann caoi ná cuma chur air ach dhá dhonacht dá bhfuil mé féin, triálfaidh mé leis.' Agus lom air agus thosaigh sé ag rá 'Amhrán Tom Neansa' é féin.

D'fhoghlaim mise ansin é, uaidh sin, mar bhínn féin agus é féin ag déanamh ceilpe san oíche; agus ag iarraidh bheith ag caitheamh na hoíche bhíodh muid ag cur síos ar gach uile shórt ní agus d'fhoghlaim mise 'Amhrán Tom Neansa' uaidh agus tá sé agamsa ó shin. Agus tá sé ag Ennis anois agus nach geall go mbeidh sé agaibh féin creidim!

COLM'S ACCOUNT OF HIS LIFE

I grew up alongside my father in Glinsce as a small child about forty-two years ago until it came about that I was able to fend for myself. And I longed for the arrival of winter. We were always watching out for its arrival, because we could go out every night to enjoy the company of the old people; for there was nothing more beautiful on this earth than listening to them singing and telling stories until it was time to go to bed. Of course, we didn't let anything they said pass our ears without trying to pick it up as best we could. So, I continued to learn in that way.

Then my father got a small boat of his own and he and I would be out at sea fishing together, and I'm not just saying it because he is my father but he was very good at his work. There was no one around here who was as clever as him for all the skills that a man could have regarding boats and much else too. They have a nickname now for me. They call me 'Colm an Bhlácaigh' [a local landlord]. The reason for this is that my grandfather, old Tomás, was a big man, he was of a very broad build, and at that time, do you know, people were not as educated as they are now and if you were seen wearing a good suit of clothes or a hat or anything special like that, or good shoes, people would wonder whether you were connected to someone of rank. And wherever my grandfather acquired it, he took to wearing a cravat. He was seen coming down the field one morning going to mass and when the old woman in the doorway didn't recognise him, she said there was a big man going down the field.

'Come out,' she said to her husband, 'until you see who it is.'

'It's surely "An Blácach",' he said.

But when my grandfather came in, he was recognised and from that day to this we have been associated with 'An Blácach'! Some people were angry at first at being likened to the landlord, thinking that it was a slur cast on them, that it was an insult, but they let that go in time.

My father and I used to work alongside each other, going out to Sceirde, fishing, to Carraige Míle, to Cruach na Caoile, Cruach na Cara, Carraig Chabhalta, Carraig Muiribhe, Béal Chuain an Dúin, Bolg Mór and Bolg Beag – everywhere over to the west catching pollock and bringing it home. Then when he died, God have mercy on him, I had a little boat of my own and I tried to follow in his ways.

I am able to trace the first Ó Caodháin – Conchúr Ó Caodháin. Have you ever heard tell of Nóra Ní Chonchúir Bháin for whom the well-known song was composed? Many people don't know which Conchúr he was. But I can tell you which Conchúr he was. He was the Conchúr Ó Caodháin who was in Glinsce. His son was called Tomás Ó Caodháin and Tomás Ó Caodháin's son was called Pádraig Ó Caodháin. And Pádraig Ó Caodháin's son was called Tomás Ó Caodháin. The first Tomás was called 'old Tomás' because of the arrival of young Tomás and young Tomás was my grandfather. My father was Máirtín Ó Caodháin and I am Colm Ó Caodháin. And I have a young lad now who is called Cóilín Ó Caodháin and he is out in the field.

When my father grew in strength and was able to earn a man's living he went with his uncle on the turf boats to County Clare and to Aran and they brought turf back to Clare to people who were called 'Na Ceatharnaigh'[10] and they worked very well together. After he had spent a long time working on the turf boats with his uncle, my father thought that he would earn more by going to Roundstone, because he had to rear the children and he had a young family. He went to Roundstone to Tomás Ó Griallais who shared a boat with Joe Clochartaigh, a shopkeeper in Roundstone. There was no one around here who was as well off as Joe and he was also very handy working on a boat. My father was always with him in his boat, as long as he was able, until his age got the better of him and he had to stay at home.

Help from the Virgin Mary

My father used to go on the boats, at the forefront, with this uncle, Máirtín Ó Caodháin, working the turf boats. They were supposed to put out to sea from the harbour and to sail to County Clare with a load of turf.

In the morning, the old man said, 'I don't want to set sail today. I would like to go to Carna, to make my confession to the Virgin Mary. Tomorrow is the feast of the Virgin Mary. I would like to confess to the Virgin Mary and to go to communion tomorrow.'

'O, well,' his wife said to him, 'leave your boat in the harbour and do that.'

He left his boat in the harbour and went to confession that evening and to communion the following day. And when he came home, they set sail with the load of turf and several boats had sailed eastwards ahead of them. When they were in Galway Bay, night fell and it became dark and foggy and dull and the night was as murky as the bottom of a pot and you would not know where to look.

'Take the fishing line down below deck,' said the uncle, 'and measure the depth under the boat. Is there much water under it?'

Well into the night, he took down the fishing line and threw out the sinker to the bottom of the sea and measured it and the spot was eight fathoms deep. After a while, he told him to test it again and he did so, and it was eight fathoms. And after another while he said, 'Test it again,' and it was eight fathoms. 'I don't know where in Galway Bay we could be except in the sound of An Spidéal, because there is nowhere else in the mouth of An Spidéal that can retain that depth so constantly except the sound of An Spidéal.'

They were sailing inwards until they were at three fathoms. They sailed until they reached a fathom and a half, and at this point they didn't have much water to spare. I heard my father, when he went to the bow to lower the jib below the boat and he heard the lapping of the water on the rocks. As they were heading out, afraid the boat would break on the rock, the light on the quay in An Spidéal lit up. They thought there was nowhere east of Galway that they couldn't see. You could take your bearings by the light at the top of the quay. He didn't have a chance to lower the jib sails at the bow – they were at the entrance to the quay – but he threw off the mainsail and continued to fumble somehow with the jib sails because they didn't have much time. It was very convenient for them, that spot. They came to the quay and there was a boat there and the crew were asleep so he woke them. My father's uncle said to him, 'This is Beairtlí Caonach's boat that was ahead of us and he must have gone out and lit a fire on the quayside as a signal to us.' But it was, in fact, a boat from Maínis.

'Did any boat come here since nightfall?' said the old man to the man from Maínis.

'No,' he said, 'ours is the only boat there.'

'Did you see any light?'

'No, because we have been asleep.'

The old man and my father went on to the quay in An Spidéal. It is a large, long, very high quay and they went from the lower part to the highest part, up the steps, everywhere you could think of. They searched here and there, to see if they could find anything that resembled a fire or something, but they could see nothing. Well, as sure as I am telling you this story, it was the Virgin Mary lit the light that night providing light to this fellow to guide him to the quay.

Another instance of help

Well, the apparition he had that night, it was a significant one. On another occasion, they were sailing from An Bheirtreach Bhuí with a load of turf, travelling eastwards, and they had gone as far as Oileán Lachan, off the coast of Maínis, when my father went up to release the sails onto the boat so that he could turn the boat around. A man appeared on the deck, but my father didn't see the man. The man put his two hands on my father's chest and the man pushed him back; and my father released the sails nevertheless, and on his return: 'I won't manage this boat any longer for you,' my father said to the uncle.

'What would you have me do?' said the uncle.

'I am asking you to turn her back around again,' he said.

The uncle was a man of few words, a sensible man and no one ever gave him advice that he didn't follow. 'All right,' he said, 'I won't go against you.'

They turned her around and as they were approaching a place called Bealach na Srathrach they saw the Roundstone boats on their way to Galway. They saw them stripped to the mast without cover, and the sails blown away to sea and the storm was increasing – higher than a hill – and the waves as high as the sails. 'Ah! You rogue!' said the old man to my father. 'See if you can take down the sails to protect them, to tie them!'

My father went and began to take down the sails and they had nowhere to go where they could survive, they thought, apart from Cuan na hAirde, to the east in a place they call Faoi Tigh Shiobháin. It is located between Maínis and An Aird Thoir. And when the swell came and hit the boat, my father had tied up all the sails, except the boom and the gaff and there was a mighty gale, so strong that it hit the spars of the boat that had no cloth on them. The gale blew water on three or four sods of the mounds that were above board, it had blown so high, and the seaweed was spread on the turf.[11] At that time, they always spread seaweed on the turf so that people's feet wouldn't destroy the turf and they thought that they were also protecting the turf to some extent from the rain. I heard my father say there was seaweed on the rick of turf for a long time because of rain and bad weather, and it was as wet as seaweed you would gather on the seashore. Nevertheless, when the gale hit the boat, it carried off the wet seaweed as if it were burnt paper! They continued until they reached Tigh Shiobháin and came to anchor there. Some of the other boats arrived and others went astray. Weren't they given great help that time as well? If they had gone ahead that day – if it weren't for the guidance my father received at Oileán Lachan – if they had gone ahead, neither of them would ever be seen again.

Well, when I grew up alongside my father – I was the eldest in the family and there were eight of us – but when they began to be able to fend for themselves I tried to earn a living, just as my father did, bringing money home as well, to help my father rear the rest of them. And the first place I went to earn a living was to Roundstone, mackerel fishing. And we made a great deal of money whenever we got the weather. One night I was out fishing, and I was to receive fifteen pounds for the night and let me tell you it was Sunday morning by the time we had cleaned the nets and I drank my fill in Roundstone that day. My father came on Sunday and collected me, and I brought my father to the pub and we went in and drank our fill and sang and had fun.

And I went from there, when autumn came, to Galway to fish herring because it was the law then, do you understand, any boat that was fishing mackerel, when the autumn came she would go to Galway as well for the herring season.

I was fishing in Roundstone one night and we went to sea. It was a calm night and there was no wind. And we set our nets and at the end of the night there was a watchman who would wake you, at the right time to get up to begin drawing in your nets, and the man woke us, he told us that there were so many dogfish and that it was a wonderful sight.[12] We settled ourselves, put on our clothes and began drawing in the nets and indeed there were several of them in the nets. And when we were sailing in to land, the man in charge of the boat told me to see to helming the boat, that he would go to sleep. I took charge of the boat and another lad stayed up with me, because if you had been on a night-spree you couldn't be sure that you wouldn't fall asleep if you didn't have a watchman, because it was very dangerous for people to be asleep on a boat. If everyone in her fell asleep, it was a very bad thing at sea, between the waves and shoals.

I was in charge of the boat and as I came into Sceirdí, I looked into the cabin and saw the man who had stayed up with me about to fall asleep. 'Oh damn it!' I said, 'get up and mind you don't fall asleep, for fear I might feel in any way sleepy. Put on a tin can of tea and the fire!'

He began preparing the tea at any rate and through the talk I heard a shot outside. But I didn't pay any heed to it. We often heard a '*rath*-bounce'[13] of great noise at sea, and I came in.

When we were going in to Cruach na Caoile, the boatman came up when the tea was made. 'You have spent long enough there now,' he said to me, 'so go to sleep for a while.' Of course, I couldn't wait to get some sleep and I did so. And when the anchor was thrown out on the way in to Roundstone the chain made a fine noise, but if it did itself, it didn't wake Colm! Colm never heard it!

But when I had been asleep for a long time one of the lads came to me in a little boat and shouted to wake me and he said, 'Get up, you rogue! Tommany has drowned!' Well! The most unfortunate thing anyone ever did to a man was to give him bad news while he slept. It is a very bad thing. Because I was half asleep when he gave the bad news, I spent a long time when I had no idea what I was doing, but I went above deck and looked in towards the quay and I have rarely seen such a large crowd of people. The reason for the crowd of people on the quay was that a long boat had come in and one of the fishermen who was out in a small boat said that he himself had seen this boat coming up alongside the boat that sank – Tommany Thomáis Hughie's boat from An Aird Thoir – and he and his two sons and his relations drowned, God between us and all harm.

A man who had seen it from the other boat said that this boat came alongside and he thought that what was thrown in was like a small barrel containing ammunition, but I believe he wasn't entirely sure what it was. Whatever it was, the boat sank; and the boat was torn asunder, and it was after the Great War, before this war.[14] Everyone thought at the time that the Germans had come and done this, whether this is true or not. The lighthouse keeper on An tOileán Iathrach (Aran)[15] said that he had seen the crowd of people going out to the forefront of the boat, and had seen the boat explode and sink.

In any event, we were so disheartened that time, because of the danger that arose for all the boats, that no boat ventured out afterwards. But when everything had passed and they went out again searching, there wasn't a mackerel to be had. For whatever reason, there were no mackerel and they have never been fished since, and the boats were broken up and they fell apart in the creeks and nothing was done. There have been no mackerel since, and I don't know why but it could be because of the great damage; because I heard the old people say long ago, there was no better harbour in the world for herring than Cuan na Beirtrí Buí, and the old people made their own nets, you know, and they used to catch very large quantities of fish and herring.

But herring is a very sensitive fish. There was a woman in Leitir a hArd long ago and she was due to marry. She thought that her man had a mind to marry her, and he told her to come to Roundstone and that they would marry there, and that even he was to get money there.[16] And what did he do only take the woman in a small boat. The woman's name was Bríd Bairéad. And beyond Inis Srathair, somewhere in a deep hole there, he drowned the woman. And when he came ashore in Roundstone, he and the man who accompanied him, wasn't she a bright, clever woman, the woman at the pub there, when they went in to have a drink she said, 'There is a man who has committed murder, certainly,' said the woman of the house. I believe she saw it from his appearance.

But since that day and since that happened, it is very hard to find herring around here; you might sometimes catch fifty, sometimes twenty, and on plenty of other occasions you would catch none. And the old people used to say that it was because of the harm that was done, the harbour was left to the fish at that time.

To Scotland

When the fishing failed then, nothing would do me but to head for Scotland because several of my relations had gone to Scotland and had great time for it. And I went to Scotland; my brother was there as well, and I received a great welcome. I would go out in the evening after supper and everyone would bring me in, and every man bought a drink for Colm. And, I am telling you that I was able to drink a good number of them, if the porter was going very cheap.

Things were fine. 'You came to a bad place!' some of them said, 'there is not a stroke of work available here!'

There were a few old navvies there and they said there were no jobs to be had in Scotland, apart from a job that was in Cloigeann Dóran,[17] 'but even if there is,' they said, 'no man can stand that; the work is too heavy. I see many people going there and they have a high opinion of themselves and some of them work for an hour and some half an hour; and some of them are not able to do a stroke there and they pretend they can.'

When I went to my landlady that evening, I asked her, 'What kind of place is Cloigeann Dóran?'

'Oh damn it!' she said, 'stay clear of Cloigeann Dóran,' she said, 'don't have anything to do with it! It is terrible.'

'Indeed,' I said, 'there is no other job to be had and wake me tomorrow morning at six o'clock so I can find out what kind of place Cloigeann Dóran is.'[18]

The next morning I simply caught the train and travelled as far as Cloigeann Dóran and we arrived there, me and nine others; and we made our way and the day was somewhat cold and there was some light rain but even so, none of the men who were working there wore a hat or a cap. We saw steam rising from the men which was the result of sweating and they were saying to one another that this place was where you got nothing for nothing!

I stood up beside a small bothy there, that's what they called the place where they had their dinner and they had a small fire inside; I stood up beside it and I had put on a bad suit, old shoes that had concrete on them – cement – and bad old clothes because it wouldn't show the people over there that you were a workman if you went looking for work in your Sunday suit. They would ask you, the gaffer would ask you if you were looking for his job if he saw you coming in a good suit of clothes. But he saw me dressed for work and asked me if I was looking for work and I said I was. 'Well, in that case,' he said, 'I have a place for you, but I don't have a place for anyone else.' You'd think I would prefer above anything else if one of the men along with me could start so that we would be company for each other, some of the day. That was not how it was and I worked away.

I'm telling you, if I did, it was hard work; we were working with coal, pulling coal out of train wagons at first and putting it into bags and loading it onto a big car. And there was a big horse there to draw that down to wooden quays. Sixty bags went on every one of those carts and drawing it down to a pleasure boat for the amusement of the gentry. And there were shifts and a shift involved preparing three boats and you would get sixteen shillings.

But at night, at the end of my day, there was nothing left for me to do but to put my fingers up to catch my shirt, trying to pull my shirt out of the holes made in my shoulders and I could see the blood on my shoulders. But I said I didn't mind. I had nothing heavy or warm that time and I was strong without a doubt. I came home, and I was going up the stairs in my lodging house – I had to climb several flights of stairs, around four or five storeys – and I hated that more than anything else, trying to go from flight to flight. My legs were so tired that in the end I had to catch the bottom of my trousers trying to lift my feet to go up the stairs.

And all the same, when I came in the landlady said, 'Well, I think you came here to die.' But that was all right and I was working away there until the job was almost finished. To shorten my tale, when a boat came in late in the day and this Johnston person said that it needed coal and these old navvies, they were 'well up', they were there longer than I was. I said nothing. If they got a shift out of it, they said they would do it, a shift was three boats, but if they didn't get a shift out of it they wouldn't do it. And he said they wouldn't.

'Well,' he said, 'I don't expect to let you go. Go to work because the job will only last another three days.'

'If that's the case,' I said, 'God help me!' I realised that I was a man on the road looking for another job.

But when I went east to Dumbarton that night and met my own mates I asked them if there was any chance of work anywhere and a man who is related to me said that there was a chance in Barney's yard; that a man was about to leave work the following day and that there would be a place for me. I went along the following day and didn't bother with the three days in the other place. I went in and a man from Donegal, Barney Boyle, was there and he was certainly a kind man. And I asked him if there was any chance of a start and he said there was.

'Come in tomorrow,' he said, 'if you have books.'

I went in the following day and I was working there. I hadn't worked very long with him when he began to value me greatly and another man from Donegal, a man called Paddy Harkin. We were working away, and in the end he trusted us completely. He felt that we were working diligently because we wanted anything we did to look well. (You are taking care of yourself when you are being a friend to yourself.) In the end – I wasn't happy with the pay. I was counting on the money so I went off to Clydebank to another job where I had a mate, who was punching plates for a vessel. As he and his men had been let go the week before that and he blamed the men for it he got this new squad. But to shorten the tale, we went along with him and we had only worked a day there when we were let go as well. The man wasn't able to do the business, the man who was in charge of the machine for punching; the word they have in English for the tool is 'punch'. But we got 'the sack' this evening and we came back again, and I was too afraid to tell my landlady what had happened to me, because I thought she would kill me. But after a while, I had to tell her.

But we got eighteen shillings for the day and I was out on the road then the next day not knowing what to do, but I watched the people who were coming out of Mac Mullen's yard to see if I might have a chance; because there were relations of mine there and a man they called 'Seán na Corann', he was an assured person. I asked him if he had any influence to get me a start and he said he would do his best. He and I drank the eighteen shillings together; it didn't take us long! And we went in to look for the job and in the end we were turned away. I went off and went to my own job because I was drunk and didn't care. And I was walking among the people and there was a thousand men there, and you wouldn't be noticed going among them, but I was too ashamed to go to my own man, I thought, because he was paying people off from the job – the job was almost finished.

However, he saw me, I don't know how, and he approached me and asked me what happened to me.

'Oh,' I said, 'I was unlucky. I took my books and my money here the other day in order to go home as I was asked to go home and I met some relatives on the street and we went for a drink and the money I would have brought home, I drank that money; and now I am like a one-year-old colt, with nothing at all, and as badly off as ever.'

'Ó Caodháin,' he said, 'I was asking round about you because I missed you. And I was given a reliable report about where you went. But why didn't you have the courage to come to me the following day?'

'Oh, thank you very much,' I said.

'Well, come in in the morning,' he said, 'at any rate. I have let many men go since then,' he said, 'but nonetheless,' he said, 'as long as I am alive and you stay with me, you will have a job. I am about to set up a job now,' he said, 'in Glasgow, when I have finished this job, and don't bother about home, or make any other plan. Stay with me and you will have a job for life.'

Well, that was fine. I was very grateful to him and we were working together until I got word from home to come for the spring and I told my brother to go and to let me stay; and he said if I had any regard for home to go there, but I think it was time for me to head home anyway. I came home and did the spring sowing; and what happened during that time, only the coal strike! There was no good fortune over there after that.

The first chance I got, however, I went over again and the effect that the coal strike had, it had caused havoc everywhere. I was a long time looking for a job and there was no job to be had. I came home again, and I am working the fields now and doing a day's fishing at sea and saving my hay and sowing my potatoes and the odd time I meet Séamus Ennis. And it's not just because I say it, and don't think I'm praising him just because he is present – I'm not! I am someone who speaks the truth just as it is, I don't care who is listening to me. He is the easiest company I have ever encountered. I have tested the mettle of many young people and I frequently had to instruct them to 'do this and do that' while they may have been fumbling. But this young man doesn't hesitate, and he does the business immediately.

Well then, this land in Glinsce, everyone has their own field, you know. And that land was not divided up or managed. You might have a field here and a field there. But the Congested Board came then,[19] and they divided the land and they gave everyone their own share.[20] And that said, they didn't do the fairest exchange. The big man was always big. There was something about the appearance of the poor man, that he didn't get his just rights.

There was an engineer from the Land Commission who came, a man called O'Grady, and he was an honest, intelligent, nice man who would treat everyone fairly. He died since, of heart trouble. God have mercy on him! But he asked me if I were to vacate the old house where we were living, as he believed I was too near another man's boundary, that he would give me a good grant to build a house. And I asked him what the grant was, and he said he would give me one hundred and forty pounds. I said it to my father that evening.

'Oh,' my father said, 'it's not a good thing for you,' he said, 'when you think of all the hardship you have had breaking stones since the day you were able to do so, and that now, just as you are finished with the work, that you should start it again.'

I said as much to O'Grady the following day.

'Well,' said O'Grady, 'I will give you a hundred and sixty pounds.'

And when I said this to my father: 'Bydad,' he said, 'that's a lot of money. You'd better go ahead with it, because we have spent long enough in this old place anyway.' And I went ahead, and I built this house myself.

I am a person who got no schooling and who has learned no English and I was able to build the house, thanks be to God. I had never put a slate roof[21] on a house when I was building it and I began to think it through, to consider it and to work it out in my head what I should do. At night, when there was nothing else bothering me, I would take down my cardboard, get my scissors, begin to draw wedges and cut them and put them together. But thanks be to God, I immediately saw a way of putting on the slates and I put them on and built the house.

I continued building houses then. I worked near Bun na gCnoc, up at Recess, Seanadh Chaola and Maínis, and Inis Ní, An Caiseal, building houses until most of the houses were built and there were no more to build. But I have become so old now, I believe if I were asked to build a house, that I wouldn't be able to oblige because of all I have to do at home. I left marriage too late in life and the children won't be able to give me any help until I am a crock.[22]

There is a place here, Mám Éan, that Saint Patrick left when he was blessing Ireland, he left a fine well at the gap of Mám Éan and he left the bed, the image of a bed, cut into it like a *chaise longue* into the side of the cliff. And people who are seeking a cure, they sleep in that bed at night and the following morning, at daybreak, it is almost like the sound of workmen on the road and hammers on the go, the noise you would hear as they hammer the bed taking pieces from the bed and bringing them home for the cure. They have hammered the bed so much that the bed is all broken now. And I was there because there was no occasion of fun that I wouldn't want to attend, or anywhere like this. There was a lot of *poitín* there and lots of singing at night. I was singing until morning and in the morning, after I had done my pilgrimage, I was singing as I was coming down and my mother was with me. And two women from Iorras Mór – two fine, young, pretty women – came down after me and they came either side of me and they put an arm around my neck. And they told me I was to come along with them! But, unfortunately, they seized their opportunity and I headed off with them. I didn't stop until I went on the train at Recess with them, and then I went from there to Baile na hInse and I walked from Baile na hInse into Inis Ní. I came back in my little canvas curach in the evening and I was very tired. I'm telling you I didn't admit to them at home that I was tired because they wouldn't have much sympathy for me.

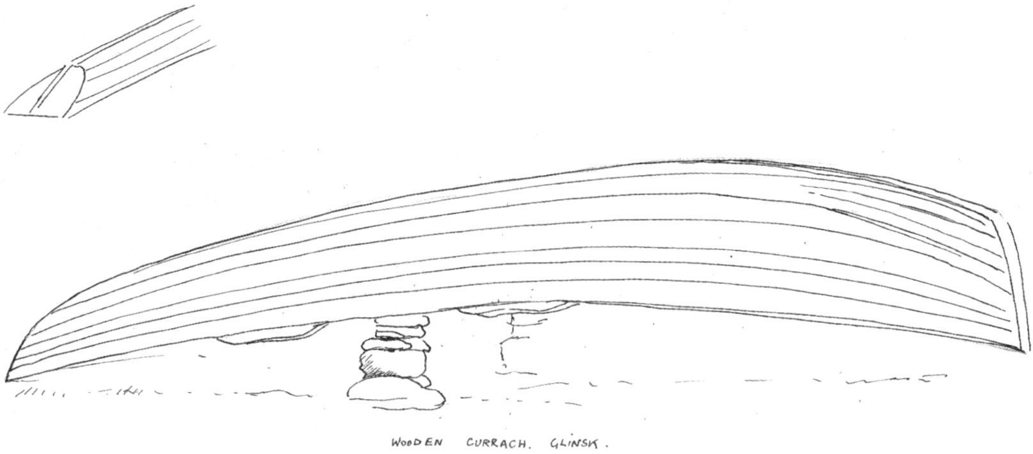

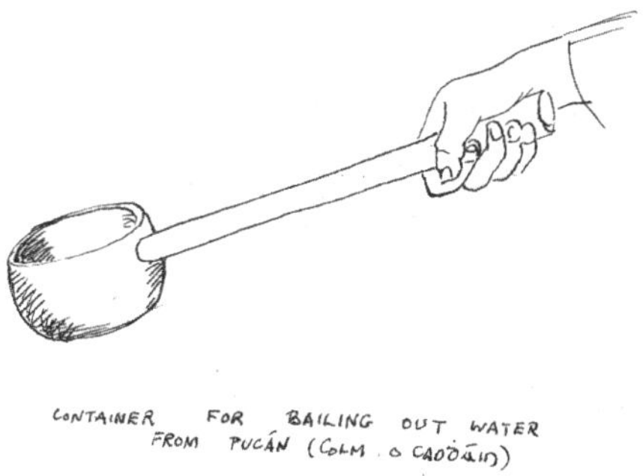

Fig. 6: Wooden *curach*, Glinsce, and Colm's container for bailing out water. Drawings by Simon Coleman, 1959.
COURTESY NFC

People talk a lot now about lore and songs and everyone says that he is correct and some are saying that they aren't correct. I am sure, however, of what I am saying. I never heard among the people here, and I heard my father say the same thing, and I heard every one of the old people saying that the man from Glinsce was always … the man who was the best, when all was said and done. He was the best, he never came across a person anywhere that the man from Glinsce was not his equal for songs, fun and sport. The Caodháin family (my father was called 'Boatman Caodháin' because he was a boatman). At that time, I was around and immersed in picking up songs and I used to sing and my father guided me; and he wouldn't leave me for long if I made any mistake that he wouldn't say it to me. He wouldn't care if there were a thousand men listening to him but if he saw me go astray in the song – I often had drink taken when I was singing and he would announce that I was wrong there. Because if you have taken a lot of drink when you are singing it is very easy to make a mistake.

There was another man who was his cousin here whom they called Pádraig na Corann. The reason he was called Pádraig na Corann was because he was living inside on a rounded hill that the tide used to encircle.[23] And there was another man beside him in Glinsce, who was called Tomás Ó Uaithnín and there was another man there, my father's father, Tomás Ó Caodháin. Well, there wasn't anyone better than Tomás Ó Caodháin to be found anywhere who was a better singer. They used to think that Tomás Ó Uaithnín was the better singer and some of the old people would say, 'Oh damn it! How can you say that Ó Uaithnín is better?' Of course, I never drank to Ó Uaithnín. But I wasn't like that with Ó Caodháin, I often drank to him, and more than once!

Well, my grandmother then was the same way. She had so much lore that it was endless. She was my father's stepmother,[24] and if I knew it would ever come about that I would want to talk of all this, I would have a thousand times more lore. I only had some of it. I forgot it; I thought I wouldn't need it, but if I had any inkling that I would meet Séamus Ennis (or this old man,[25] and that I would put words into its belly with a pitchfork), I am telling you I would have lore to give it as well. In my youth, I didn't see anything other than bags of periwinkles, old twigs and old apples.

Fig. 7: Colm with his sisters Nóra (left) and Neansaí (right), Glinsce, Carna, County Galway, 1974. COURTESY MARGARET CLOHERTY

There was a man around here some time ago who was called Peaitsín Mháirtín Shéamuis and no one could compare to his singing. (Please excuse that as this child had a pitchfork and was about to puncture me!)[26] This Peaitsín Mháirtín Shéamuis spent a great deal of his time over in America and he had so many songs and was so well liked in America that the leader of the band wanted him to be with the band during the day. But he came to Ireland, and the poor devil, he somehow became impoverished so that he was going from house to house in the end. But he was in the house of a cousin of my father's this night and, because he had good songs and the lads knew he had them and the poor man had a cold and was hoarse, the lads came in. And they knew he wasn't able to sing any song, but despite that, they wanted to get a song from him. And what did they do with '*Amhrán Tom Neansa*' ['Tom Neansa's Song'] only start a verse of it, and the verse they sang first was a verse from the middle of the song. And they put the final verse at the beginning.

'Oh, dear God!' he said, when he saw how they were treating the fine song. But when they had spent a long time singing it: 'Oh! shut up!' he said, 'you are unable to put any shape or form on it but however bad I am, I will give it a try.' And he started and began to sing '*Amhrán Tom Neansa*'. I learned it then, from him, because he and I used to make kelp at night.[27] And as we were passing the time at night, we would talk about everything and I learned '*Amhrán Tom Neansa*' from him and I have it ever since then. And now Ennis has it and it won't be long, I think, before you have it yourselves.

> This chapter, describing as it does Colm's life experience, prepares us for the next chapter, where we can listen to some of his songs and stories.

CHAPTER 2

'Some of Them Long and Some Short'[1]

This chapter presents a selection of sound recordings from Colm Ó Caodháin, all of which are included on the accompanying compact disc. They offer an insight into the variety of Colm's repertoire in Irish and English. Songs, tunes and stories illustrate Colm's unique style. Additional information from Colm is indicated in square brackets in the text.

Fig. 8: Colm at his sister Neansaí's house in An Caiseal. COURTESY MARGARET CLOHERTY

1. The Mountain Top[2]

In many parts of Ireland, music for dancing was often provided by *portaireacht bhéil* or lilting, or by whistling. Musical instruments were often not owned by an individual and were shared within a community. Colm was a proficient melodeon player and a lilter. He possibly played 'The Mountain Top' on the melodeon as well as lilting it. Versions of this reel appear in many of the major collections of Irish music, indicating that it was well known and also well documented throughout Ireland.

2. *Bean Pháidín*[3]

Ara, is trua ghéar nach mise, nach mise,
Agus trua ghéar nach mise bean Pháidín!
Trua ghéar nach mise, nach mise,
Is an bhean atá aige bheith caillte!

Óra, rachainnse siar Tóin an Roisín,
Is rachainn aniar Barr an tSáilín;
Rachainn tigh Mhaitiais Uí Chathasaigh,
Mar shúil is go bhfeicinn bean Pháidín.

Trua ghéar …

Ó go mbristear do chosa, do chosa,
Go mbristear do chosa, a bhean Pháidín!
Go mbristear do chosa, do chosa,
Go mbristear do chosa is do chnámha!

Trua ghéar …

Óra rachainn go Gaillimh, go Gaillimh,
Agus rachainn go Gaillimh le Páidín;

Rachainn go Gaillimh, go Gaillimh,
Agus thiocfainn abhaile insan mbád leis.
Trua ghéar …

Ó rachainnse siar ar an gClochán,
Is aniar thrí Bhéal Átha na Báighe,
Bheinn ag breathnú isteach thríd na fuinneogaí,
Mar shúil is go bhfeicinn bean Pháidín.

Trua ghéar …

Fig. 9: *Bean Pháidín*. NFC MUSIC MANUSCRIPTS (MMS) 19

Tosnuigheadh scríobh 18adh Bealtaine 1944 le Colm Ó Caodháin.

Bean Pháidín — (Ráiméis Poirt)

'S nach truagh géar nach mise, nach mise,
Nach truagh géar nach mise bean Pháidín!
Nach truagh géar nach mise, nach mise,
'S a' bhean atá aige bheith caillte!

Rachainn-se siar Cúinn a' Roisín
Is rachainn anuas Bárr a' tSáilín;
Rachainn tigh Mhaitias Mhic Cathasa'
'Súil is go bhfeicinn bean Pháidín.
'S nach truagh géar srl.

Rachainn go Gaillimh, go Gaillimh,
'Gur rachainn go Gaillimh le Páidín;
Rachainn go Gaillimh, go Gaillimh;
'S 'gur thiocfainn abhaile 'sa mbád leis.
'S nach truagh géar srl.

Go mbristear do chosa, do chosa,
Go mbristear do chosa, 'bhean Pháidín!
Go mbristear do chosa, do chosa,
Go mbristear do chosa is do chnáma!
'S nach truagh géar srl.

2. Páidín's Wife

What a great pity, what a great pity it is,
What a great pity I'm not Páidín's wife,
What a great pity I'm not Páidín's wife,
And that his wife is not dead.

I would go to Tóin an Roisín,
And back by Barr an tSáilín;
I'd go to Maitias Ó Cathasaigh's house
Hoping to see Páidín's wife.

What a great pity …

I'd go to Galway, to Galway,
I'd go to Galway with Páidín;
I'd go to Galway, to Galway,
And I'd come home with him in the boat.

What a great pity …

May you break your legs, your legs,
May you break your legs, Páidín's wife,
May you break your legs, your legs,
May you break your legs and your bones!

What a great pity …

I would go to the hillock,
And return by Béal Átha na Bóidhe,
I would look in the windows,
Hoping to see Páidín's wife.[4]

Facing page: Fig. 10: *Bean Pháidín*, written on 18 May 1944. NFC 1281:169

Colm said that his father told him he heard a piper, McDonagh Mór, play the tune 'long ago' and that it was a wonderful experience. Ennis noted in his transcription that the song was *ráiméis poirt* – a 'nonsense tune'.[5] In this recording, the sense of enjoyment comes through when the company joins with the chorus.

Although Colm sings the song in a lighthearted way, as is generally the case, the thrust of the song is about a woman's jealousy and her desire for Páidín's wife to die so that she might take her place. The song is especially associated with Conamara, where it originated, as is evidenced by personal names and placenames. In jig form, it is often played as a piece of instrumental music.

3. *Bríd Thomáis Mhurchadha*[6]

Ó is a Bhríd Thomáis Mhurchadha, molaim thú ar mhná óga
an tsaoil,
Le do mhúinteacht, le do dheiseacht, is go deimhin, le do dhea-,
dhea-méin,
Má shíl tú mé mhealladh le glórtha bog binn do bhéil,
Is rí-mhór tá mo ghean ort ar a bhfaca mé de mhná óga an tsaoil.

Is chuaigh mo 'daddy-sa' go Sasana, is cheannaigh sé gairdín úll;
Chuir sé loing ar an bhfarraige le haghaidh bheith ag déanamh spóirt,
Ach ag filleadh ó Shligeach dúinn, siolla ar bith fháilt den chóir,
Dheamhan a gcónód faoi bhealach, nó go mblaisfead de phóg mo stór.

Is tá gairdín mín milis ag Bideog taobh thall den chuan,
Le go bhfásann úll cumhartha air a baintear faoi dhó sa mbliain;
Tá na ródánaí meala ag na meachain gach áit faoin sliabh,
Is go bhfuil siúcra donn craite ar a mblaiseann mo ghrá den bhia.

Is nach milse póg Bhideog ná uisce Loch Éirne ar fad,
Is ná an chéad scoith den chruithneacht a bheadh fuintí as sú na
mil-mheach,

Óra, a cúilín deas triopálach fite ina thrilseán óir,
An té bheadh gan amharc go ndéanfadh sé soilse dhó.

Cá bhfuil ní ar bith níos deise ná an eala ar an toinn is í ag snámh?
Sin, ó, nó an spideog a bhíonns ag seinmt ar bharr na gcrann?
Ní liachtaí, ó, titim a níonns an t-uisce ná intinn mná,
Nach fear gan aon mhisneach nach rithfeadh naoi n-uaire an cás.

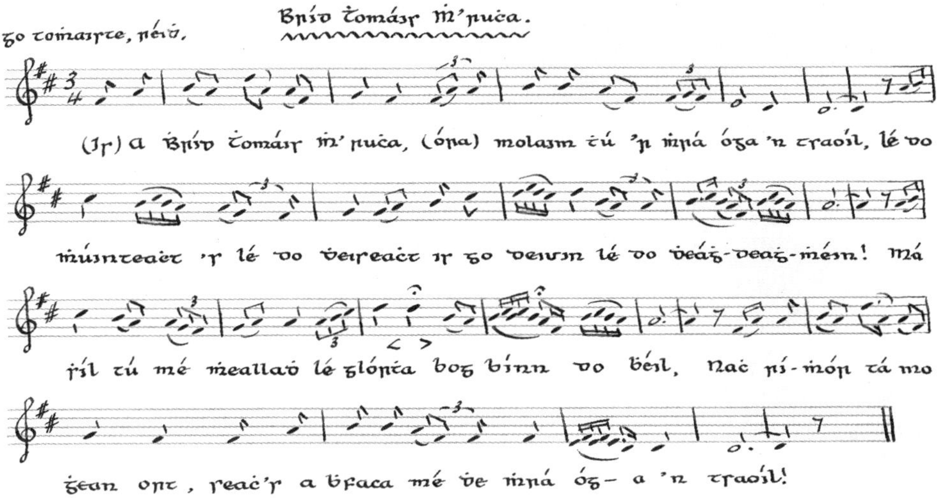

Fig. 11: *Bríd Thomáis Mhurchadha.* NFC MMS 19

3. Bríd Thomáis Mhurchadha

Bríd Thomáis Mhurchadha, I praise you above all young women
 in the world,
Your grace, your beauty, and indeed your good nature,
You thought to entice me with your gentle singing,
I am fonder of you than of all the young women I have seen.

My father went to England, where he bought an apple orchard;
He sent a fleet to sea for amusement,
But returning from Sligo, if there is any draught of a fair wind,
I won't stop along the way until I get a kiss from my darling!

My Bideog has a smooth, sweet garden on the far side of the bay,
Where a fragrant apple grows which is picked twice a year,
The bees have honeyed routes everywhere on the mountain,
And everywhere my beloved tastes food, it has brown sugar
sprinkled on it.

Bideog's kiss is sweeter than all the water of Lough Erne,
Than the best of wheat kneaded with the juice from the
honeybee,
Her lovely keen locks plaited in golden tresses,
She would give brightness to a blind person.

Is there anything in this world more beautiful than the swan as
it swims?
Or the robin singing on treetops?
A woman's mind changes as swiftly as water flows,
Only a cowardly man would not pursue the prize.

> The song is a popular love song and typical of lyrical love songs in Irish in which images from nature praising the beloved feature prominently. In this instance, representations include apples, bees, the swan and the robin. The song expresses a man's love for a young woman, Bríd Thomáis Mhurchadha. Ennis wrote that Bríd Thomáis Mhurchadha was a sister of Colm Ó Caodháin's great-grandfather.

4. Soldier, Soldier, Will You Marry Me Now?[7]

'Soldier, soldier, will you marry me now,
With a hey, with a ho, with the sound of your drum?'
'No, fair maid, I couldn't marry you,
I have no shoes for to put on!'

She ran to the shop as quick as she could run,
With a hey, with a ho, with the sound of a drum.

And she brought him the boots of the very, very best:
'And here my small man, put this on.'

'Soldier, soldier, will you marry me now,
With a hey, with a ho, with the sound of your drum?'
'No fair maid, I couldn't marry you,
I have no jacket for to put on.'

She ran to the shop as quick as she could run,
With a hey, with a ho, with the sound of a drum,
And she brought him a jacket of the very, very best,
'And here my small man, put this on.'

'Soldier, soldier, will you marry me now,
With a hey, with a ho, with the sound of a drum?'
'No, fair maid, I couldn't marry you,
I have no trousers for to put on.'

She ran to the shop as quick as she could run,
With a hey, with a ho, with the sound of a drum.
And she brought him the trousers of the very, very best,
'And here my small man, put this on.'

'Soldier, soldier, will you marry me now,
With a hey, with a ho, with the sound of a drum?'
'No fair maid, I couldn't marry you,
I have no hat for to put on.'

She ran to the shop as quick as she could run,
With a hey, with a ho, with the sound of a drum,
And she brought him the hat of the very, very best.
'And here my small man, put this on.'

'Soldier, soldier, will you marry me now,
With a hey, with a ho, with the sound of a drum?'
'No, fair maid, I couldn't marry you,
I have my own wife at home.'

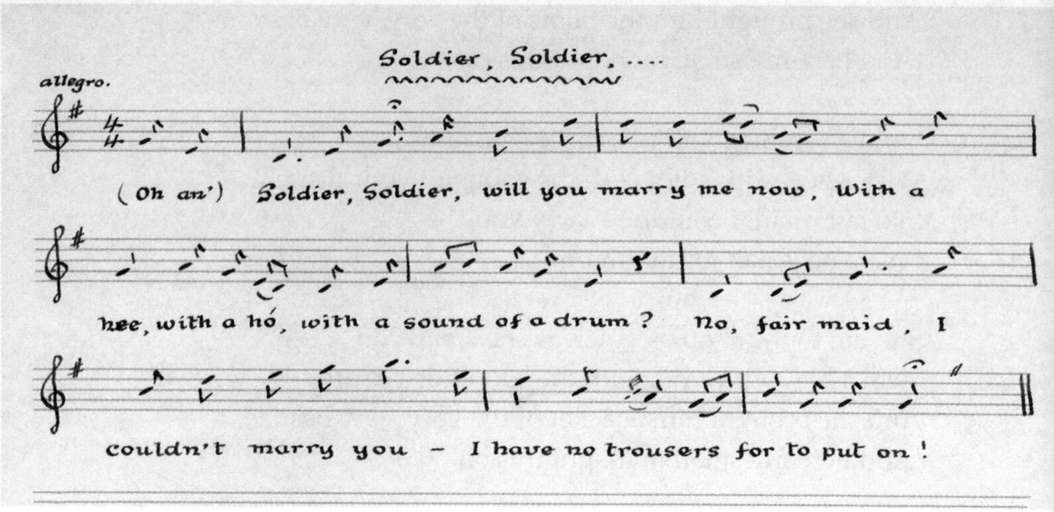

Fig. 12: Soldier, Soldier, Will You Marry Me Now? NFC MMS 19

The song is a conversation between a man and a woman who wishes to marry him. At his request, she buys him boots, a jacket, trousers and a hat only to discover that he is already married. The song has been recorded in Britain, Ireland, the United States of America and Canada. It may well have been sung as a children's song. Alan Lomax collected a version of Colm singing the song in 1951, which was released on the record *The Columbia World Library of Primitive and Folk Music* in 1955.[8]

Facing page: Fig. 13: Soldier, Soldier Will You Marry Me Now? NFC 1281:142

42

Soldier Soldier will you marry me now?

(Féac Claiscreadal: "A Ṡaiġdiúir in a Ċnoí")

Soldier, soldier will you marry me now
With a hee, with a ho, with the sound of ~~your~~ a drum?
No, fair maid, I couldn't marry you —
I have no jacket(e) for to put on!

She ran to the shop as quick as she could run,
With a hee, with a ho, with the sound of a drum,
And she bought him a jacket an the very, very best,
"An' here my small man'(a) put this on"

Soldier, soldier, will you marry me now
With a hee, with a ho, with the sound of ~~your~~ a drum?
No fair maid, I couldn't marry you —
I have no waistcoat(e) for to put on!

And she ran to the shop as quick as she could run,
With a hee, with a ho, with the sound of a drum
An' she bought him the waistcoat and the very, very best,
"An' here my small man (a) put this on"

Soldier, soldier, will you marry me now,
With a hee, with a ho, with the sound of ~~your~~ a drum?
No, fair maid, I couldn't marry you —
I have no trousers for to put on!

5. *Oileán Mhic Dara*[9]

Tá oileán sa gceann thiar den áit seo agus is é an t-ainm é Cruach na Cara – Oileán Mhac Dara – agus tá daoiní ann Lá Fhéile Mhic Dara ag tabhairt turasachaí i bfad agus i ngearr ariamh ón seanreacht. Agus tá oileán eile taobh thiar dhe insa bhfarraige a dtugann siad Cruach na Caoile air. Naomh Caolán a bhí ansin agus bhí beithígh ag Mac Dara agus caoirigh, ach ní raibh aon tarbh ná aon reithe aige agus d'iarr sé ar Naomh Caolán an tarbh a ligean chuig a chuid beithíoch agus an reithe a ligean chuig na caoirigh agus dhiúltaigh an fear thiar é, dúirt sé nach dtabharfadh. Ach le toil Dé, buíochas le Dia, chuaigh an reithe aniar thríd an bhfarraige agus shnámh sé aniar go dtáinig sé isteach insan mbruth. Well, is é an áit é is fiáine a d'fhéadfá cur síos air. Tá an bruth mór geal ag éirí suas an lá is breáichte ar bith, ach mar sin féin, tháinig an reithe aníos as an bhfarraige agus nuair a bhí sé ag baint teannta as a leic le thíocht isteach ar a talamh chuir sé áit a ghlúiní insan leic. Well, is é an t-ainm atá seandaoine a tabhairt ariamh ó shin air 'Léim an Reithe'. Tháinig an tarbh dhá léir aniar agus tháinig sé isteach insan mbruth gar go leor don áit agus is é an t-ainm a thugann siad ar an áit sin 'Spout an Tairbh' agus tháinig siad aníos go dtí beithígh agus go dtí caoirigh Mhac Dara.

Well, tá báid mhóra anois in ann a dhul isteach is amach ins an mbealach idir Cruach na Cara agus an tOileán Máisean, agus tá báid mhóra in ann a dhul idir Maínis agus an tOileán Máisean. Well, sa seanreacht sin ní raibh aon bhlas ann ach dá mbeadh fear scafánta ann bhí sé in ann a dhul de choisméig mhaith thar chaon cheann acu isteach go Cruach na Cara. Agus anois tá sé chomh mór, míleach ar bhealach. Creidim gurb é oibriú na farraige agus an aois, na haimsire, is ciontaí leis.

5. St Mac Dara's Island

There is a small island to the west and it's called Cruach na Cara[10] – *Oileán Mhac Dara* (St Mac Dara's Island) – and people have been visiting from near and far on St Mac Dara's feast day since olden times. And there is another island to the west of it that is called Cruach na Caoile.[11] St Caolán was there[12] and Mac Dara had cattle and sheep, but he had no bull or ram and he asked Saint Caolán to let the bull come to the cattle and the ram to the sheep but he refused, he said he would not allow it. But by the will of God, thanks be to God, the ram went away over the sea and swam until he came to the swell. Well, that is the wildest place you could imagine. The great, white swell erupts there even on the finest day, but nonetheless, the ram came out of the sea, and as he was getting a foothold on the rock to come on to dry land he went on his knees on the rock. Well, the old people have called it 'Léim an Reithe' ('The Ram's Rock') ever since. The bull accordingly came and entered the swell near to the spot and they call that place 'Spout an Tairbh' ('The Bull's Spout') and they came to Mac Dara's cattle and sheep.

Well, the big boats now are able to go in and out on the passage between Cruach na Cara and An tOileán Máisean, and big boats can travel between Maínis and An tOileán Máisean. Well, in olden times it was only possible if there were a vigorous man who was able to go smartly past both of them in to Cruach na Cara. And now, in a way, it is quite enormous. I believe it is the working of the sea and years of weathering have caused it.

> Cruach na Cara (St Mac Dara's Island) is just over 2 km south-west of An Más, near the village of Carna. The annual pilgrimage takes place on 16 July when mass is celebrated on the island at the stone oratory dedicated to Saint Mac Dara, who is reputed to have lived in the sixth century. The oratory, which was originally stone-roofed, is now a national monument and was re-roofed in 1975. The current custom of boats lowering their sails three times in homage to the saint as they visit the island on the saint's day was also observed at least as early as 1684, as recorded by Roderick O'Flaherty in his book *West or H-iar Connaught*. The annual pilgrimage also includes boat races, athletic competitions and music, song and dance.

6. The Keel Row[13]

This fling has been noted in England, Scotland, Ireland, Canada and the United States and takes the various forms of an air, a lament, a listening piece, a fling, a highland, a reel and a strathspey. Although most often associated with Scotland, where it has been linked with Jacobite times in the late seventeenth into the eighteenth centuries, 'The Keel Row' is also strongly connected with Tyneside, in north-east England, where the popular traditional folksong 'Weel May the Keel Row' has been sung to the melody. Here it is:

As I came thro' Sandgate,
thro' Sandgate, thro' Sandgate,
As I came thro' Sandgate,
I heard a lassie sing.
O weel may the keel row,
the keel row, the keel row
O weel may the keel row
That my laddie's in.

The keel refers to the working boat used by the keelmen to transport coal from the banks of the Tyne to the waiting collier ships. The tune has appeared in numerous collections since the eighteenth century including the William Vickers manuscript collection in 1770. Also known as 'The Duke of Northumberland's Favourite', it was printed under that title in 1815 in Nathaniel Gow and Son's publication 'Ancient Curious Collection of Scotland'. Other titles for the Keel Row include 'Jennie's Frolics' and 'The Cat's Got the Measles'. In O'Neill's *Waifs and Strays of Gaelic Melody* the tune is called 'Johnny When You Die'[14] and O'Neill indicates that the version came from the Rice-Walsh manuscripts, a collection of the music of the blind north Kerry fiddle teacher Jeremiah Breen which was given to O'Neill in Chicago by fiddler Paddy Stack. 'The Keel Row' was also published as a *schottische* in the 1870s in *Kerr's First Collection of Merry Melodies for the Violin.*[15] The tune has always been popular with military and marching bands.

7. *Port na Giobóige*[16]

Is é Port na Giobóige é agus is é an t-údar atá leis seanbhean a bhí san áit seo fadó agus bhí beirt mhac aici agus bhíodar an-ghéimiúil, an-chuideachtúil, an-spraoiúil, Tadhg is Dónall, agus bhíodar amuigh sa ngarraí ag stucadh agus ag baint eorna. Agus dúirt fear acu, chuaigh sé amach go ngabhfaidís isteach go dtí an mháthair go ndéanfaidís píosa spraoi. Agus d'fhiafraigh sé dhe cén chaoi agus dúirt sé go ndéanfadh sé fear bréige agus go ndéanfadh sé báinín agus hata agus ghléasfadh sé amach é ar nós fear ar bith di. Agus go ngabhfadh sé isteach agus go n-inseodh sé dhá máthair é go raibh fear a bhí dhá hiarraidh le pósadh.

Ghléasadar suas an stuca eorna chomh maith is d'fhéadadar é agus chuaigh sé isteach sa teach agus dúirt sé leis an máthair, 'Tá fear amuigh sa ngarraí thall do d'iarraidh,' a deir fear acu agus bhí sí ag sníomh lena túirne lín ag an am chéanna. Agus bhreathnaigh sí amach go bhfeicfeadh sí an í an fhírinne í agus chonaic sí an fear agus tháinig an-chroí agus an-mhisneach chuici is dhá mhéid fuaim dhá raibh sí a bhaint as an túirne riamh, bhí sí baint dhá fhuaim as an 'trip' seo, nuair a chonaic sí an fear agus an-spóirt aici ann agus is é deir sí:

'Grá mo chroí-sa,' a deir sí, 'Tadhg agus Dónall, agus an tríú fear eile atá i stuca na heorna.
Grá mo chroí-sa Tadhg is Dónall, agus an tríú fear eile atá i stuca na heorna,
Grá mo chroí-sa Tadhg is Dónall, Tadhg is Dónall agus an tríú fear eile atá i stuca na heorna.'

Fabha da dúdail aidhdil dea, daighdil údail aighdil dum,
Haighdil í údail aighdil údail aighdil údail aighdil um,
Didil í dúdail aighdil dum, didil í dúdail aighdil um,
Didil í dúdail aighdil, dúdail aighdil, údail aighdil um.

Fabha daighdil, údail aighdil, dabh, daighdil údail aighdil,
Dabha, daighdil údail, aighdil údail aighdil um,
Dabha daighdil, údail aighdil, dabh, daighdil údail aighdil,
Abha daighdil údail aighdil údail aighdil údail aighdil um.

'Maise, cén spré a gheobhaidh tusa, a chailleach?' a deir sé.
'Ó maise,' a deir sí, 'gheobhaidh mise pluid agus leaba agus an méid a cheap Dia agam.'

Forúdail …

'Cén spré a gheobhfas d'iníon, a chailleach?' a deir sé. Well, níor mhaith léi caint ar an iníon ar chor ar bith mar cheap sí go mb'fhéidir go mbainfeadh an iníon as cor í féin agus dúirt sí, 'maise,' deir sí, 'ceirt an phota agus dheamhan blas ach sin.'

Fabha …

Didilí údail, aighdil, um, didilí dúdail, aighdil, um,
Didilí údail, aighdil, údail, aighdil, údail aighdil, um. x 2

Well, theastaigh uaidh anois, mar ó Dhia, fios a bheith aige cé mhéad cuta a shníomhfaidís insa ló agus é ag cur a chuile cheist a bhí uathu seo uirthi, go bhfeicfeadh sé céard a gheobhadh sé aisti.
'Cé mhéad cuta a shníomhfá insa ló, a chailleach?' a deir sé.
'Well, anois,' deir sí, 'shníomhfainnse cuta, agus dhá chuta agus dhá chuta déag, dhá dtogróinn é.'

Forúdail …

'Cê mhéad cuta a shníomhfadh d'iníon insa ló a sheanbhean?' a deir sé. Níor mhaith léi anois caint ar an iníon ar chor ar bith le faitíos tada, go gcuirfeadh sé trioblóid uirthi féin.
'A, maise,' a deir sí, 'shníomhfadh sí cuta is dhá chuta is mar sin.'

Fabha …

Fabha …

'Ó, is a phisín a rún cé gcodlóidh tú anocht, cé gcodlóidh tú anocht?' a dúirt an tseanbhean, an dtuigeann tú, nuair a cheap sí gan an fear le bheith aici.

'Óra, cloisfidh do chluais an síodramán suan,
A bheidheas insa leaba seo thuas anocht.'

Fabha ...

Sin é anois é.

Fig. 14: *Port na Giobóige.* NFC MMS 18

7. The Unfortunate Widow's Tune

This is '*Port na Giobóige*' ['The Unfortunate Widow's Tune'][17] and it was made because of an old woman who lived here long ago and she had two sons and they were full of mischief, very friendly and full of fun, Tadhg and Dónall, and they were in the field stooking and reaping corn and one of them said he was going into his mother to have some fun. And he asked how and he said he would make a figure of a man and make a homespun suit and hat and he would create him like any man for her. And he came in and he said to their mother that there was a man out in the field who wanted to marry her.

They dressed up the corn stook as well as they could and he went into the house and he said to his mother, 'There is a man out in the field over there and he is looking for you,' said one of them and she was weaving with her flax loom, and she looked out to see and saw the man and her heart lifted and she got great courage from it. And all the sounds she was getting from the loom before this, she was getting twice as much this time when she saw the man and she enjoyed this very much and said:

'Tadhg and Dónall,' she said, 'are my darlings, and the third man who is in the corn stook.
Tadhg and Dónall are my darlings, and the third man who is in the corn stook.
Tadhg and Dónall are my darlings, and the third man who is in the corn stook.'

Fabha da dúdail aidhdil dea, daighdil údail aighdil dum,
Haighdil í údail aighdil údail aighdil údail aighdil um,
Didil í dúdail aighdil dum, didil í dúdail aighdil um,
Didil í dúdail aighdil, dúdail aighdil, údail aighdil um.

Fabha daighdil, údail aighdil, dabh, daighdil údail aighdil,
Dabha, daighdil údail, aighdil údail aighdil um,
Fabha daighdil, údail aighdil, dabh, daighdil údail aighdil,
Abha daighdil údail aighdil údail aighdil údail aighdil um.[18]

'Well, what dowry will you get, old woman?' he said.
'Oh, indeed,' she said, 'I will get a blanket and a bed and all God ordained for me.'[19]

Forúdail …

'What dowry will your daughter get, old woman?' he said. Well, she didn't want her daughter mentioned because she thought the daughter might take precedence over herself, and she said, 'Well, the pot cloth and nothing else at all.'[20]

Fabha …

Didilí údail, aighdil, um, didilí dúdail, aighdil, um,
Didilí údail, aighdil, údail, aighdil, údail aighdil, um. x 2

Well, he wanted to know then, how many skeins they would weave in a day and he asked all the questions of her that were required, to see what information he would get.
'How many skeins would you weave in a day, old woman?' he said.
'Well, now,' she said, 'I would weave a skein and two skeins and twelve skeins, if I were so inclined.'

Forúdail …

'How many skeins would your daughter weave in a day, old woman?' he said. She didn't want any mention of her daughter at all in case it might cause her trouble. 'Oh indeed,' she said, 'she would weave a skein and maybe two skeins.'

Fabha …

Fabha …

'Oh, dear little kitten where will you sleep tonight?' said the old woman, you understand, when she thought she would not have the man.

'Oh, your ear will hear the slumber talk in this bed above tonight.'

Fabha …

That is it now.

[Chuala mise m'athair agus mo mháthair mhór ag casadh an phoirt seo agus mé i mo leaid beag, tá dhá fhichead bliain ó shin ann. Bhíodh sé ag mórán chuile sheanduine i nGlinsce an t-am sin le píosa dhe a rá nuair a bhídís dallta le poitín le gáirí a bhaint amach. Ach chonaic mé m'athair dhá rá ag banais a bhí anseo tá dhá fhichead bliain ó shin ann agus ní fhaca duine píosa ariamh ab fhearr déanta ná é, leis an ealaíon a bhí ag gabháil leis an bport. D'abraídís go minic é i dteach a mbeadh cruinniú ann le spraoi a dhéanamh agus daoine nach bhfaca déanta cheana é, deirimse leat go mbíodh an-iontas orthub faoi – bheadh éan beo in ann a ghabháil siar ina mbéal le méid is d'osclaídís iad le hiontas agus le rachtaíl gháirí.

An té bheadh ag casadh an phoirt sheasadh sé suas agus bhíodh sé ag aithrist ar a chuile shórt dhá raibh an tseanbhean a déanamh – ag tarraingt an tointe ón bhfiorsaid agus ag casadh an rotha agus dá mbeadh aon chnapóg ar an snátha, ag fliuchadh a mhéarachaí ina bhéal le é shleamhnú anuas agus ag breathnú thríd an bhfuinneoig ag an am chéanna ar an bhfear bréige a bhí amuigh. Shiúladh sé go dtí an fhiorsaid agus ar ais aríst siar uaidh, go léir mar bheadh fad sa tointe ag an bpointe sin.

Chuala mé m'athair a rá, agus go leor nach é, ná raibh aon duine b'fhearr ag casadh 'Poirt na Giobóige' ná Micil Ó Ceannabháin as Leitir Mealláin. Ní fhaca mise ariamh é. Duine é sin de na 'Ceannabháin Bhána' atá i gceist sa ráiméis 'Goirim péin, goirim péin, goirim péin, Goirim péin Micil is Máire' agus a fágadh ag Baibín (iníon) Ghriallais nuair a báthadh a fear; dhá dhílleachtaí a fágadh is iad ina ngasúir.]

[I heard my father and grandmother singing this tune when I was a small lad, forty years ago. Almost all the old people in Glinsce had it then and said some of it to raise a laugh when they were drunk from *poitín*. But I saw my father reciting it at a wedding here twenty years ago and no one ever saw a better composition, there is such art in the tune. They often said it in a house where people were gathered for sport, and people who had never seen it performed previously,

I'm telling you, they marvelled greatly at it – a live bird could enter their mouth as it was wide open with wonder and shouts of laughter.

The person singing it would stand up and he would act out everything the old woman was doing – pulling the thread from the frame, and turning the wheel and if there was a knot in the wool, he would wet his fingers in his mouth to smooth it out and he would look out the window at the same time at the figure of a man outside. He would walk to the spindle and back again as if it had the length of the thread at that point.

I heard my father telling, and others also said it, that no one could beat Micil Ó Ceannabháin from Leitir Mealláin reciting '*Port na Giobóige*'. I never saw him. He was one of the '*Ceannabháin Bhána*' ['Fairhaired Ceannabháins'] mentioned in the rhyme 'I acclaim, I acclaim, I acclaim, I acclaim Micil and Máire' and who was left to Baibín (daughter of) Griallais when her husband drowned; two orphaned children were left.][21]

> The first part of this recording is a historic piece, as it is the first known sound recording of Colm, recorded by Séamus Ennis on an Ediphone machine on 27 July 1945. The recording was transferred from Ediphone to acetate disc on 7 November 1945.[22] Track 7 then proceeds to the 1951 BBC recording, demonstrating the development of sound-recording technology.
>
> The lilting of the nonsense vocables closely resembles the second part of a tune known as 'The Old Concertina Reel'.

8. *An Sceilpín Draighneach*[23]

Ó, agus maidin chiúin dhár éirigh mé amach faoi bhruach na gcoillte,
Táim cinnte gur buaileadh saighead orm mar leigheas is níl le fáil,
Faoi bhruach na Sceilpe Draighní is ea dhearc mé an bhruinneall bhraonach,[24]
Is gheit mo chroí le meidhg di, níor éirigh liom í fháil.

Is nach minic a d'ól mé pionta, ar leathchoróin is sé pighine,
Ach feasta beidh mé críonna mar tá mé óg go leor,
Nach minic mé gabháil timpeall ach ariamh níor fhéad mé inseacht,
Is gurb í do mhéin bhreá chloígh mé, nó dtabharfá dhomsa bó?[25]

Ó, is a stóirín tabhair do lámh dhom, i ngan fhios do do 'father',
Agus aithris do do mháithrín is na háiteachaí a bhfuil tú tinn,
Tá do chúilín soilsiúil fáinneach is tá do bhéilín tanaí tláth-deas,
Más fíor a bhfuil tú a rá liom, leig do láimhín faoi mo cheann.

Ó, a stór nach breá nach scríobhfá go dtí mé cúpla líne,
Cén clúid nó caladh a mbíonn tú faoi dhraíocht nó cén áit?
Tá na torthaí boga ar coillte ann, tá mil ar feadh do radhairc ann,
I ngleanntán bán má théann tú, nach mé an cladhaire nach dtéann ann.

Ó, is a stór go deo ná tréig mé, mar gheall ar bha ná ar chaoirigh,
Is a ghairdeacht is bheidís ag éaló uaim in imeacht bliain nó dhó,
Tá do mhuintir ins gach taobh dhíot, ní fhéadaim comhrá a dhéanamh,
Ach go leanfaí cuntas géar orm dhá dtéinn amach san oíche.

[Ó maise, tréigfidh mise an tír seo sin agus mo mhuintir,
Is rachaidh mé seal insan arm Gallda san áit ar beathaíodh fir mhaithe insan tír,
Ní fhillfidh mé aríst choidhchin nó go labharfaidh an chuach sa ngeimhreadh,
Nó Caisleán Rinne Mhaoile bheith dhá dhéanamh ar bhruach na trá.

Dhá mbeinnse i mo smóilín nach deas mar shiúlfainn ród leat,
Bheinn ag seinm cheoil duit gach maidin chiúin lae bhreá.

Ach i gcinniúint fearabh Éireann, ba tú mo roghain dhá bhféadfainn,
Is gur i mbrollach geal do léine ba mhian liom codladh d'fháil.]

8. The Thorny Little Rock

On a quiet morning I went out to the woods,
A dart was certainly thrown at me and I cannot be cured,
I saw the sorrowful maiden at the edge of the thorny little rock,
And my heart jumped for joy, yet I could not entice her.

I often drank a pint, for half a crown and sixpence,
I will be wise from now on as I am still young!
I have been a long time meandering and could never reveal it,
That your beauty has destroyed me, or would you give me a cow?

My darling, give me your hand, without your father's knowledge,
And tell your mother where you go, where you are distressed,
Your hair is bright and ringleted and your little mouth is soft and pretty,
And if what you tell me is true, put your little hand under my head.

Oh, my darling why don't you write a few lines to me,
To tell me in what nook or harbour you are under a spell?
There are soft fruit in the woods there and honey as far as you can see,
And if you go to a barren valley am I not the rogue that does not follow?

My darling do not abandon me ever for the sake of cattle or sheep,
How quickly they would vanish from me within a year or two,
Your people are on every side of you and I cannot converse,
And there would be a harsh account given of me, if I were to go out at night.

[I will leave my family and home,
To join the foreign army which sustained many of my
countrymen,
I will not return until the cuckoo sings in winter,
And until Renvyle Castle is being built on the shore.[26]

If I were a small thrush, I would go along with you,
I would play music for you every fine calm morning,
Above all, you would be my choice,
And it's on the bright breast of your shirt I would fall asleep.][27]

> The song tells of a young man who falls in love with a beautiful girl as he sets out one morning in the woods. Her beauty defies description and much of the imagery is based in nature. The song is widely sung today.

9. *An Súisín Bán*[28]

Tá mo cheannsa liath is a Dhia cé hiontas dom é?
Mo chairde gaoil atá ag moladh mná liom gan spré,
Mar gheall ar chúpla crupach síofróg mná a bhí gan chéill,
Nach minic a bhain duine slat a bhuailfeadh é féin.

Tá mé ar meisce is a Dhia ní náire dom é,
Ní bheathaíonn briathra na bráithrí bána uilig go léir.
Ach tá mé in do dhiaidh le bliain is gan fáil agam ort féin,
Ach is í an uaigh mo leaba, an bhean, ó sháraigh sí mé.

Is dá mba min í an raithneach shiúlfainn féin é leis na mná,
Mar níl siad leath chomh dona agus bhíonns muid a rá.
Óra duine bocht mise a d'imir is a d'ól mé leob mo sháith,
Nó gur chuireadar an cluiche orm le bogadh an tsúisín bheag bhán.

Óra, threabhfainn is d'fhuirsinn is chuirfinn síol insa gcré,
Agus sheolfainn na ba ar an bpáirc is míne a bhfaigheadh siad féar,

Chuirfinn crú ar an each is áille shiúil an féar,
Agus d'éalódh bean le fear nach ndéanfadh é sin féin.

Is má bhíonn tú liom, bí liom de ló geal is d'oíche,
Má bhíonn tú liom bí liom os coinne lán an tí,
Má bhíonn tú liom is gur liom gach orlach in do chroí.
Mo bhrón go trom ní liom Dé Domhnaigh thú mar mhnaoi.

[Tháinig mé isteach i dteach dhá uair roimh an lá,
Is bhí bean ar meisce ann is a cúilín gruaige fúithi ar lár,
Níor bhreathnaíos fúm ná tharam go híseal ná go hard,
Is gur chuir mé cos lena cois agus gur bhogamar an súisín geal bán.

Thíos i Sligeach a chuir mé eolas ar mo ghrá,
Is thuas i nGaillimh, d'ól mé léithi mo sháith,
Dara brí mo bhaiste: mura ligfidh sibh domsa thar mar atá,
Déanfaidh mise cleas a bhainfeas siúl as na mná.

Ó agus cén cat mara a chas chun na tíre seo mé?
Is a liachtaí cailín deas a d'fhága mé i mo dhéidh,
Tháinig mé isteach i dteach a raibh rún is searc mo chléibhe,
Is chuir an chailleach amach le casadh an tsúgáinín mé.

Is nach iomaí cor is cleas a bhíonns insna (in intinn na) mná,
Cé go sílfeá seal gur leat an croí bheadh ina lár,
Mara mbí tú bríomhar, spreacmhar, neartmhar faoi do lár,
Óra, fan sa mbaile ag bogadh an tsúisín gheal bháin!

Rinne mé cleas tigh Mhac Uí Dhónaill aréir,
Is an darna cleas i dteach an ósta lena thaobh,
Ach an tríú cleas, cén gar dhom tá ag áireamh mo scéil,
Ach go meallfá bean dá gcaithfeá dúthrachta mhaith léi.

Is é sú an ghráinne eorna a tharraingíonns bruíon agus cath,
Agus luach an óil go deo ní bhfaighfidh muid ar ais.
Nó go n-aithrí an chóir is go dté sí an ghaoith ó thuaidh is ó dheas,
Óra is liomsa an phóg go deo na díle agus an bhean.

Is dhá mbeadh spré ag an gcat nach deas a pógfaí a bhéal?
Is an cat nach mbeadh, nach fada ó bhaile a seolfaí é?
Tá iníon na caillí, smearthaí póstaí ó aréir,
Is a liachtaí cailín deas gan fear a phógfadh a béal?

Tá rud go (chomh) deas le cat ar íochtar na mná,
A bhuailfeadh poc ar fhear dhá uair roimh an lá,
Séard a dúirt sí: 'A stóirín, iompaigh liom anall,
Tá muid tuirseach den chodladh ach bogfaimid an súisín geal bán.']

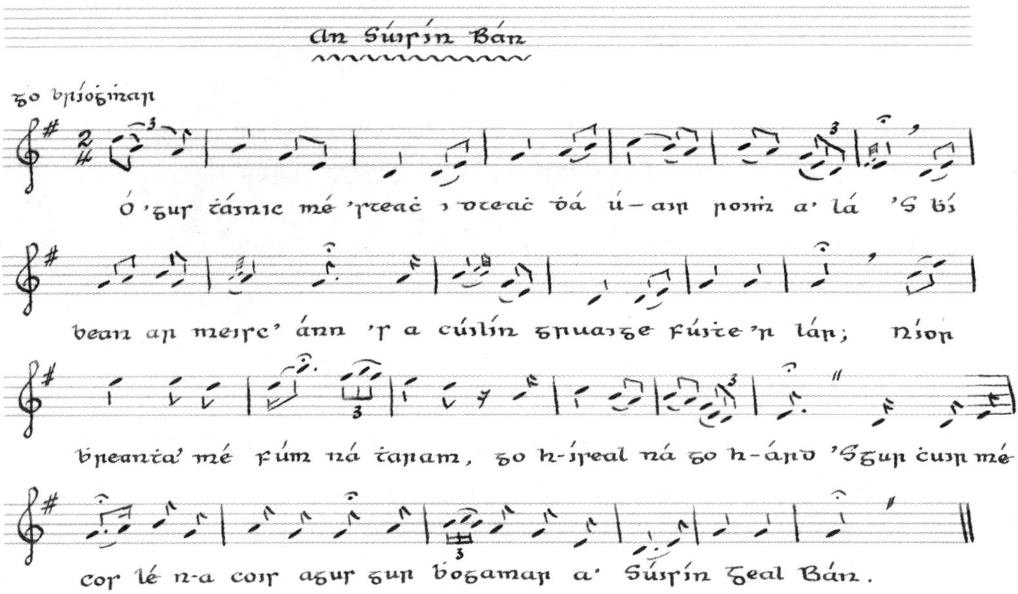

Fig. 15: *An Súisín Bán.* NFC MMS 19

Facing page: Fig. 16: *An Súisín Bán.* NFC 1281:179

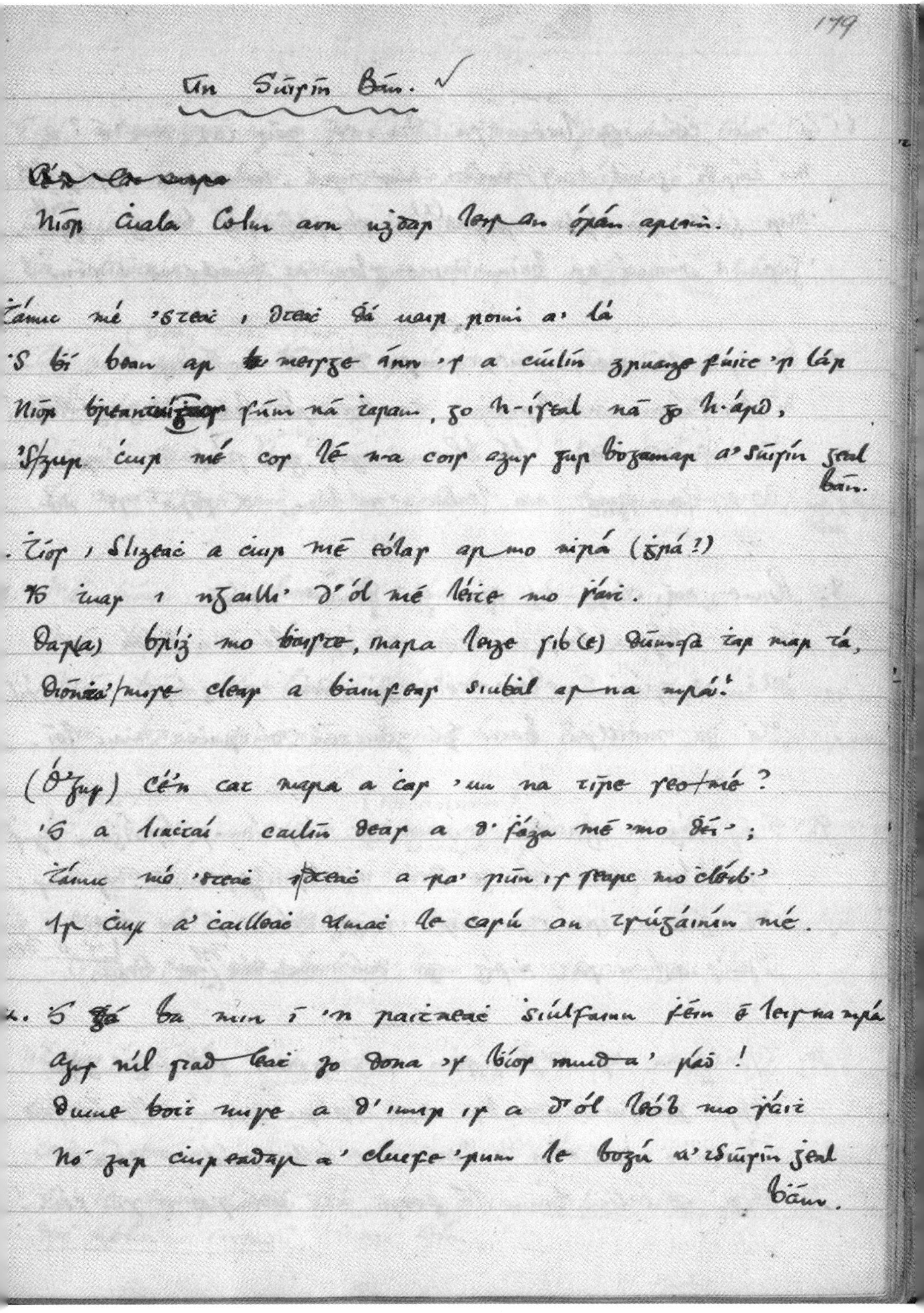
179

An Súisín Bán. ✓

Níor chuala Colm aon ughdar leis an amhrán arís.

Tháinic mé 'steach i dteach dhá uair roimh an lá
'S bhí bean ar meisge ann 'is a cúilín gruaige fúithe 'r lár
Níor [illegible] fúm ná thairis, go h-íseal ná go h-árd,
'S gur chuir mé cos léi na cois agus gur bhogamar a' súisín geal bán.

Thíos i Sligeach a chuir mé eólas ar mo shráid (ghrá?)
'S thíos i nGaillimh d'ól mé léithe mo shá.
Dar(a) bhrígh mo bhaiste, mara leigh sí(e) dúinn-sa thar mar tá,
Dionfaidh/muise clear a bainfeas siubhal ar na sráid!

(Ó gur) Cé'n cat mara a chuir 'un na tíre seo/mé?
'S a liachtaí cailín deas a d'fhága mé 'mo dhéidh;
Tháinic mé 'steach isteach a ra' fúm is seaipe mo chlóca
Is chuir a' chailleach amach le casú an trúgáinín mé.

2. 'S [illegible] ba mhian 'n paiteach siúlfainn féin ó leis na sráid
agus níl fad leat go dona 's bíos mud a' fad!
Duine bocht mise a d'imir is a d'ól leób mo sháith
Nó gur chuireadar a' cluiche orm le bogadh a' tsúisín geal bán.

9. The Little White Blanket

My head is grey, and, God, it is no wonder,
My friends and relatives are recommending dowryless women to me,
Because of a few shrunken, jabbering women[29] who were without sense,
And how often does a person cut a rod that will beat himself?

I am drunk, and God, I am not ashamed,
Words alone do not feed all the friars.
I have been seeking you for a year and cannot entice you,
But my bed is the grave, since the woman has got the better of me.

If the fern were powder, I would walk there with the women,
And they are not half as awkward as we say,
I am a poor person who sported and drank my fill with them,
Until they played a game with me letting out the bright white little blanket.

I would plough, and harrow and sow seed in the earth,
And I would drive the cattle into the smoothest field for grass,
I would shoe the most beautiful horse that ever walked the ground,
And a woman would go away with a man who would not even do that.

If you will be with me, be with me in the bright day and at night,
If you will be with me, be with me in everyone's presence,
If you will be with me, and I have every inch of your heart,
My deep sorrow is that you are not my wife on Sunday.

[I came into a house, two hours before daybreak,
And there was a drunken woman there and her hair was awry,
I didn't look under me or past me, up or down,
Until I put my foot to her foot and we stirred the bright white little blanket.

I met my love in Sligo,
And I drank my fill with her in Galway,
I swear that if you don't leave me be as I am,
I will do something that will disperse the women.

And what mischance brought me here?
I left many a nice girl behind me,
I came into a house where the love of my heart was,
And the old woman put me out by the twisting of the straw rope.

Don't women's minds carry many a twist and trick,
Although you might think sometimes their heart is yours,[30]
If you are not lively, sprightly, strong in constitution,
Stay at home stirring the bright white little blanket.

I played a trick in Ó Dónaill's house last night,
And the second trick in the inn beside it,
But the third trick, what good is it to me who is declaring my
story,
But you would entice a woman should you strive.

The juice of the barley causes rows and fighting,
And we never recover the price of drink,
Until the fair wind changes course and comes from the north and
from the south,
The kiss and the woman are mine until the end of time.

Were the cat to have a dowry, wouldn't his mouth be nicely
kissed?
And the cat without one, wouldn't he be sent far from home?
The woman's daughter is besmirched, married since last night,
And isn't there many a nice girl without a man to kiss her?

Women have something very nice in the lower part of their body,
Which could catch a man out two hours before daybreak,
What she said was: 'Darling, turn around to me,
We are tired of sleeping and let us stir the bright white little
blanket.'][31]

The song '*An Súisín Bán*' was also documented by Séamus Ennis elsewhere in Conamara.[32] On the island of Fínis the song was called '*Sú an Ghráinne Eorna*' ('The Juice of the Barley Grain').[33] Seáinín Choilmín Mac Donncha in Fínis said that an tAthair Dónall Ó Loideáin, a priest from Headford, County Galway, brought the song to Carna.[34] In Donegal, the singer Máire Mhór Nic Pháidín near Gort an Choirce remarked to Ennis that the song '*Casadh an tSúgáin*' was part of the singing tradition. Ennis wrote that the phrase which an older generation in the district used, *ní chuirfeadh muid amach le casadh an tsúgáin thú* (we would not put you out with the twisting of the rope), meant that it was not intended to send someone out of the house as they were welcome to stay.[35] On Tory island, Donegal, Ennis wrote the words of the song from Róise Nic Ruairí who called the song '*Casadh an tSúgáin*' and also '*Taobh Thiar de Shligigh*' ('West of Sligo Town').[36]

Dubhghlas de hÍde (Douglas Hyde, 1860–1949) wrote a play called *Casadh an tSúgáin* which was later translated by Lady Gregory. Performed in the Gaiety Theatre, Dublin, in October 1901, it was the first play in Irish ever publicly staged. In it, a suitor calls to the house of the girl he desires and is asked by the girl's mother to assist with the twisting of hay, and in so doing the rope lengthens and the man finds himself outside, at which point the door is closed.

Séamus Ennis noted that Colm Ó Caodháin never heard an origin for this song. Ennis transcribed the music for this piece '*An Súisín Bán*' from Colm and introduced the staff notation with the words *go bríomhar* or 'in a lively fashion'.

10. *Ceann gan Arann*[37]

[Fear a bhí dhá lua le bean agus bhí athair is máthair na mná ag iarraidh ar an mbean é phósadh, agus níor cheap an bhean óg go raibh sé sách meabhrach is ní raibh sí sásta é phósadh. Thosaigh sí ag déanamh amhráin di féin ansin agus dúirt sí:]

Tá ceann gan arann anois dhá lua liom,
Le naoi n-uaire agus a bhfuil ó Shamhain;
Bhí sé i mo chinniúint gur chuir mé suas dó,
Is gur cuireadh ruaig orm i bhfad ó bhaile.
Ach ar fhilleadh abhaile dhom aríst ar cuairt,
Cuireadh de chluain orm a bheith dhá mhealladh,
Más é sin fortún a gheall Mac Dé dhom,
Go siúlfad Éirinn mura bhfágha mé a mhalairt.

Gheall mo mháithrín a chuile shórt dom,
I dtús an fhuaicht ach a bheith dhá mhealladh,
Gheall sí gé dhom agus mailí bána,
Agus dúirt go mb'fhearr dom an fear a sheasfadh.
Labhair mo 'daddy' liom, de chomhrá chéillí,
Is é go tréithlag ina luí ar a leaba,
Nach deas é a bhuaile is a scata caorach,
Ach cén mhaith in Éirinn bheith geallta don arann?

Is nach mór an truaigh anois, cailín spéiriúil,
A chuir chun tíobhais ar bheagán eallaigh?
Is nach mór an truaigh, ó, na créatúir,
Tá ag iarraidh a ndéirce ó bhaile go baile,
Nach mór an truaigh bean a chaillfeadh,
A fear is a clann agus í bheith ina baintrigh,
Nach mór an truaigh uilig ná an méid sin,
An cailín spéiriúil seo a bheith ag ceann gan arann.

Fig. 17: *Ceann gan Arann.* NFC MMS 18

10. An Unfeeling Suitor

[In this song, a man was reputed to be associated with a woman and the woman's father and mother wanted the woman to marry him and the young woman thought he was not sensitive enough and she was not prepared to marry him. She started composing a song for herself then and she said:][38]

An unfeeling person has been associated with me now,
Nine times since November;
And it was my fortune that I refused him,
And that I was sent far away from home,
But when I returned to visit,

I was tricked into enticing him,
If that is the destiny that the Son of God has destined for me,
I will walk throughout Ireland unless I get an alternative.

My mother promised me everything,
At the start of the cold season, if only I would entice him,
She promised me a goose and white swans,[39]
And said that a man who would last would be better for me,
My father spoke to me, in a sensible fashion,
Although he was lying weak in bed,
He has fine summer pasturage, and a flock of sheep,
And what on earth good is it to be engaged to an unfeeling
   person?

Isn't it a great pity for this beautiful girl,
To be forced into thrift with few cattle?
And isn't it a great pity, to see the poor creatures,
Who are going to beg from village to village,
And isn't the woman who loses her husband and children,
And is left a widow, to be greatly pitied?
And isn't it a greater pity than all of that,
To see this beautiful girl with an unfeeling suitor?[40]

> This song appears to be relatively unusual in the local living tradition, although singer Micheál Ó Cuaig of Aill na Brón, Cill Chiaráin, sings it (2020) and it was released as sung by Seán Chóilín Ó Conaire (1913–91) of Ros Muc on the long-playing record *Seoda Ceoil* (CEF0018) in 1968, re-released on compact disc in 2013 (CEFCD203).x

11. *Neainsín Bhán*[41]

A Neainsín Bháin cé is 'fancy' leat fear eile ná mé féin?
A Neainsín thug mé 'fancy' dhuit i dtosach ar mhná an tsaoil.
Mar shíl mé go mba bhreáichte thú ná bean ar bith fón saol.
Smid chainte ná raibh i gceann an té nach molfadh leatsa mé.

Is an chéad lá d'earrach tóigfidh mé talamh, agus beidh áras agam péin,
Agus séard a dúirt mo mhuintir liom nach bhfuil aon mhaith in mo scéal.
Óra, níl ach a toghadh ar óigmhná an domhain is beidh mo
roghain agam péin,
Ní as cuid ná as maoin a molfar í, ach as a cáilíocht is a dea-mhéin.

Is dá mbeadh tosuithe ar mo bhrógaí is cóir mhaith bheith ar na boinn,
Ó rachainn gach uile Dhomhnach leat san áit a mbeadh an spraoi.
Ní thóigfeadh an t-aos óg orm gach cor dá gcuirfinn dhíom,
Dá mbeadh mo stór ar cheann an stóil agam níorbh fhada liom an oíche.

Ach má théann tú chun an aonaigh, bíodh an chaora agat is an t-uan,
Is má théann tú a déanamh tíobhais, bíodh do mhian agat ar dtús.
Óra, bíodh sí maíorthaí macánta is í moltaí as a cliú,
Is ní barr maoine a chuirfeas chun tíobhais thú, is ná mealltar le sraoill
thú.

Is a tíocht na Nollag nach dona í m'obair a' síorchur insa gcré,
Mar bheadh seabhac ann ar bharr sceichí, ó, nó barr glas na sútha
craobh,
Mo mhallacht go deo anois a bhéarfainnse d'aon fhear beo insa saol,
A thóigfeadh ormsa a bheith a cogarnach le stóirín geal mo chléibh.

Ach a théagairín, dheamhan a féidir dhuit gan duine eicíneacht fháil,
A nífeas do chuid éadaigh, is a fhuinfeas do chuid aráin.
Óra a phéarla atá breá gléigeal, de chích, de chois agus de láimh,
Is nach é mo léan gan mé faoin éadach leat, is cead éid ag fearabh Fáil.

Fig. 18: *Neainsín Bhán.* NFC MMS 19

11. Fair Neainsín

Fair Neainsín, do you prefer another man or myself?
Fair Neainsín, I first took to you before all the women in the world,
Because I thought you were more beautiful than any other woman,
May the person who would not recommend me to you be speechless.

The first day of spring I will find land, and will have my own house,
And my family told me that mine is not a happy tale,
They can choose from all the young women but I will make my own choice,
Her wealth and possessions will not recommend her, but rather her qualities and good appearance.

And if my shoes had uppers and the soles were in good shape,
I would go with you every Sunday to the place where the fun is,
The young people would not blame me for any steps I might take,
And if my darling were seated by me on the stool I wouldn't feel the night passing.

If you go to the fair, bring the sheep and the lamb,
If you are setting up house, have your heart's desire beforehand,
She should be dignified, honest and praised for her renown,
Wealth will not set up a home for you, and do not be tempted by a slattern.[42]

And when Christmas comes, it's not pleasant for me constantly sowing seed,
Like a hawk on top of a bush, or the green top of the raspberry bush,
My curse now forever on any man alive,
Who would blame me for whispering with the darling of my heart.

My darling, you cannot fail to find someone,
Who will wash your clothes or who will knead your bread,
Oh my pearl, who is bright and fine of breast, of foot and of hand,
My great sorrow I am not under the covers with you and let all the men of Ireland be jealous.

> This lyrical love song is typical of the pastoral imagery portrayed in songs of this kind in Irish. In this instance the song tells of the young man expressing his love for Neainsín Bhán, a girl who has all the desirable qualities of character and appearance.

12. *Sail Óg Rua*[43]

Dhá mbeadh a' fhios ag mo mhuintir-sa leath mar bhímse,
San am a smaoiním ar mo Shail Óg rua,
A bhíodh sínte síos liom de ló agus d'oíche,
Is gur idir a dhá chíoch gheala a bhíodh mo lámh.
Ach an am a smaoiním nach bhfaighfidh mé choidhchin í,
Ó, i gcionn mo thí dhom, ná i mo leanbh bán,
Is é fuil mo chroí istigh atá ag tíocht ina braíona,
Agus a Dhia, ní hiontas dom é, i ndiaidh mo ghrá?

Ó is ar Oileán Éidí, is ea d'fhága mé aréir í.
Nach é mo léan is mo mhíle trua.
Is go bhfuil triúr ar aon chéill ag gabháil dhá hiarraidh,
Gan bean a mbréagaithe, faraor, le fáil.
Óra, tá mé tréithlag, is níl gar dhá éileamh,
Agus níl mé ar aon chaoi ach mar an ceo.
Is a ghrá bán, Éireann is tú d'fhág liom péin mé,
Nuair a chuaigh tú i gcré uaim, is tú i do chailín bhreá.

Ó is dhá bpósfainn Máibleoig de chailleach ghránna,
Ní thóigfeadh a lán orm a bheith ag gol ina diaidh.
Ach mo chailín breá, deas, le go dtug mé grá dhi,
Is gan í ach ina páiste nuair a fuair mé í.
Óra, b'fhearr liom go mór, mór i mo dhiaidh insa ród í,
A bleáint na bó dhom nó i gcion mo thí.
Ná saibhreas Sheoirse, is é fháilt ina scórtha,
Is gur faoi na fóidí atá stór mo chroí.

[In aois a sé déag is ea fuair mé féin í,
Is nár dheas an féirín í ag fear le fáil,
Bhí a grua is a héadain a' tíocht le chéile,
Is a leicíní gléigile mar an sneachta bán.
Mo ghrá do bhéilín, nár chum na bréaga
Agus do mhéin deas ná raibh ag fear le fáil,
Do dhá chích gheala le do leana a bhréagadh,
Is a stór dhá bhféadainn é, ní bhfaighfeá bás.]

[Fear ar cuireadh ina leith gur mharaigh sé a bhean agus nuair a tugadh os comhair an bhreithimh é, dúirt sé an t-amhrán agus dúirt an breitheamh ansin nach ndearna sé ariamh aon bhlas uirthi, agus shaor sé é.]

Fig. 19: *Sail Óg Rua.* NFC MMS 19

12. Red-Haired Sail Óg[44]

If my family had any idea of how I am,
When I think of my red-haired Sail Óg,
Who used to lie beside me day and night,
And my hand between her two white breasts,
But when I think I will never have her,
In charge of my house, or as a fair child,
My heart's blood flows in drops,
And my God, little wonder, because of my beloved.

I left her in Islandeady last night,
My great and deep sorrow,
And there are three of one mind who are going to seek her,
And sadly, no woman can be found to refute them.
For I am greatly weakened, there is no use in denying it,
And I am only like the mist at any rate,
And my fair love, dearest in all Ireland, you have left me alone,
When you died when you were a fine girl.

If I married Máibleoig, the ugly old woman,
Many would not blame me for weeping after her,
But my fine, beautiful girl whom I loved,
And she only a child when I got her.
I would far, far prefer her after me on the road,
Milking my cows or in charge of my house,
Than King George's wealth, and to receive it in scores,
And my darling is lying in the clay.

[She was sixteen years of age when I got her,
Wasn't she a lovely present for a man to receive,
Her cheek and her face were matched,
And her bright cheeks like snow.
My love is your little mouth, that never lied,[45]
And your fine looks that a man could not have,
Your two white breasts, to entice your beloved,
And darling if I could have prevented it, you would not die.][46]

[A man was accused of murdering his wife and when he was brought before the judge, he sang the song and the judge then said he had never done anything to harm her and he set him free.][47]

> The song is a lament by a man whose wife, Sail Óg Rua, has died. She was from Oileán Éadaigh [Islandeady], west of Castlebar in County Mayo. The earliest known reference to the song dates from 1824 and appears in a manuscript in the Royal Irish Academy (RIA 23E1, p. 84), where it is stated that John McHugh, Seán Mac Aoidh, from Oileán Éadaigh was accused of murdering his wife Sail Óg, although the reasons given are not clear. The writer says that Mac Aoidh composed the song while he was in prison in Castlebar as he tried to clear his name. The song and associated lore appear to concur with the account, as the narratives recount that Sail Óg Rua's family came to Mac Aoidh's house to kill him, but when they arrived there they heard him sing the song and they left.[48]

13. The Rocks of Bawn[49]

And my curse to you dear Sweeney you have me nearly robbed,
You are sitting by the fireside with your dúidín[50] in your gob,
You are sitting by the fireside from clear daylight til dawn,
And I'm afraid you'll never be able to plough the rocks of bawn.

Arise up lovely Sweeney and come along with me,
To give your horse a field to work, before you start away,
Don't feed her off wood turnips, take her down at yon green lawn,
And then you might be able to plough the rocks of bawn.

And I wish the Queen of England had sent for me in time,
For when I was in humour, in my youth and prime,
I'd fight for Ireland's glory from clear daylight til dawn,
And I'm sure I wouldn't be able to plough the rocks of bawn.

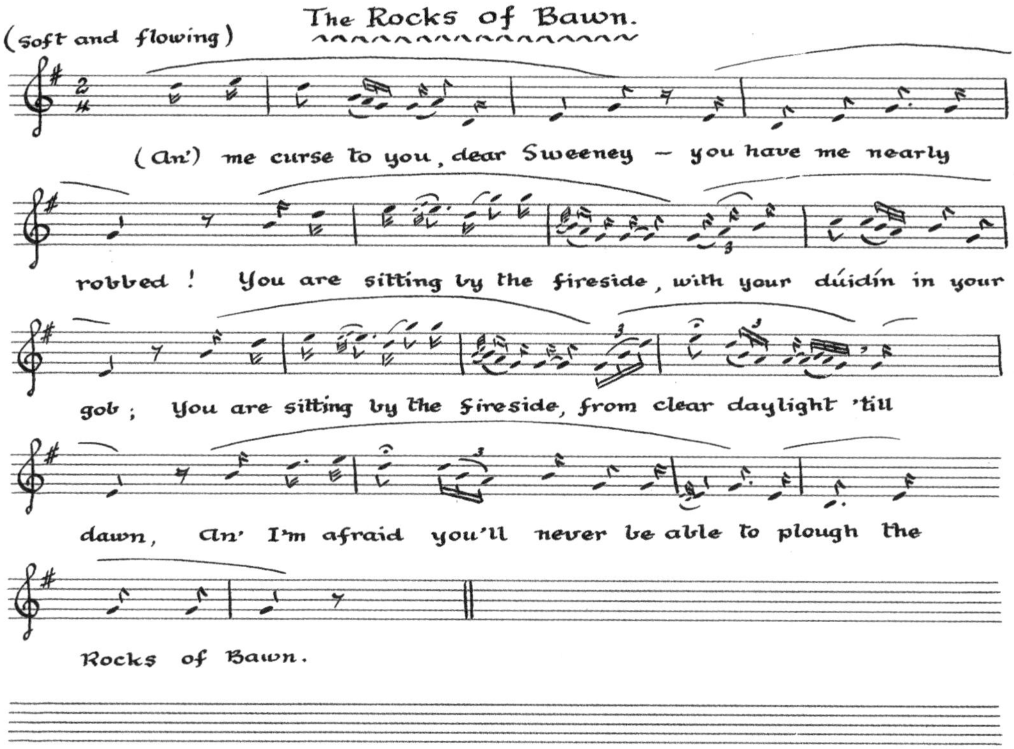

Fig. 20: The Rocks of Bawn. NFC MMS 19

The song was very popular among Conamara singers and was a particular favourite of Seosamh Ó hÉanaí who recorded it on the Topic label released in 1963: *Joe Heaney: Irish traditional songs in Gaelic and English*. The song appears to relate to the driving out of native Irish farmers from their lands during the time of Oliver Cromwell in the seventeenth century. The Clare singer Tom Lenihan believed that the reference to the 'Queen of England' was incorrect and that it was originally 'Patrick Sarsfield'.[51] The song is classified under Roud 3024.[52]

14. Colm's Welcome to Séamus Ennis[53]

I wish that Séamus Ennis would come to me in time,
When I was in humour, in my youth and prime,
I would sing for him the old songs, I would sing them loud and long,
And Colm is the man to sing them when he'd get his humours on.

15. Séamus Ennis' Collecting[54]

The first time I called up to Colm's,
I was welcome as the flowers of May,
He asked me would I come down to the stable,
It wasn't to look at his hay.

There was bags in it filled to the neck up,
Some of them long and some short,
And he opened one of the longest,
And the first thing came out was a song.

> The two compositions, tracks 14 and 15, by Colm reflect his creative talent and his deep engagement with the collecting process and exchange. His sense of fun is exemplified in the songs, their rhythm, the style of singing and his enthusiasm is especially evident in the laughter at the end of the song about Ennis and his visits to Colm.

16. A Competition Between Two Singers[55]

Colm: My grandfather was the best singer you could ever hear. And there was another man in the village called Greene, Tom Greene was his name. And they were about a hundred yards anyways from one another, the two houses, and after their day's work always my grandfather comes in, he stretched back by the fireside, and he used to smoke his pipe and start singing. And when the old fellow abroad heard him singing, when he had the song ready, always himself would start. Both of them was hearing one another and it was about a hundred yards, anyways or more, if I were to say it,[56] from one another.

Séamus Ennis: It was a competition between them all the time?

Colm: It was, they were trying which of them would be the best. There was no end to any of them.

> The tantalisingly brief account above underlines the central role of song and describes a picture of Colm's singing community.

17. Séamus Ennis[57]

Tháinig Séamus Ennis chun mo thí-sa,
Amach san oíche is é faoi dheifir mhór,
Bhí comhra airgid ina lámha míne,
Is bhí sé ag iarraidh é a líonadh le nótaí ceoil.

Thug sé buidéal fuisce dhom agus bhain mé braon as,
Gur fhliuch mé mo chroí leis agus mo scórn',
Agus chuaigh mé ag casadh dhó ar feadh na hoíche,
Agus bhí an comhra líonta agam nuair a bhuail sé an dó.

Nach mór an truagh nach raibh Ennis i nGlinsce,
Nuair a bhí na seandaoine ann agus m'athair beo,
Ag éisteacht le seanamhráin is le poirt bhreá chroíúla,
Bheadh an bás gan daoine agus bheadh chuile fhear beo.

Ach anois a d'fhágadar i dtaobh na n-amhrán,
Nárbh ait an fear mé iad a choinneáil beo,
Is an chuid acu théanns faoin talamh síos, is mór an jab a gcuimhniú,
Lena gcasadh ar phíopaí ná ar aon ghléas ceoil.

17. Séamus Ennis

Séamus Ennis came to my house,
Late at night and he was in a great hurry,
He carried a silver chest in his fine hands,
And he wanted to fill it with notes of music.

He gave me a bottle of whiskey and I took a drop,
To wet my heart and my throat,
And I sang for him all night,
And by two o'clock I had filled the chest for him.

Isn't it a great pity that Ennis wasn't in Glinsce,
When the old people and my father were alive,
Listening to old songs and fine lively tunes,
Death would have no hold and everyone would be alive.

But now the songs that they have left us,
Wasn't I an odd person to keep them alive,
And those that are buried in the ground, it is a difficult job to recall them,
To play them on the pipes or any instrument.

> This song is an example of Colm's talent for songmaking. The song underlines the friendship between singer and collector. The singer felt it was a pity Ennis hadn't been around a few generations earlier when the older people were alive and had more songs. The idea that the living tradition of today cannot be compared to that of the past is still very common among storytellers and singers.

18. *Ciste Mhic Uí Cheallaigh*[58]

[Búsar (Boozer) a bhí ann agus creidim go raibh sé ag caitheamh cuid is mó ná raibh sé ag breith air; agus ansin bhí fear san áit arbh ainm dó Mac Uí Cheallaigh agus bhí sé cruinniú ciste mhóir airgid agus gan é ag caitheamh tada agus d'imigh an t-airgead go dona ar deireadh uaidh. Ach siod amhrán a rinne an Búsar seo.]

Ag éirí dhomsa ar maidin is mé siúl go moch cois leasa,
Tharla orm an ainnir ba háille ar bith gnaoi;
Ó cheap mé riamh nár ceapadh i gceard na naomh a samhail,
Ba cosúil í le aingeal san áit úd ina suí.
Ba caol é a com is a pearsa; bhí dlaofa donn go taltha,
Na réalta bhí dá dearcadh is a grua mar bhláth na gcraobh;
Ach nár mhór an chabhair ar thalamh an té gheitheadh póg ón ainnir,
Go dtóigfeadh sí na mairbh beo as an gcill.

Muise, d'fhiafraigh mé go faiteach, cén cheard arb as an ainnir?
Nó cé na trí ní is gastaí fuair an úchta le roinnt?
Ó páirt as na trí ranna sa gceard lér shíolraigh m'athair,
Ón gcéirseach is ón gCeallach, mo mháithrín ar gach taobh,
Ach is é a hainmse Peige Ní Fhlathartaigh, a chaill a meabhair is a haithne,
Is go gcónaíonn sí i gCnoc Chathail Óig lena saol.

Is nach mór an truaigh buachaill cliste, i dtús a shaoil is a mhisnigh,
Ag súil le bheith gan rath, mar tá mé faraor,
Agus an nós a cheap Dia dhomsa, mo phócaí bheith folamh,
Is go mb'fhearr liom beo insa taltha ná bheith os a chionn.
Mar bhí croí agam lena chaitheamh agus gan slí ar bith lena ghlacadh,
A Chríost nach bocht an galra le gur fhága tú mé.
Ach dhá ba liomsa casfaí ciste Mhic Uí Cheallaigh,
Is daoibhse a mhná an leanna, a thabharfainn é le roinnt.

Muise d'ólfainnse mo scilling le mná deasa na fine,
Ní fearr ná d'imreoinn cluiche ar barr mo chúig méar,
Mar punt ariamh ná scilling ní chuirfinn féin sa gciste,

Ach dá scaoilfinn insan uisce é síos le mo thaobh,
Ach anois ó tá mé ag imeacht is nach bhféadfaidh mé féin filleadh,
Mo chúpla gabhairín bhainne a fhágfas mé i mo dhéidh,
Is mura bhfaighfidh mé suaimhneas feasta ó dhaoine uaisle an ghleanna,
Rachaidh mé anonn thar caladh is ní fhillfidh mé go deo.

Fig. 21: *Ciste Mhic Uí Cheallaigh.* NFC MMS 19

18. Mac Uí Cheallaigh's Treasure

[He was a drinker (boozer) and I believe he was spending more than he earned; and there was a man there who was called Mac Uí Cheallaigh and he was collecting a big store of money and spending nothing and his money went against him in the end. But this is a song the boozer composed for him:][59]

When I got up in the morning and walked early along by the fairy
mound,
I encountered the most beautiful maiden in her appearance;
I didn't ever believe that her like could be found in the world of
saints,
And she was like an angel sitting in that place.
Her waist and form were slim; her brown locks curled to the ground,
Her eyes were like stars and her cheek like the blossom on the
branch,
But it would be a gift for the person who would get a kiss from the
beautiful girl,
And she would resurrect the dead in the graveyard.

I timidly enquired, where did the beautiful maiden come from?
Or what were the three cleverest things the testament had to share?[60]
A part of the three parts where my father's people came from,
From the female blackbird,[61] and from Ó Ceallaigh, my dear
mother on both sides,
But her name is Peige Ní Fhlathartaigh, who lost her mind and
reason,
And she has lived in Cnoc Chathail Óig all her life.

It is a great pity to see a clever lad, at the start of his life's experience,
Expecting to be unfortunate as I am, sadly,
And as God has ordained for me, my pockets are empty,
And I would far rather be alive under the ground, than above it,
Because I had a heart to give away and no way to accept it,
Christ, did you not leave me with a terrible affliction?
But if I had Mac Uí Cheallaigh's treasure,
I would give it to you, women of the alehouse, to share.

I would drink my shilling's worth with the fine women of the group,
No better would I play a game on the tips of my five fingers,
Because I would place neither pound nor shilling in the store,
But would let it into the water down beside me.
Now as I am leaving and am unable to return,
I will leave a few milk goats after me.

If I do not get peace henceforth from the gentry of the valley,
I will depart from the quay and I shall never return.

> The first stanza of the song is similar in form to the *aisling* or vision poetry prominent in Ireland in the eighteenth and nineteenth centuries, especially in Munster. In the *aisling*, the poet meets a woman as he is out walking. Her beauty defies description and frequently a conversation occurs in the poem in which he tries to entice her. In the second part of the song the young man seems to have fallen on hard times and is about to emigrate.

19. *An Bhó Bhán*[62]

[Níl aon údar cloistithe agam don amhrán ach go léir mar dhéanfainn amach, bó í a ceapadh a tugadh as.]

Agus cuirí scéala chuig Féilim go bhfaca mé an bhó bhán
Aréir is mé tíocht ó chuartaíocht, is bean uasal dhá bleán,
Nuair a theann mé faoina tuairim go meallfainn uaithi an bhuarach,
Rinne sí coire guairdill is chuaigh sí isteach san aill.

Is ar thóraíocht na bó báine a chaith mé an oíche aréir,
Dheamhan blas a bhí dhá barr agam ach cnámhannaí a géill.
Gabháil siar ag Leic an Treilseáin, is ea lig sí an ghéim ab airde,
Bhí banríon na hAille Eidhní dhá 'driveáil' go Cnoc Meá.

Is bhí seanbhean insa gclúid ann ag tabhairt diúl don bhuin bháin,
A raibh galún aici is buarach is snaidhm buaice ar a ceann;
Nuair a shíl mé féin í mhúscailt, bhí sramaí ar a súile,
Agus d'fhiafraigh sí go múinte, an é an púca a bhí ann.

Is níor mhór leis an mbuin bháin Oileán Árann di féin,
Iorras Bheag is An Máimín is Gleanntaí Mhám Éan,

Thart thrí Uachtar Ard is i gCois Fharraige bhí a nádúr,
Is i bhfeilm Sheáin ab fhearr léi mar is ann a bhí an féar.

[Thart faoi Uachtar Ard is Cluain Meala le haghaidh clóbhair,
Agus gine d'fhear a seolta le n-ól gach uile lá.]

[Bhí an t-amhrán ag aint a athar, dúirt Colm, agus an méid seo thuas fuair a athair uaithi é. Ba mhinic Colm ag troid lena athair, deir sé, faoi nár thóig sé uilig go léir é uaithi. Níor chuala Colm ariamh a aint ag gabháil fhoinn, ná duine ar bith eile a raibh an bhó bhán aige.

Chreid an tseanmhuintir agus creideann cuide den dream atá suas anois, má dhíolann tú bó ag an aonach, nach ceart an bhuarach a dhíol leis an mbuin. Má thugann tú uait chor ar bith é, ní sheasfaidh an t-ádh ort le beithígh, creideann siad. Deallraíonn sé go raibh an fear seo ag iarraidh an bhuarach fháil den mbuin bháin le faitíos go gclisfeadh an t-ádh air feasta – sin nó bhí sé 'gabháil a mealladh na buaraí ón mnaoi uasail agus an bhó ar a ceann b'fhéidir'! (m'fhoclaí féin) [Séamus Ennis]. *Colm a mhínigh dom.]*

Fig. 22: *An Bhó Bhán.* NFC MMS 19

19. The White Cow

[I haven't heard an origin for the song but as far as I can make it out, it was about a cow they thought was 'taken away' [by the fairies].][63]

Send word to Féilim that I have seen the white cow,
Last night as I came from visiting, and a fairy woman was
milking her,
I approached her to entice the stall-rope from her,
And she turned around suddenly and entered the large rockface.

I spent last night in search of the white cow,
And nothing to show for it but the bones of her jaw.[64]
As I passed by Leic an Treilseáin, she lowed loudly,
The queen of An Aill Eidhneach was driving her to Cnoc Meá.

There was an old woman in the corner feeding the white cow,
She had a gallon and a stall-rope and a knotted halter on her head;
When I went to wake her, she had sleep in her eyes,
And she asked politely was it the *púca* that appeared before her.

The white cow would want the Aran island for herself,
Iorras Bheag, and An Máimín and the valleys of Mám Éan,
Around by Oughterard and Cois Fharraige was her wont,
And she would rather be in Seán's farm because that is where
the grass was.

[Around by Oughterard and Clonmel in search of clover,
And a guinea for the man who drove her for drink every single
day.][65]

Séamus Ennis wrote that Colm said his father's aunt had the song, and his father got the foregoing from her. Colm said that he often disputed with his father that he didn't learn it all from her. Colm never heard his aunt singing the song, nor anyone else who knew 'The White Cow'.

Colm told Ennis that the old people believed, and some of the people around at the time he was speaking believed, if you sell a cow at the fair you should not sell the stall-rope with the cow. If you give it away at all, you will have no luck with cows, they believe. It appears this man was trying to take the stall-rope from the white cow for fear he would be unlucky afterwards – either that or he was trying to entice the stall-rope from the fairy woman and the cow from its head perhaps. Ennis noted these are the collector's notes taken down from Colm's explanation.[66]

The Iorras Aithneach poet Féilim Mhac Cumhaill is said to have composed this song. Féilim's father Labhcás was also a poet and they were from Inis Ní, near Roundstone, County Galway.[67] Irish oral tradition is rich in beliefs related to otherworldly encounters. Humans and animals often appear in narratives of the Otherworld. A cow may be taken away to the Otherworld to supply milk for the fairies, for example. These beliefs underline the parallel worlds of mortals and fairies. In nineteenth-century rural Ireland, cattle were an essential part of farming life and the economy, and protective measures such as keeping the rope when selling a cow provided a connection with the cow that had just been sold and offered assurance that future transactions would be fortunate.

20. *Hóbhá, a Dhiarmuidín!*[68]

Bean ar goideadh banbh uaithi, agus bhí sí ag imeacht ag tóraíocht an bhainbh agus céard a dhéanfadh bean eile ach an banbh a chur aniar ar a droim, i seál, agus í ag ligean uirthi féin gur páiste a bhí aici agus í dhá corraí féin anonn is dhá corraí féin anall mar ó Dhia go raibh sí ag cur an pháiste a chodladh. Agus casadh an bhean di a raibh an banbh imithe uirthi

agus chuir sí tuairisc uirthi an bhfaca sí an banbh.
'An páiste seo, ar mo chruit agam,' a deir sí,
'Ná raibh sé bliain ó inniu agam.
Má chonaic mé do mhuicín,
Nó má bhí sí riamh agam.
Is hóbhá, a Dhiarmuidín, is hóbhá, a Dhiarmuidín!'

20. Howa, Diarmuidín

A piglet was stolen from a woman and she went in search of it and another woman put the piglet on her back in a shawl, pretending that it was a child, and she began rocking herself from side to side pretending to put the child to sleep, and she met the woman who had lost the piglet, who asked her if she had seen the piglet.
'This child I carry on my back awhile,' she said,
'May I not have him a year from today,
If I saw your little pig,
Or if I ever had her,
And howa, Diarmuidín, howa, Diarmuidín!'

21. *Micheál Mhac Suibhne*[69]

Séamus Ennis: Tá scéal anois ag Colm faoi Mhicheál Mhac Suibhne a raibh sé ráite faoi go mba é an duine a b'fhearr de na filí é.

Colm Ó Caodháin: Well, bhí Micheál Mhac Suibhne cheana agus creidim go raibh marc ag an sagart air le gur mhaith leis caint a bhaint as. Ach casadh an Suibhneach an lá seo dhó go tráthúil agus dúirt sé leis:

'Ní raibh tú ag an aifreann inniu, a Mhichíl?' a deir an sagart.

'Ó ní rabhas,' a deir Micheál, 'ach má chaill mé an t-aifreann, níor chaill mé an t-eadra.'

Ba geal leis an Eaglais a bheith an-chruinn.

'Má chuireann tú turas orm go Cruach Phádraig, tá mé sásta ar é chur dhíom.'

'Cuirimse turas na Cruaiche ort,' a deir an sagart.

Well, go cliste anois, bhí Micheál ag faire an tsagairt ariamh nó go bhfaca sé a tíocht an bóthar é an lá seo. Agus sheas Micheál ag cruach mhóna, agus ba í an chruach mhóna í féin cruach le Pádraig eicínt. Pádraig a bhí ar máistir na cruaiche, agus nuair a chonaic Micheál an sagart a tíocht bhain sé dhe a hata agus thosaigh sé gabháil timcheall na cruaiche. Agus nuair a tháinig an sagart:

'Céard tá tú dhéanamh ansin, a Mhichíl?' a deir sé.

'Tá mé tabhairt turas na cruaiche, a athair,' a deir sé 'a chuir tú orm.'

'Agus, ar ndóigh, ní shin í an chruach í,' a deir an sagart.

'Ó, m'*anam, gur shíl mise,' a deir Micheál, 'go ndéanfadh cruach Phádraig ar bith mé.'*

'Well, anois a Mhichíl,' a deir sé, 'baist an hata sin.'

Rug Micheál ar hata an tsagairt agus thosaigh sé ag breathnú síos ann:

'Muise, baistim thú,' deir Micheál, 'gan cois, gan ceann,
Gan uisce, gan salann, gan deoir, gan leann,
Fios d'ainm do leinbh ní fhéadaim fháil,
Agus níl a fhios agam an tú an olann a bhí ar an gcaora dhubh nó ar an gcaora bhán.'

21. Micheál Mhac Suibhne

Séamus Ennis: Colm has a story now about Micheál Mhac Suibhne who was said to have been the best of the poets.

Colm Ó Caodháin: Well, Micheál Mhac Suibhne was about and I believe the priest wanted to hear his clever talk. But he met Mhac Suibhne one day by chance as he was going along and he said to him:

'You weren't at mass today, Micheál?' said the priest.

'Oh, I wasn't,' said Micheál, 'but if I missed mass I didn't miss milking time.'

And the Church was wont to be very punctilious.

'If you make me undertake a pilgrimage to Croagh Patrick [literally St Patrick's Stack] I am prepared to do it.'

'I demand that you undertake the pilgrimage,' said the other fellow.

Well, Micheál was cleverly watching the priest until he saw him coming along the road one day and Micheál stood by a stack of turf, owned by a man called Patrick. Patrick owned the stack and when Micheál saw the priest approaching, he took off his hat and began going around the stack. And when the priest arrived:

'What are you doing, Micheál?' he said.

'I am doing the pilgrimage of the croagh [stack], father,' he said, 'that you instructed me to do.'

'And of course, that isn't the croagh I meant,' said the priest.

'Oh, dear,' said Micheál, 'I thought any Patrick's croagh would do me.'

'Well, now, Micheál,' he said, 'baptise that hat,' he said. Mícheál grasped the priest's hat and said:

'Indeed, I baptise you,' said Micheál, 'without foot or head,
Without water, without salt, without a drop, without ale,
I cannot discover the name of your child.
And I don't know if you are the wool that was on the black sheep or the white sheep.'

The poet Micheál Mhac Suibhne was reputedly born near Cong, County Mayo, in the mid-eighteenth century. He spent most of his life in Conamara and died in Fahy, Clifden, around 1820. According to a manuscript compiled and written by James Hardiman and held in the Royal Irish Academy, Micheál worked for a landlord called Steward near Moyard, County Galway, and became a blacksmith. His composition '*Murchadh Ó Maoláin*' (track 22) and the song '*Amhrán an Phúca*' ['The Song of the Pooka'] are among his better-known songs. Another well-known song is an amusing song cursing a place called Errislannan in County Galway because of its inhospitality to him as a wandering poet.[70] The recording was made for broadcast and Ennis introduces Colm, who goes on to give the account.

22. *Murchadh Ó Maoláin*[71]

Fadó, deineadh amhrán do Mhurchadh Beag Ó Maoláin. Bhí sé gabháil a phósadh. Agus bhí Micheál Mhac Suibhne, filí, bhí sé titithe ar meisce insa teach agus bhí iallach ar chuile duine dhá raibh sa teach amhrán a rá. Ach d'éirigh Micheál as a chuid óil. Caithfidh tú a rá go mba mhaith meabhrach an cloigeann a bhí air agus a bheith in ann a dhul a filíocht tar éis a bheith titithe ar meisce dhó agus chuaigh sé a rá an amhráin 'Murchadh Ó Maoláin'.

Ó is tá buachaill insa tír seo mar Murchadh Deas Ó Maoláin,
Tá sé molta ar fheabhas na tíre, agus tá sé i gceist go mór ag mná;
Agus cá bhfuil aon bhean sa tír óra a d'iarrfadh sé, nach bhfaigheadh sé,
Agus leithchéad ghine bhuí, ó, le leagan ar an gclár.
Séard dúirt an iníon ós ísle lena maimín insan oíche:
'Díol na ba is na caoirigh is cuir na pingneachaí le fáil.
Is níor mhór liom os a chionn sin, óra, culaith dheas i mo thimpeall;
Crios den tsíoda is míne agus bíodh snaidhm air faoi mo lár.'

Óra, siúd mar bhí sé gléasta, faoi bhúclaí is faoi éadach,
Bhí a charabhata gléigeal air is a léine dheas bhreá.
Bhí a veist de thogha an éadaigh, ó, is a chasóg mar an gcéanna,
Is a chóta mór den 'bhearskin' air ab éadroime le fáil.
Ó bhí a bhríste as an bhfaisean déantaí air, den bheilbhitín ab aeraí,
Bhí stocaí 'cotton' gléigeal air agus féachaigí ar a bhrágha.
Bhí a bhróga daití géar air, óra, de dhéanamh Sheáin Uí Bhéarra,
Agus dúshlán fearabh Éireann más bréag atá mé a rá.

Ó, is nach deas an moladh ar óigfhear a bheith múinte, measúil, tóigthe,
I gcliú is i gean a chomharsan i gcónaí ins gach am;
Agus d'aithneoinnse is ba chóir dhom, óra, do choisméig ar an mbóthar,
Nach iomadh bean sa tóir ort ach ní dhóib atá tú i ndán.
Ba lách i dteach an ósta é, ní air a thagadh stróbh ar bith,
Go nglanfadh sé na scórthaí agus 'Ólaigí bhur sáith!'
Bhí ór buí ina phócaí agus píosaí garbha crónach,
Nach gearr go mbí sé posta lena stóirín, Jenny Bhán.

Tá mo hata le trí Dhomhnaigh is é dhá cheainteáil le haghaidh mná an ósta,
Nuair a shílim é bheith cóirithe cén chaoi mbíonn sé ach bán,
Ní áirím ar mo chóta nuair a bhím a gabháil an bóthar,
Níl foscadh ná díon deoir ann, nuair a dhoirteanns an lá.
Tá mo léine is mo bhríste an chuid díobh nach bhfuil scaoilte,
Mo veist de thogha an tsíoda is gan ach roinnt di le fáil,
Tá mo bhróga lán le píosaí agus mo stocaí titim síos díom,
Is mo charabhata roinnte faoin tír idir mná!

[Siod é an fear nár choigil riamh an ball socair a cheap Dia dhó,
Nó go meallfadh sé le aighneas aghaidh chiúin gach mná,
Mar níl bean óg ná maighdean nach uirthi bhíodh an t-oibriú,
A' gabháil a luí dhó san oíche agus ag éirí gach lá.
Níl áit ar fud na poiblíocht nach gcluinfeá bean dhá fhiafraí siúd,
Ag cur tuairisc cá fhaide siar é nó go dtéadh sí féin ina cheann.
Má bhí scata acub dhá chuibhriú is an chuid eile 'gabháil a' luí leis,
Mar bhí sé go breá meidheagach[72] *agus a 'phint' aige ina láimh.]*

22. Murchadh Ó Maoláin

Long ago, a song was composed for Murchadh Beag Ó Maoláin, when he was getting married. The poet Micheál Mhac Suibhne became drunk in the house and everyone in the house had to sing a song. But Micheál stopped drinking. You must admit that he was very clever indeed to be able to compose poetry in his state of inebriation and he began to sing the song 'Murchadh Ó Maoláin'.

There is a lad in this district called Murchadh Deas Ó Maoláin,
His praises are sung everywhere and women are very interested in him.
There isn't a woman he would seek in these parts that he wouldn't get,
And fifty gold guineas as well, to put on the counter.

Fig. 23: *Murchadh Beag Ó Maoláin*. NFC MMS 19

The daughter said secretly to her mother one night:
'Sell the cows and sheep and provide the pennies,
And I would want a bright dress to wear, as well.
A belt of the finest silk knotted at my waist.'

O, that's how he was dressed, with buckles and fine cloth,
With a bright neck-tie and fine white shirt,

His waistcoat was made of the best cloth, and his jacket as well,
And his overcoat was made of the lightest bearskin available,
His trousers were of the latest fashion, the most pleasing velveteen cloth,
He wore bright cotton socks and just look at his figure,
He wore pointed, coloured shoes made by Seán Ó Béarra,
And a challenge to the men of Ireland, should I lie.

It is a virtue in a young man to be polite, respectable and well reared,
Always held in regard and loved by the neighbours around,
And I would recognise, as I should, your footstep on the road,
Many a woman seeks you but you are not destined for them.
He was kind in the inn, he would remain even-tempered,
He would settle the debt and then say 'Drink up!'
He had bright gold in his pockets and rough crown coins,
And soon he will marry his darling, Jenny Bhán.

For the last three Sundays my hat is being auctioned to pay the women of the inn,
When I think it has been repaired, it appears to be threadbare,
I don't even include my coat as I walk the road,
Where there is no shelter nor protection when it pours rain,
My shirt and my trousers those parts which are not in tatters,
My waistcoat is of the best silk and only some of it endures,
My shoes are heavily patched and my stockings are falling down,
And my neck-tie has been shared around among women.

[This is the man who never tended the quiet spot God ordained for him,
Until he enticed every quiet woman with attention,
Because there is not a young woman or maiden that he had not stirred,
When he went to bed at night and got up every morning,
There is nowhere you would go that a woman wasn't enquiring after him,
Asking where he was so that she could seek him out,

Some of them were luring him and the rest going to bed with him,
Because he was full of fun when he had a pint in his hand.][73]

For a note on the poet Micheál Mhac Suibhne, see notes to track 21 'Micheál Mhac Suibhne'.

23. *Johnny Seoighe*[74]

Bhí fear insan áit seo fadó agus is é an t-ainm a bhí air Tomás Shiúnach. Filí a bhí ann. Agus bhí sé ag imeacht ag súistéireacht, ag bualadh cruacha arbhair ó áit go háit. Well, ba é an drochshaol a bhí ann san am seo anois agus bhí daoine go leor a fáilt an-chrua, an-chrua. Ach duine ar bith a bhí ina chainteoir mhaith, bhí sé ag baint an-bhearradh amach lena theanga. Agus bhí fear thiar i Maíros a dtugaidís Johnny Seoighe air. Agus bhí sé ina cheannphort ar mhin bhuí le haghaidh déirce a thabhairt do na boicht de réir mar a bheadh sé ag teastáil, de réir mar a bheadh sé ag teastáil. Agus ní dhearna Tomás ach a dhul go dtí Johnny Seoighe an lá seo agus a dhul ag … á thriáil féin amach le go mbainfeadh sé bearradh dhe. 'Anois,' a deir sé:

A Johnny Seoighe, tuig mo ghlórtha,
Is mé ag tíocht le dóchas faoi do dhéin.
Nach tú an réalt eolais is deise lóchrainn,
As mo shúile ag teampall Dé.
Is tú bláth na hóige is deise glórtha,
Dhearc mo shúil ó rugadh mé,
Agus as ucht Chríost, tabhair dom 'relief',
Nó go gcaithtear oíche Nollag féin.

Ó, agus lá arna mháireach fuair mé an páipéar,
Is nach mé bhí sásta agus chuaigh mé chun siúil,
Is ní bhfuair mé freagra ar bith an lá sin,
Ach mé féin agus mo pháistí bheith amuigh faoin drúcht.
Tá mé bruite, sciúrtha, feannta,
Liobraithe, gearrthaí, ó neart an tsiúil.

Is a Mhister Joyce, tá an 'workhouse' lán,
Is ní glacfar ann isteach níos mó.

Is nach mór an chliú do bhaile Charna,
An fhad is tá an lánúin seo gabháil thríd,
Mar is deise agus is breáichte dreach na mná,
Ná an 'morning star' nuair a éiríonn sí.
Tá an bhanríon tinn is í go lag ina luí,
Is deir dochtúirí go bhfaighfidh sí bás,
Agus is é fios a húdair, de réir mar deir siad liomsa,
Nuair nach bhfuil sí póstaí ag Mister Joyce.

23. Johnny Seoighe

There was a man here long ago and his name was Tomás Shiúnach. He was a poet. And he was travelling around threshing corn with a flail going from place to place. Well, it was the time of the Great Famine and many people found life very hard, very hard indeed. But anyone who was a good speaker, they had to rely on their eloquence. And there was a man in Maíros called Johnny Seoighe. He was in charge of the yellow meal to be given to the poor according to their needs, according to their needs. And Tomás simply went to Johnny Seoighe one day to test him. 'Now,' he said:

Johnny Seoighe, understand what I say,
As I come in hope to you.
You were the star of knowledge with the finest light,
That my eyes could see at God's church,
You are the flower of youth with the finest voice,
That I have ever seen, since the day I was born,
And for the sake of Christ, give me relief,
At least until after Christmas eve.

Facing page: Fig. 24: *Johnny Seoighe.* NFC 1281:182

Johnny Seoige

(Ṫomás Siúnaċ a Ċum)

(Ó)'s a Johnny Seoige, ~~[illegible]~~uig mo ġlóire
'S/mé/'s/ tloċt ar dóċas faoi do ḋéin;
Ba tú 'n péarla eólais ba deise lóċrainn
Ar mo ṡúile age teampoll Dé;
Ṫú bláṫ na h-óige 's/deise ġlóire
Ḋeire mo ṡúil ó rugú mé,
'Gur ar uċt Ċríost, 's tóir dom "Relief"
Nó go gcaiṫtear oiḋċe Nodlag ḟéin!

• Gur lá 's n̄a mairreaċ fuair mé/'n páipéar
'Gur ~~rí~~ mé ḃí sásta 's ċua' mé/'n siúl;
'S ní ḃfuair mé freágra/'/ḃí a' lá sin,
Aċ mé féin 's/mo páirdí ḃeiṫ 'muiġ faoi'n drúċt!
Tá mé bruiṫte, dóiġtí, gearrṫa,
Lobraiġṫe, feannta, ó neart a' tsiúil —
Aċ a' ṁistear[1] Joyce, tá/'n "Workhouse" lán
'S ní glacfar ánn aon ḟear níos mú.[2]

(Ó)'s nac mór a' clú go Línde Ċarna
'N ḟad 's tá 'n lánúin seo/'s/gul ṡíd:
'S ba deise, ḃréuċte dreaċ na mná
Ná/'n "morning Star" nuair eiriġionn sí →

(1) mistea. (2) mó

And the following day I received the piece of paper,
I was a happy person as I set off,
And I received no reply that day,
But I and my children left outside in the dew,
I am crushed, beaten, flayed,
Berated, torn, from intense walking.
Mister Joyce [Seoighe], the workhouse is full,
No one else will be taken in there.

It is a cause of great fame for the village of Carna,
While this couple is there.
Because the woman's appearance is nicer and finer,
Than the morning star as it rises.
The queen is ill and weak as she lies in bed,
And doctors say that she will die,
And the reason for this, according to what I am told,
Is that she is not married to Mister Joyce.

> As Cormac Ó Gráda has written, this song tells us little about Johnny Seoighe other than the fact that he was associated with the distribution of meal during the Famine in the Carna district. The song implies that there is no room in the workhouse for the songster and his family and Johnny Seoighe is asked to give assistance. Seoighe and his beloved are indeed praised, but the song might also be seen as a satire, as, according to local sources, the queen might be one Peig Barry who was in love with Seoighe, a man who was reputed to have been a crooked character. Peig Barry was the daughter of a bailiff or agent, on the Martin estate. Seoighe, from Oughterard, attempted to outsmart a local man, Seán Mac Donncha, who was in charge of distributing relief tickets in Carna. The reference to Peig Barry's sickly appearance may refer to her feigned ill-health at the courthouse in Roundstone where she was witness for Johnny Seoighe. Oral tradition also states that Seoighe refused a half-stone of meal to the songster but that the woman's heart was moved, as found in the third stanza.[75]

Colm Ó Caodháin told Séamus Ennis that Johnny Seoighe, a man who had neither relation, connection nor relationship through marriage with local people, was appointed to distribute the yellow meal. Colm said that poets composed songs to try to move him to be more generous and to give them a larger amount.[76]

In an account written in 1932, Pádraig Ó hÉanaí, An Aird Thoir, Carna, said that the song was composed by Micheál Mharcais (Micheál Mac Con Iomaire) from Carna when he requested a half-stone of yellow meal from Seoighe, who refused him. At that point, he composed the final verse of the song and the woman gave him a half-stone.[77]

24. P Stands for Paddy I Suppose[78]

I went out one May morning to have a pleasant walk,
I sat myself down by an old stone wall to hear two lovers talk,
To hear what they might say my dear,
To hear what they might say,
That I might know a little bit more about love,
Before I'd go away.

P stands for Paddy I suppose,
J for my love John,
W stands for false Willie-o,
But Johnny is the fairest man.

Johnny is the fairest man, my dear,
Johnny is the fairest man,
I don't care what anybody says,
But Johnny is the fairest man.

Come and sit beside me now,
Together on the green,
It's a long three quarters of a year or more,
Since together we had been.

Since together we had been, my dear,
Since together we had been.
It's a long three quarters of a year or more,
Since together we had been.

I will not sit beside you now,
Now or any other time,
You are in love with another pretty chap,
And your heart's no longer mine.

Your heart's no longer mine, my dear,
Your heart's no longer mine.
You are in love with another pretty chap,
And your heart's no longer mine.

P stands for Paddy I suppose,
J for my love John,
W stands for false Willie-o,
But Johnny is the fairest man.

Johnny is the fairest man, my dear,
Johnny is the fairest man.
I don't care what anybody says,
But Johnny is the fairest man.

I'd climb up a tall, tall tree,
To rob a little bird's nest,
And I'd come down with a leafy little flower,
To the girl that I love best.

To the girl that I love best, my dear.
To the girl that I love best.
I'd come down with a leafy little flower,
To the girl that I love best.

P stands for Paddy I suppose,
J for my love John,
W stands for false Willie-o,
But Johnny is the fairest man.

Johnny is the fairest man, my dear,
Johnny is the fairest man,
I don't care what anybody says,
But Johnny is the fairest man.

> This is a song of courtship. It is also known as 'Johnny Is the Fairest Man', the title by which Joe Heaney called it. Other titles are 'Come and Sit Beside Me Now', 'T Stands for Tom' and 'The Verdant Braes of Skreen'. It is classified as Roud 419.[79]

25. Wild Rover[80]

I am a wild rover this many long day,
I spent all my money with whiskey and beer,
And I mean to give it over and my money in store,
And I'll never be called the wild rover no more.

Wild rover, wild rover, wild rover no more,
And I'll never be called the wild rover no more.

I came into an ale house where oft times I went,
And I told the landlady my money was spent,
I called for some whiskey, the answer was no,
There is plenty of customers here like you every day.

Wild rover, wild rover, wild rover no more,
And I'll never be called the wild rover no more.

I put a hand in my pocket and me purse forth I drew,
And a handful of money on the table I threw,
She said she had brandy and plenty of the best,
And all that I said, it was all for a jest.

Wild rover, wild rover, wild rover no more,
And I'll never be called the wild rover no more.

I'll go home to my father if he lets me in,
And I hope he will pardon his beauty, fine son,
And if he will give me, it's at home I will stay,
And I'll never be called the wild rover again.

This rousing song still retains a considerable popularity. Sometimes perceived as a drinking song, it has been documented from the late sixteenth century and may well be older. Over the centuries, it has been published on broadside, in songster and in audio format and has been documented from oral tradition in North America, Canada, Australia, Ireland, Scotland and England. The ballad groups The Dubliners and The Wolfe Tones recorded it and, in more recent times, The High Kings have recorded it. It is classified under Roud 1173.[81]

26. *Finnbheara*[82]

Bhí fear sa mbaile seo fadó agus bhí garraí coirce curtha aige agus aimsir spéir ghealaí a bhí ann agus bhíodh capaill a tíocht ag déanamh mísc insa gcoirce. Ach dhúisigh sé anois, deireadh na hoíche, an mhaidin seo, agus chuaigh sé amach go bhfeicfeadh sé an raibh na capaill insa gcoirce agus ní raibh. Ní raibh na capaill thoir sa gcoirce.

'A,' deir sé, 'mura bhfuil sibh sa gcoirce, tá sibh a tíocht chuig an gcoirce agus is fearr dhomsa déanamh faoina gcoinne sibhse ná dhul a chodladh aríst go bhfeice muid.' Shiúl sé síos an bóthar achar fada go bhfeiceadh sé an raibh na capaill ag triail air agus ní fhaca sé capall ar bith. Agus chas sé abhaile aríst agus nuair a bhí sé ceathrú míle aníos an bóthar chuaigh fear capaill amach lena chluais agus léim sé i leataobh an bhóthair agus scanraigh sé.

'Ná scanraigh,' a dúirt an fear a bhí ar an gcapall. 'Ó ní scanróinn,' a deir sé, 'ach níl sé noiméad ó bhreathnaigh mé síos an bóthar agus ní raibh duine ar bith le feiceáil ann. Agus tá mé scanraithe mar ghealll ar chomh tobann is tá tú tagthaí orm.'

'Well,' a deir sé, 'mise,' a deir sé, 'Finnbheara. Mise an Finnbheara,' a deir sé, agus bhí sé ag: 'breathnaigh soir anois,' a deir sé, 'sna garrantaí sin is sna portaigh sin thoir.' Bhreathnaigh. 'Bhí mucaí, beithígh, caoirigh, jabaireacht, ceannacht is díol ann agus tá mise, agus tá mise agus na síogaí ag troid le chéile go géar,' a deir sé, 'i gcónaí. Tá na síogaí ag iarraidh bheith ag baint na bhfataí dhíbhse agus tá mise ag coinneáil na bhfataí daoibh. Agus "elec" ... tá vótannaí againn, vótannaí againn, an ceann a bhíonns istigh i mbliana ní hé bhíonns istigh an chéad bhliain eile.'

D'imigh an fear capaill agus na spoir a bhí air, bheifeá in ann thú féin a bhearradh iontu, leis an 'shine' breá a bhí iontu. Ghlan sé siar in éadain cnoic agus leacrachaí agus bhí sé ag baint aithinneachaí dearga as na leacrachaí a dhul suas in éadain an chnoic, agus tháinig an fear abhaile.

26. Finnbheara

There was a man in this place long ago and he had planted a field of oats and it was a bright night[83] and horses used to come and do damage in the oats. But he woke, at daybreak, one morning, and went out to see if the horses were in the oats and they weren't. The horses were not in the oats.

'Ah,' he said, 'if you are not in the oats, you are coming to the oats and I had better watch out for you rather than going to sleep again and we will see what happens.' He walked a good bit down the road, to see if the horses were coming in his direction and he saw no horse. And he turned home again and when he had travelled a quarter of a mile down the road, a man on a horse came just by his ear and he jumped out of the way, and took fright.

'Don't be afraid,' said the man on the horse.

'O, I am not afraid,' he said, 'but not a minute has passed since I looked down the road and there was no one to be seen. And I got a fright because you came on me so suddenly.'

'Well,' he said, 'I,' he said, 'am Finnbheara. I am Finnbheara,' he said, and he was. 'Look now,' he said, 'in the fields, where the oats are planted.' He did so. 'There were pigs, cattle, sheep, a jobber, buying and selling there and the fairies and I,' he said, 'are always fighting. The fairies are trying to take the potatoes from you and I am keeping them for you. And we have elec … votes, we have votes, and of course, if one is in this year they won't be in the following year.'

The man on the horse headed off and as for his spurs, you could shave yourself in them, they had such a wonderful shine on them. He sped off up the hill and the rock faces and he rose red sparks from the flagstones going up the hill and the man came home.

> Finnbheara is the king of the fairy realm and is said to have dwelt in Cnoc Meá, near Tuam in County Galway. He is reputed to bring good crops to people but his absence may be the cause of poor crops. The narration underlines the importance of saving the harvest, and also the fear of losing it. Contact with Finnbheara in this narration underlines his power and presents a positive image of Finnbheara supporting the local farmer.[84] It appears from this recording that Colm may have seen Finnbheara's role as the result of an election and that the fairies took a vote.

27. *Brá Thír Locha*[85]

Tá seanfhocal ag seandaoine insan áit seo agus is é an focal é féin dá gcuirtí brá thír locha fútsa is tú tá ann i gcónaí. Well, is é an míniú eile atá leis sin – dhá mbeadh deartháir agat, ná deirfiúr, ná duine ar bith a bheadh insa teach, contráilte, ag déanamh rudaí as bealach, déarfá gur brá thír, go raibh … is tú atá ann i gcónaí dá gcuirtí brá thír locha fút. Agus is é an fáth é sin, dhá gceapfá go mbeadh do pháiste, ná duine ar bith a bheadh sa teach, tugthaí as ag na siógaí, deir seandaoine dhá dtugtá leat do bhrá thír locha, a bheadh curtha ag taoille mór thar éis fuarlach mhór a dhéanamh, agus na fiógaí locha a bheadh curtha isteach i mbarr na talthúna ón bhfuarlach a thabhairt leat agus a chur insa … faoin duine go ndéarfadh … go gcaithfeadh sé imeacht, más rud ar bith é a bhí fágthaí in áit an duine saolta. Agus marab ea, bheadh an duine saolta ansin i gcónaí.

27. Lakeside Waste

The old people here have a saying and the phrase is, if you were to put lakeside detritus under you it would always be there. This is what it means: If you had a brother or a sister, or anyone who was misbehaving, doing things wrongly, you would say that you are still here if you were to have lakeside waste under you … at first, lakeside waste would be placed under you. And the reason for that is that if you thought your child, or anyone else from your house, was taken away by the fairies, and the old people would say to bring your lake-side waste which the high tide would have formed, following very heavy rain, and to bring that waste with you that would have been thrown into the upper shore because of the heavy rain, and to put it in … there under the person until he would say … he would have to leave, if there was anything at all that was left instead of the mortal person. And if there wasn't, the mortal being would be still there.

The saying *Is tú tá ann i gcónaí dhá gcuirtí brá thír locha fút* ['It is you all the same even if there were waste from the lake placed under you'] is, as Colm explained on another occasion, said to someone who did something against you, and you did nothing about it. If the person did something against you a second time then the phrase would be said to him, stating that he is not a good person.

Colm described *brá thír* as the reeds that grow in the lake and the moss and everything that the wind would gather in the lake and would form a tide line at the lakeshore.

This led Colm to explain to Ennis that if a child were born that was different in appearance to other children and did not have the ability to thrive, if the child could not speak properly or had other disadvantages, the parents thought their own child had been taken by the fairies and that they had left a creature somewhat like their own child in its place. And if they were in doubt about it they would bring this waste from the lake and place it under the child in the bed. And they knew if they found the child dead in bed that it was not their own child. Ennis wrote that Colm understood this belief to be a part of life, but that there was protection against the fairies leaving a changeling behind them. The protection was lakeside waste or reeds that grow in a lake and the moss and everything that the wind would gather and would form a tide line at the lake.[86]

The belief in the existence of a changeling, or fairy child, left in place of a human child was common in Irish vernacular belief. This meant that protective steps were in place to prevent such an occurrence. There were also traditional methods for identifying a changeling. The natural materials such as reeds and algae that collect at the point of contact of water and the lakeshore were believed to have special properties to protect against preternatural misfortune. This belief is very much in keeping with beliefs associated with thresholds and borders that were places of liminality, allowing for special contact between the mortal and the Otherworld.

28. *An Mharthain Phádraig*[87]

Glaoitear suan fial feart in aithne is i gcéill,
Agus go mba bua an braon glas de shú na gréine, Gréige gile,
Agus ní fhaigheann súch do shluaite D-,
Go mba súch, sách duitse agus go Surlaí Solamghlas,
Mise agus Surlaí Solamghlas, dís nach ionann dúinn rún creidimh,
Agus gan aon ní ar an talamh dhá ngráú ach Anna Áille.

Beannacht leis an anam a bhí i gcorp Anna Ní Mhóráille,
Agus beannacht le gach anam dhá ndéarfaidh mo mharthainse agus
dhá ngrá;
Mar níl ar an domhan dallaba[?] ní bith níos breáichte,

Ná folt breá banartha[?] faoina haghaidh corportha,
Chumhartha, sean-chumhartha, go béal chrua chogaille,
A ghlanfas na s-, f-, f- a chléibhe.

Siod iad na buannaí c-, l-,
A chuirimse ar an aithne agus ar aon fhear go deo ná ceiltear í.
Míse Pádraig t- a léanns gach aithne,
Agus fágaim an bua ag an aithne seo,
Mar tá bua treise, bua feasa, bua cúnta le fionnmhná,
Do na trí rí rialta bhí i mb- leis an anam a bhí i gcorp Anna Ní Mhóráille,
Agus má tá cion ar d'aithrí agat, ní éistfear comhrá.

Tá sé scríofa sna f-, f-, fírinne,
Go lá dheireadh an domhain agus i bponc an bháis,
Go bhfuil pearsa as a gcionn nach gcloífear.
Tá sé léite sna s- gach ní dhá ndéarfainn,
An Mharthain Phádraig agus a hainm i nGaeilge,
Tá sí agamsa anonn le chéile,
Agus is é mo thrua ghéar dheacrach gan í ag fearabh Éireann
Mura mbeadh agat ach na trí phearsanaí deireanacha déanacha dhi,
Go dtabharfadh sí as Ifreann go dtí flaithiúnais Dé thú.

Ag éisteacht le mo laoi luirc nó le m'fhírinne ghlan-uasal,
Ghabhfadh an t-aingeal ar neamh agus níor bhaol dó Rí an Uabhair,
An té déarfadh mo mharthain a gabháil ag ionsaí mná oíche.
Is maith an áit a gcuirfí é i gcionn séan agus clainne.
An té déarfadh mo mharthain a gabháil ag ionsaí mná oíche,
Slán a thiocfadh sé agus gan d- na saothar.

An té déarfadh mo mharthain do chiontaí na hÉireann,
Má b'ísle b'osclaithe ó ghlais is ó ghéibheann.
An té déarfadh mo mharthain a gabháil i mbannaí ná i bhfiacha,
Gheobhadh siad a gheastal agus bheadh roimhe go rialta,
An té déarfadh mo mharthain a gabháil i gcogadh ná i gcliara,
Thiocfadh sé abhaile faoi arm lasta agus bheadh feoil iata air.

An té déarfadh mo mharthain a gabháil chun tí an óil.
Ba ghlór bodhar, searbh do lucht airm in ailt chrua;
An té déarfadh mo mharthain, a gabháil i dteach nua,
An corp ní fhágfadh é gan ola shagairt chúns bheadh cleith faoi dhíon air,
An té déarfadh mo mharthain a dhul chun toinne ná farraige go dtiocfadh sé,
Abhaile slán gan bá toinne ná anachain.

Mise Pádraig na bhfeart, an chéad easpag a tháinig go hÉirinn,
In mo léinteán glan uasal agus ba mhaith an bua dhom a bheith léithe,

Crios Muire mo chrios,
Crios na gceithre crois,
Crios lé ar geineadh Críost,
Críost a geineadh as.
Fóir ar an mbean, a mháthair, atá in airticil an bháis.
Fóir féin a Mhic, uirthi, ós ar do láimh atá,
Baiste a thabhairt don leana agus an bhean a thabhairtean slán.
Beir do leana a bhean,
Mar rug Anna Muire,
Mar rug Muire Dia,
Mar rug Naomh Sibéal Naoimh Eoin Baiste,
Gan matra, gan daille,
Gan easpa coise ná láimhe
Ach in ainm an Athar, an Mhic agus an Spioraid Naoimh.

[Seanchas ar An Marthain Phádraig

D'abraíodh seandaoine An Mharthain Phádraig nuair a bhíodh daoine tinn, le go dtiocaidís slán as an tinneas. (Tá dornán cásannaí cloiste agam féin, daoine a leigheasadh thar éis an mharthain a rá ar a son agus gan aon tsúil roimhe sin go n-éireoidís go brách. Creidtear gur an mharthain a shlánaigh iad. SMacA.) Deir Colm go ndúirt sé an mharthain agus é a siúl an bóthar lá do bhean a bhí tinn, ach gur cailleadh í.

Dhá dtéadh na seandaoine dhá rá do dhuine bheadh tinn, ba mhaith leob dhá n-éireodh leob é rá gan aon lúb síos ó thús go deireadh agus dhá n-éireodh leob é sin a dhéanamh shílfidís go mbeadh chuile shórt ceart, ach dhá dtéidís amú ann, ba sórt taispeánadh dhób é nach leigheasfaí an duine sin – níor mhaith leob é.

Tá sé creidte freisin, dhá mbeadh an mharthain scríofa síos agus í ina phóca ag bádóir, nach mbáifí go deo é. 2.12.1944]

28. Saint Patrick's Sustaining Prayer

A generous, wondrous sleep is called in knowledge and in
  wisdom -[88]
And may the soft drop of a drink from the bright, Greek sun be
  triumphant,
And does not beget succulence for the hosts of D-,
May you and Surlaí Solamghlas[89] live in luxury and be content,
I and Surlaí Solamghlas will be content, a pair whose religious
  resolve is not the same,
And nothing on earth loving us except Anna Áille.

A blessing to the soul that was in Anna Ní Mhóráille's body,
And a blessing to every soul that says this sustaining prayer
  with love;
For there is nothing more wonderful in the dark world,
Than her beautiful feminine hair framing her face,
Fragrant, most fragrant, to the firm mouth -
That will purify the [?] of the breast.

These are the attributes,
That I place on this commandment, not to be concealed from any
  man,
I am Patrick who reads every commandment,
And I give the victory to this commandment,
Because fair women have the gift of strength, a gift of knowledge
  and of assistance,
For the three ruling kings – with the soul in Anna Ní Mhóráille's
  body,
And if you have respect for your penance, there will be no
  conversation.

It is written in truth,
Until the world's last day and the moment of death,
That there is a figure above them who will not be overcome,
Everything I would say can be read,
Patrick's sustaining prayer and its name is in Irish,
And I know it in sequence.
And it is my bitter, hard sorrow that the men of Ireland do not know it,
If you knew only the last, final three figures of it,
It would bring you from Hell to God's paradise.

Anyone who listens to my verse or to my noble truth,
The angel would go to heaven and would not be in danger from the devil,
The person who says my sustaining prayer while setting about women of the night,
Would be in a good place regarding happiness and family,
The person who says my sustaining prayer while setting about women of the night,
He would return safely and without any [?] in his work.

The person who says my sustaining prayer for Ireland's sins,
If humble, he would be freed from fetters and incarceration,
The person who says my sustaining prayer taking up bonds or in debt,
It would be worth the trouble and would sustain him regularly,
The person who says my sustaining prayer going to war or to conflict,
He would return home laden with weapons, and his wounds healed.

The person who says my sustaining prayer going to the inn,
It was a deaf, bitter voice for those in arms in a difficult place,
The person who says my sustaining prayer going to a new house,
A body would not be left without the anointing of a priest as
long as there was a beam beneath the roof,

The person who says my sustaining prayer going to sea, he would return
Safely without being drowned by the waves or by disaster.

I am Patrick of the miracles, the first bishop who came to Ireland,
In my clean, fine shirt and it was a good victory for me to be with her [Ireland].

Mary's belt is my belt,
The belt of the four crosses,
The belt of which Christ was conceived,
Christ was conceived of it.
Help the woman, mother, who is on the point of death,
Help her, Son [of God], as you have the power,
To baptise the child and to save the woman,
Give birth to your son, woman,
As Anna gave birth to Mary,
As Mary gave birth to God,
As Elizabeth gave birth to John the Baptist,
Without disability, without obscurity,
Without lack of foot or arm,
But in the name of the Father, the Son and the Holy Spirit.

[Lore of Patrick's Sustaining Prayer

The old people used to recite Patrick's Sustaining Prayer when people were ill, so that they would recover from the illness. (I have heard of a handful of instances where people were cured after the Marthain was said for them and where there was no hope beforehand that they would ever get up again. It is believed that they were cured by the Marthain. Séamus Ennis.) Colm says he recited the Marthain as he was walking along the road one day for a woman who was ill, but that she died.

When the old people began reciting it for someone who was ill they wanted to recite it without hesitation from start to finish and if they succeeded in doing so, they believed everything would turn out well, but if they went astray in it, it was a kind of sign that that person would not be cured – they did not like that. It is also believed that if the Marthain is written down, and a boatman carries it in his pocket, he will never drown.][90]

Irish oral tradition includes prayers for many occasions, that were part of the daily and nightly routine. Many of these prayers were not part of the official church practice nor were they part of normal ecclesiastical occasions. They offered hope in ill-health and in times of duress. This 'sustaining prayer' is an example of a prayer in a form of incantation.

It is difficult to interpret some of the words and to determine their precise meaning. As it was believed that the prayer was especially powerful, obscure words added to the sense of mystery. Some words in Colm's version are indecipherable and are represented with a dash: '-'.

Versions have been documented from oral and manuscript tradition. For example, a version of the prayer, taken from oral tradition, was included in a late-nineteenth-century manuscript which was probably written on the small island of Inis Bearachain, Leitir Móir, County Galway.[91]

In her article 'The Legends of the False God's Daughter', Máire MacNeill has described the importance of the prayer in popular tradition, referring to it as 'the strangest of our traditional prayers'. She also wrote that the prayer was particularly prized by those who had to cross the sea. She refers to different versions, and one in particular by a Conamara man working in Scotland who wrote it down on two pieces of a cardboard box which he brought back home. The Conamara man in question was the father of the singer Joe Heaney, a second cousin of Colm Ó Caodháin.[92]

29. *Barr an tSléibhe*[93]

Ó, is nach deas é barr an tsléibhe nuair a bhíonns an ghrian ag éirí,
Níl duifean insa spéir ann, ná gangaid insa ngaoith,
Tá an broc ar thaobh an tsléibhe ann is tá an sionnach rua ina phéice,
Tá an giorria réidh a pocléimneach ann le pléisiúr insa bhfraoigh.
Tá úth na mba ag pléascadh a tíocht abhaile ag géimneach,
Is nach deas é ceol na n-éanlaith insa ngleann a tíocht na hoíche;
Tá an fear is a bhean in éineacht, a gabháil i mbannaí le chéile,
Is an seanfhear bheadh na céadta bliain is ní chrapfadh sé le aois.

Ó is a Mháire, ná bíodh díchéille ort, ach teanam chun an tsléibhe,
Ná fulaing mé bheith i m'aonraic insa ngleann a tíocht na hoíche.
Mar tá do theach dhá dhéanamh agus tá rúmaí deasa ina éadan;
San áit a mbeidh tú aerach, is tá an sliabh ar bheagán cíos;
Tá na comharsanaí ar gach taobh dhíot is fearr ar bith in Éirinn,
Dhá mairteá beo na céadta bliain níorbh fhada leat do shaol.
Ach go mb'fhearr liom ann ar aon chor ná dá ngealltá arán is tae dhom,
Ní feicfear mé go héag ag an ngeata mór aríst.

Ó tá an lacha agus tá an naosc ann, óra tá an chiorc is tá an chearc fhraoigh ann,
Tá londubh ar bharr na gcraobh ann agus gach ní eile faoina bhláth,
Tá luachair ghlas is cíob ann is iad ina sraitheachaí breátha, míne ann,
Is ní hionann é sna tíortha le go dtéann na ba ó dháir.
Tá an páiste in aois a mhíosa ag siúl ar fud an tí ann;
Tá macras gach uile oíche ann, ar fhir agus ar mhná,
Tá gabhair bhreátha ghlana agus caoirigh is iad a tíochtain chun an tí ann,
Is ní baolach díbse choidhchin go ngabhfaidh a gcuid chun fáin.

29. The Top of the Mountain

Isn't the top of the mountain a fine place as the sun is rising,
There is no darkness in the sky, nor bite in the wind;
The badger is on the mountainside and the fox is at his swiftest there,
And the slender hare is jumping in the heather for sport,
The cows' udder is bursting as they come home lowing,
Isn't the birdsong pleasant at nightfall in the valley?
The man and woman are making pledges to each other,
And an old person, hundreds of years old, would not bend with age.

Máire, do not be silly, let us go to the mountain,
And don't leave me alone in the valley at nightfall!
Because your house is being built; it has fine rooms to the front;
Where you will be lighthearted, the moor is free from dues,
On either side, you have the best neighbours you could find in Ireland,
If you lived hundreds of years, you wouldn't find your life tiresome,
I would much rather be there than if you promised me bread and tea,
And, until I die, I will never be seen again at the big gate.

The duck and snipe are there, and the hen and the grouse,
The blackbird is on top of the branches and everything else is in bloom,
There are green rushes and sedge and they are in good, fine rows there,
And it is not like the country where cattle become barren,
The one-month-old child is walking throughout the house;
There is revelry every night, of men and women,
There are fine clean goats and sheep coming to the house there,
And you are never at risk they will go wild.

In the accompanying notes to the song in '*Amhráin Ghaeilge an Iarthair*' it is stated that Séamus Coscar, a Mayo poet, wanted to bring his wife from An Geata Mór, Iorras, County Mayo, to another house they owned, and she refused to accompany him until he composed the song '*Barr an tSléibhe*' praising her. She accompanied him when she heard the song. Micheál Ó Tiománaidhe collected the song from Séamas Mac Enrí of Dumha Thuama, Iorras.[94]

Ennis wrote that Colm sang this song to the same air as '*Murchadh Beag Ó Maoláin*' (track 22).

30. Captain Wedderburn's Courtship[95]

There was a gentleman's fair daughter walking down a narrow lane,
She met with William Dixon, the keeper of the game,
He said unto his comrade boy 'Only for the law,
I'd have that girl and lie with me and she lying next to the wall.'

'Go your way, young man,' she said, 'and do not bother me.
Before I lie one night with you, you must answer me questions three.
Three questions you must answer me as I repeat them all,
Before I lie one night with you at either stock or wall.

'For my breakfast you must get for me a bird without a bone,
For my dinner you must get for me a cherry without a stone,
For my supper you must get for me a bird without a gall,
Then you and I, and one good lie and you lying next to the wall.'

'And when the bird is in the egg I'm sure he has no bone,
When the cherry is in blossom, it really has no stone,
The dove it is a gentle bird, that flies without a gall,
Then you and I, and one good lie and you lying next to the wall.'

'Go your ways, young man,' she said, 'and do not me perplex,
Before I lie one night with you, you must answer me questions six,
Six questions you must answer me, as I repeat them all.
Before I lie one night with you at either stock or wall.

'What is rounder than a ring? What's higher than a tree?
What is worse than woman's kind, what's deeper than the sea?
What bird sings best, what tree buds first, and where does dew first fall,
Before I lie one night with you at either stock or wall.'

'The globe is rounder than a ring, heaven is higher than a tree,
The divil is worse than woman's kind and is deeper than the sea,
The lark sings best, the oak buds first, and on earth the dew first falls,
Then you and I and one good lie, and you lying next to the wall.'

Séamus Ennis: You can't remember any more of it, Colm?

Colm Ó Caodháin:
The sparrow's horn, the priest isn't born,
To join us one and all
Before I lie one night with you on either stock or wall.

No, I had that verse, all, but 'tis out of my mind now.

SE: Well, where did you hear the song?

CÓC: I heard it about sixteen or seventeen years ago at an old man, and he was an old man and he said that he had it with ages. That song.

SE: Where was he from?

CÓC: He was from Glinsce and there was some of them talking about songs and he said that it was one of the oldest songs he had.

SE: Well, was he a sailor man?

CÓC: He was a sailor man. He used to be working with the sail boats.

SE: Sailing up and down to Galway?

CÓC: Yes, and land and every kind of work.

SE: Do you think he learned it from some people he met sailing?

CÓC: Oh, I'm sure he got a lot of songs from the Galway fellows and from County Clare side. He used to be in it drinking with them in, with bad weather [?], when he wasn't able to sail home you know.

SE: Yes, and he'd have to spend his time … among the people.

CÓC: He'd have to spend his time, yes, among the people. And they used to … the people knows him well, do you see, and were pulling together[96] and singing and playing.

SE: They'd spend their time singing?

CÓC: He was a good singer, do you see, and they all liked him. If he hadn't money himself he'd have … if he didn't have enough money in the morning, he would have it in the evening, do you see, because there was good company and singing.

> The international ballad is classified as Roud 36 (Child 46).[97] It is a Scottish ballad dating from as early as the 1780s. Recorded in North America, Australia and Scotland, it is also known as 'The Riddle Song' in which the young man, by answering each of her riddles, marries the girl or takes her to bed. In Ireland it is also known as 'Either Stock or Wall'.
>
> When Séamus Ennis asked Colm how he acquired the song, Colm described how the song came to Glinsce and also underlined the importance of singing within the local community.

31. *Oíche Shamhna*[98]

Séamus Ennis: A Choilm, is gearr ó bhí muid ag caint le seanfhear cheana agus bhí seanchas éigin aige dhúinn faoi oíche Shamhna. Creidim nach bhfuil tú féin gan roinnt seanchais a bheith agat ar do sheanmhuintir.

Colm Ó Caodháin: Well, tá seanchas agamsa faoi oíche Shamhna, an méid dhe a chonaic mé féin agus an méid nach bhfaca mé féin, chuala mé m'athair agus mo mháthair, agus mo sheanmhuintir uilig a rá, ag cur síos ar oíche Shamhna. Well, b'fhada liomsa ná a bhfaca mé riamh nuair a bhí me óg go bhfeicinn oíche Shamhna tagaithe le go bhfeicinn an obair seo a bhí acu. Agus, bhí mé a faire agus oíche Shamhna thugadar isteach gabáiste, trí bhileog gabáiste ar an urlár agus thugadar créafóg isteach agus chuireadar ar bhileog acub é agus thugadar isteach uisce glan agus thugadar ar bhileog eile é. Thug siad isteach uisce salach agus chuir siad ar bhileog eile é. Bhí mise a faire. Anois, gearr go dtáinig na daoiní seo isteach a bhí ag iarraidh an fios agus dúradh leo go gcaithfí púicín a chur ar a súilí. Cuireadh púicín ar a súilí, na bhfear óg, agus iad a déanamh a n-aghaidh ar an ngabáiste agus dhá gcuiridís lámh insa salachar, ba baintreach a bheadh acu mar bhean agus dhá gcuiridís san uisce glan é, ba bean óg é agus dhá gcuiridís insa gcréafóg é, bhí siad ag déanamh amach go raibh a dhuine caillte. Well, chonaic mé féin a tíocht anuas iad agus ag cur a láimh insa ngabáiste ach níl mé an-dearfach[?] anois cé acu ar chuir siad a lámh insa gceann glan nó sa gceann salach go háithrid an t-am sin. Well, nuair a bheadh na fir óga ansin triáilte ar an mbealach sin, thriáilfeadh na mná óga iad féin freisin dhá léir.

Nuair a bheadh 'chaon cheann acu sin déanta ansin acu, ghabhaidís amach agus ghabhaidís go dtí sruthán teorthann a bhí idir dhá bhaile. Agus thabharfaidís lán béil den uisce leo agus thiocaidís go dtí an teach is mó a gceapaidís sioscadh cainte a bheith ann. Agus thiocaidís sa doras dúinte, duine i ndiaidh duine agus fébí caint a déanfaí istigh bheidís a faire, féachaint a gcainteofaí ar ainm duine eicínt dá ba iad na fir a bheadh insa … ann agus an doras dúinte agus iad a faire cén t-ainm mná a gcainteofaí uirthi. Ba shin é an t-ainm a cheapadar a bhí ar an mbean a bheadh acu. Nuair a bheadh an duine sin réidh ansin, d'imeodh sé agus thiocfadh ceann eile agus thiocfadh an tríú ceann dhá léir go bhfaigheadh sé féin a chuid feasa féin agus d'imeodh leo. Well, bhí beagán eile ansin acu nuair a bheidís a dhul a chodladh insan oíche thléis an oíche a chaitheamh ar an obair sin. Agus nuair a bhainidís a gcuid éadaigh san oíche díob, chuiridís an treabhsar i gcoirnéal den leaba agus chuiridís an drár i gcoirnéal eile den leaba, agus chuiridís an veist i gcoirnéal eile den leaba, agus chuiridís an léine i gcoirnéal eile den leaba. Well, bhíodar ag déanamh amach dearfa cinnte ansin an té a mbeifeá ag brionglóidí air insan oíche gurb shin é an t-ainm a bheadh ar do chéile, a bheadh agat – pósta. Agus bhí na seandaoine a rá go raibh sé sin cinnte, siúráilte.

SE: Well, an gcreideann tú féin a raibh aon fhírinne ann?

CÓC: Creidim go maith go raibh fírinne ann, mar chonaic mé féin go leor Éirinn más mé is óige, de na rudaí seo.

SE: Well, an mbídís ag goid ghabáiste nó ag déanamh aon ní mar sin?

CÓC: Bhídís ag goid ghabáiste, ag imeacht insan oíche ansin, ag goid ghabáiste agus dhá chaitheamh ar an mbóthar, ag taispeáint go mba í oíche Shamhna a bhí ann.

SE: Well, ar chuala tú go raibh údar ar bith le bheith ag caitheamh an gabáiste ar an mbóthar?

CÓC: Níor chuala mé go raibh aon údar leis ach go mba sórt, go raibh sé, ná raibh aon dlí insan oíche sin ar aon fhear a bheadh a déanamh spraoi mar sin. Cuir i gcás nach dtaitníodh sé le fear an ghabáiste go mór lá arna mháireach nuair a d'fhághadh sé ar an mbóthar é. Ach féacha, théidís ag déanamh spraoi in aon turas ag tabhairt anall as garraí fear eile. Agus dhá scaradh in aice garraí an fhir seo le go gceapfadh an fear seo gurb é a chuid gabáiste féin a bheadh tugthaí chun bealaigh. Agus nuair a d'éireodh fear an ghabáiste sin ar maidin agus nuair a d'fheiceadh sé na bileogaí seo, d'imeodh sé, ó, ní raibh fear ar bith a bhí chomh fiáin leis mar gheall ar a chuid gabáistí. Agus gan blas ar bith tugthaí as an ngabáiste ach na leads ag déanamh spraoi ag caitheamh an ghabáiste i bhfianaise an gharraí ar an mbóthar.

SE: Is ea.

31. Hallowe'en

SE: Colm, recently we spoke with an old man who had some lore for us about Hallowe'en. I think you are not without some lore that you got from the old folk.

CÓC: Well, I have lore about Hallowe'en, what I saw myself. And what I did not see, I heard my father and mother, and all the old folk saying it, describing Hallowe'en. Well, when I was young I couldn't wait for Hallowe'en to come to see what they were doing. And I was on the lookout, and at Hallowe'en they brought in cabbage, three cabbage leaves on the floor and they brought clay in and they put it on one of the leaves and they brought clean water in and they put it on another leaf. They brought in dirty water and they put it on a leaf. I was watching. Now, it wasn't long before these people came in who wanted to know their destiny and they were told they would have to be blindfolded. They were blindfolded, the young men, as they approached the cabbage and if they put their hand in the dirty water, they would marry a widow and if they put it in the clean water, they would marry a young woman and if they put it in the clay, it was supposed that a relative would die. Well, I saw them myself coming to the cabbage and putting their hand in it but I'm not sure now if they put their hand in the clean one or the dirty one especially that time. Well, when the young men had been tested in that way, then they would test the young women accordingly.

When they were both done, they would go out and they would go down to a boundary stream between two places and they would take a mouthful of water with them and would come to the house they thought most likely to have a buzz of talk. And they would come to the closed door one by one, and whatever talk was happening inside, they were watching out to see if someone would be named if it was the men who were in the … And the door would be closed and they would watch out to see what woman's name would be mentioned, that they would discuss. That was the name of the woman they thought they would have. When that person was ready, then he would leave and another would come and accordingly a third would come to discover his own destiny and they would leave. Well, they had a little more then as they were going to bed that night having spent the evening with this practice. And when they took their clothes off at night they would put the trousers in one corner of the bed, the drawers in another corner of the bed, and they placed the vest in another corner of the bed and they would put the shirt in another corner of the bed. Well, they thought then, for sure, that the person you would dream about that night, that that was the name of your future spouse, that you would marry. And the old people said that that was definite, it was certain.

SE: Well, do you believe there is any truth in it?

CÓC: I certainly believe there was truth in it because I saw a vast number of these things as I am the youngest.

SE: Well, used they steal cabbages or do anything similar?

CÓC: They used to steal cabbages, going around at night stealing cabbages and throwing them on the road, to show that it was Hallowe'en.

SE: Well, did you ever hear a reason for throwing cabbages on the road?

CÓC: I never heard there was a reason for it but that it was a kind of, that it was, that there was no law enforcement that night for anyone who caused that kind of mischief. Say, for example, that the cabbage owner did not like it at all when he found it on the road the following morning. But see, they made mischief on purpose, taking it from another man's field and spreading it in another man's field, so that this man would think they were his own cabbages had been taken. And when that cabbage owner got up the following morning and when he saw the leaves he would go ... no-one would be as angry as he would be about his cabbages. And nothing happened about the cabbages except that the lads caused mischief throwing the cabbages from the field, on the road.

SE: Yes.

> In Irish tradition, Hallowe'en or 'Samhain' in Irish is a time of tricks, disguise and divination in celebration of one of the four quarter days. The eve of Samhain, the 31st of October, as Colm describes it, is the time for tricks and prophecy and a time when general rules do not apply.[99]
>
> When asked by Ennis about his recollections, Colm communicates his enthusiasm for the fun of the occasion.

32. *Cúirt an tSrutháin Bhuí*[100]

Tá Rí na Gréige ag iarraidh scéala, cé mar dearnadh í,
Ní bhfaigheadh sé é gan tuairim is céad agus dhiúltaigh sé dhá íoc,
Tá plátaí péatair ar 'ghreen table', sin agus díol an Rí
Dhá roinnt ina dhéirce ar bhoichte Dé tá Banríon an tSáirdín.

There was a little house that was made beyond in Lettermullan long ago, with stone – it wasn't stone but sand – and the green grass was growing inside in it and that's what they made out that it was a green table – the green grass. And Wallace and Cloherty was making this song – both of them helping one another. And then Gorham was beyond in Letter … long ago, with a load of turf and they were drinking in a pub and one of the boatsmen says to Gorham that he was able to do it better, to make it better. And he went down to the boat the way that nobody would bother him and he made the song and he says to Cloherty, Mr Cloherty:

Ó, is a Mhister Cloherty nach mór mo ghrá dhuit,
Is tá mo nádúr leat as ucht mo ghaoil.
Nuair a thiocfas an t-earrach is tosóidh an ghrian ag ardú,
Rachaidh mé i do cheann isteach go ceann cúpla mí.
Mar níl aon obair bhreá ariamh a chuala mé trácht uirthi,
A mbeadh m'intinn sásta nó go bhfeicinn í.
Ach thléis a bhfaca mé is gur shiúil mé an méid údain,
Agus molaim an 'sway' le Cúirt an tSrutháin Bhuí.

Ó, is é Cormac Ó Cairt a rinne carrachaí na féile,
Agus Cúirt Bhinn Éadain, ba le Cú Chulainn í.
Mar bhí mé i nDoire thíos, san áit a raibh na séipéil bhreátha,
A raibh an t-aifreann dhá léamh iontub gach lá insa mí.
Mar a maraíodh Samson ann le troid na Gréige,
Cailleadh Páras agus Éilin ann le scrios na Draoi,
Ach ní maith liom Wallace bocht ar scáth a léigh sé,
A ghabháil a déanamh cúirt chomh tréan is tá sa Sruthán Bhuí.

Fig. 25: *Cúirt an tSrutháin Bhuí.* NFC MMS 19

Ós is nach mór an buille anois ar dhaoiní óga,
Gan caladh sách dóchasach a bheith ann le haghaidh loing agus báid,
Le bheith foghlaim 'exercise' is a caitheamh gróití,
Agus clochaí móra le spracadh cnámh.
Mar dúnfar an Daingean, is déanfar bealach cóiste ann.
Is beidh na báid i gcontúirt a gabháil os cionn an Chinn,
Is mara dtroide Wallace ar shon a gháirdín phléisiúir,
Bainfear seilbh éigin de sa Sruthán Bhuí.

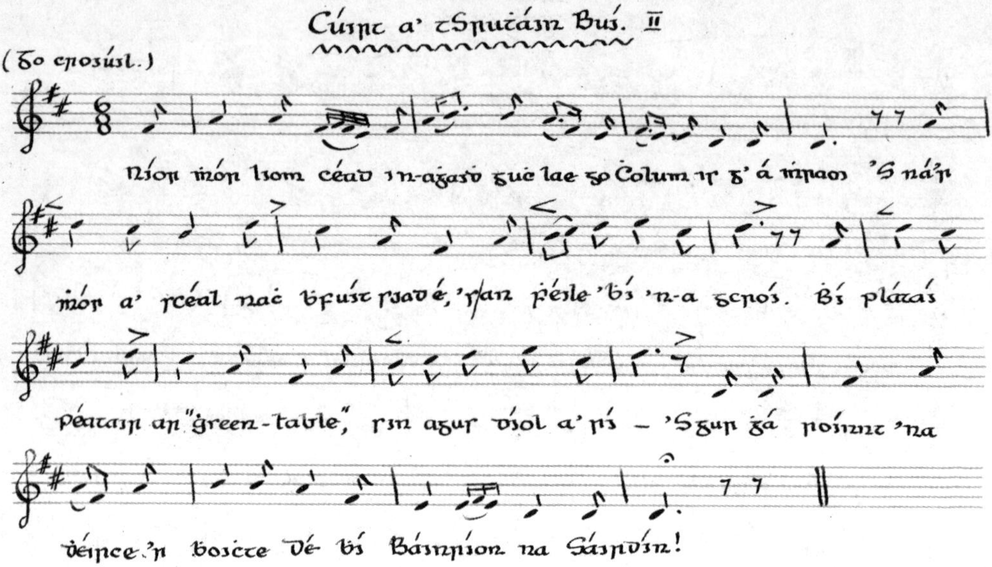

Fig. 26: *Cúirt an tSrutháin Bhuí II.* NFC MMS 19

Tiocfaidh socrú 'Government', tiocfaidh breitheamh agus méara air,
Tiocfaidh na Poles agus na Danes ann agus na Littalies,
Is beidh na Christa-Turkeys ar an mbealach céanna ann,
Agus lorg géar acub i ndiaidh an Sáirdín,
Nuair a chloisfeas an Lochlannach é lucht Tuirgéise,
Mar ba bheag an féirín dúinn é a thíocht aríst,
Nuair a chuaigh sé go na Fortaginians siar a cruinniú néigiors bhoicht,
Faoi chomhair na téisclime a bhí insa Sruthán Bhuí.

32. The Court of the Yellow Stream

The King of Greece wants to know how it was made,
He won't get it for less than about a hundred and he has refused to pay,
There are pewter plates on that green table and a regal portion,
Being shared amongst God's poor by the Queen of Sardinia.[101]

There was a little house that was made beyond in Lettermullan long ago, with stone – it wasn't stone but sand – and the green grass was growing inside in it and that's what they made out that it was a green table – the green grass. And Wallace and Cloherty was making this song – both of them helping one another. And then Gorham was beyond in Letter … long ago, with a load of turf and they were drinking in the pub and one of the boatsmen says to Gorham that he was able to compose it better, to make it better, and he went down to the boat the way that nobody would bother him and he made the song and he says to Cloherty, Mr Cloherty:

Mister Cloherty I love you dearly,
I hold you in affection because of my kinship,
When spring comes and the sun begins to rise,
I will go with you for a few months.
For there is no great work I ever heard of,
That would satisfy my mind until I could see it.
But after what I have seen and having travelled that distance,
I give the highest praise to the Court of the Yellow Stream.

Cormac Ó Cairt built the causeway of the feasts,
And the Court of Howth – it belonged to Cú Chulainn.
Because I was below in Derry where there were fine chapels,
Where mass was read every single day of the month.
While Samson was killed in the Grecian war,
Paris and Helen died there at the destruction of Troy,[102]
But I do not like poor Wallace given the extent of his reading,
Going to build such a strong court as exists in Sruthán Buí.

And isn't it a heavy blow now for young people,
Without a sufficiently secure harbour, for ships and boats.
To learn what exercise is and tossing crow-bars,
And large stones by dint of strong bones.
Because Daingean will be closed and a road for coaches will
  be built.
And the boats will be in danger going beyond the headland,[103]
And if Wallace doesn't fight for his garden of pleasure,
He will be dispossessed by force in An Sruthán Buí.

A Government solution with judge and mayor will come about,
Along with the Poles and the Danes and the Littalies.
The Christa-Turkeys will be in the same way there,
With a strong desire to possess Sardinia.
When the Viking, the people of Turgéis hear of it,[104]
Because it would be poor reward for us if he were to come again,
When he went west to the Fortaginians to collect poor black
people,
Because of the preparations in An Sruthán Buí.

The song is said to have been composed originally by the poet Colm de Bhailís (Wallace as mentioned in the song). Another poet, Micheál Ó Clochartaigh, is said to have rearranged it and it was reshaped afterwards by poet Seán Ó Guairim.[105]

33. Miss McCleod's Reel[106]

This is a very popular reel in Irish music tradition. It is known in England, Scotland, Ireland, Canada and the United States and is known by a number of other titles. It was published in 1810 in *O'Farrell's Pocket Companion for the Irish or Union Pipes*, London, vol. 4, p. 137, entitled 'Mrs McCleod', and described as 'Scotch'. It is also known as 'Mrs MacLeod of Raasay'. 'Mrs MacLeod' was published in Niel Gow's *Fifth Collection of Strathspeys, Reels &c. For the Piano Forte, Harp, Violin & Violoncello* (Edinburgh, 1809).

CHAPTER 3

'An Ediphone Machine on the Table'

PERSONAL LORE, LOCAL CUSTOM AND BELIEF

Colm Ó Caodháin not only shared his music and song, but he also allowed collectors a glimpse into his world. His life experiences shed light on his understanding of how the natural, supernatural and religious planes intersected and functioned. His accounts, which range from his reaction to the Ediphone recording machine, the singing experience and his acquisition of songs, paint a picture of life in Glinsce, County Galway, in the early and mid-twentieth century. Colm's recollections of adventures give us a context for his working life and for some of the dangers and challenges he and his contemporaries faced. His accounts of beliefs and customs echo aspects of the nature of vernacular life in much of Conamara in the first and second quarters of the twentieth century.

The following are some examples from the recordings made by Séamus Ennis from Colm in the 1940s, concerning Colm's engagement with collecting, as well as examples of his personal lore and of local custom and belief.

THE EDIPHONE

Séamus Ennis wrote that he first received the Ediphone recording machine from the Irish Folklore Commission on 10 June 1944 and used it thereafter when collecting from Colm. At first, Colm was afraid of the machine and thought his voice was weak, but he gradually became accustomed to it.

Colm ag sciollaíocht leis an Ediphone[1]

Meastú dá gcuirfinn faoi mo smig mar seo é, nach amhlaidh is fearr a bheadh glór aige? Ní thaitníonn liom an glór atá ag tíocht amach – feicthear dhom go bhfuil sé an-bhodhránta! Feicthear dhom go bhfuil mé ag cur focal breá cainte isteach ann is níl a fhios agam, beirthe ná beo, cén fáth nach labhródh sé amach breá gnaíúil mar tá mé féin ag labhairt, mar bhí an ghnaíúlacht ag plé linne riamh, is neart ceisteannaí againn. Níl a fhios agam, beirthe ná beo, céard atá air, marar ceal braon óil atá air!

Céad míle slán don am a raibh sú an ghráinne eorna againn agus buidéal breá poitín, dhá mbeifeá ag cogarnach féin is é an chaoi mbeadh béiciúch dhearg as do chionn! Ach tá sé sin stopaithe anois. Dhá siúlfá Conamara anois ní bhfaighfeá lán do bhéil de fuisce ann – 'ól pórtar, má thograíonn tú é'. Is ár ndóigh níl aon chroí ansin le haghaidh cainteannaí! Níl! Ní raibh aon cheo faoin domhan ní ba bhreáichte ná an braon. Ó mhuise, céad míle slán don bhraoinín poitín, nó an gloine fuisce féin, sin é thabharfadh an croí dhuit le haghaidh cainte labhairt. Agus an tobac.

Insan am a raibh ganntan an tobac anseo i mbliana ar ndóigh, níor léir dhomsa Cnoc an Chaisil is ba mhór é, le ceal aon ghráinne tobac. Ach mo sheacht míle beannacht ag an té a chuir chugam ar an bpost é. D'oscail mé é agus bhí mé dhá chaitheamh. Ach chaith mé é agus bhí carr asail agam ag gabháil i gcoinne carr móna is má bhí féin, ní raibh a fhios agam an é an t-asal nó an carr a gcuirfinn an mhóin ann, nuair a bhí mo dhóthain caite agam, leis an mearbhall a bhí curtha ag an tobac orm- mar gheall ar gur chaith mé seachtain gan aon ghráinne a chaitheamh an t-am sin. Ach tá mé ag cur mo sheacht míle beannacht ag an dream seo agus Séamus seo atá in éindí liom; is ar ndóigh, níl aon uair a thiocfas sé nach bhfuil neart tobac agam, neart tobac. Agus sin é an tobac is fiú chaitheamh, ní hé an tobac é a bhfuil na ceirteachaí istigh ann.

Bhí mé dhá choinneáil seo scathamh mór amach ó mo bhéal, creidim go raibh faitíos orm nuair nach raibh a fhios agam cén sórt rud é féin. Ach anois ó chuala mé ag rá na gcainteannaí seo é, feicthear dhom gur breá bláthmhar atá sé. Bláfar atá sé, bláfar atá sé, bláfar atá sé agus araile (deireadh fiteáin).

Colm scolds the Ediphone

I wonder if I put it under my chin, like this, would it make a better sound? I don't like the sound that comes out. It seems to be very deafening. I think I give it fine words of speech, and I have no idea why it can't speak properly and clearly just as I am speaking. Because we were always known to be well-mannered people, and we had lots of things to say. I have no idea what's wrong with it – unless it needs a drink.

God be with the days when we had the juice of the barley and a fine bottle of *poitín*, even if you were whispering you would have loud yelling above you. But that has stopped! If you were to travel throughout Conamara, you wouldn't get a mouthful of whiskey – but you could drink porter if you wanted to. And of course, that doesn't have the spirit that gives rise to clever talk. It doesn't. Nothing in the world surpassed the drop. Farewell to the small drop of *poitín*, or even the glass of whiskey, that would give you such heart for speaking. And tobacco too.

When tobacco was scarce here this year, it even affected my sight and I couldn't see Cnoc an Chaisil and it is a big hill, because I didn't have a grain of tobacco. But seven thousand blessings to the person who posted it to me. I opened it and I was smoking it. I had a donkey cart to fetch turf and if I had itself, I didn't know if I should put the turf in the donkey or the cart, as I was so dizzy after I had smoked so much tobacco because I had spent a week before that without smoking a grain. I send seven thousand blessings to these people and to Séamus here who is beside me; and always whenever he visits I always have plenty of tobacco. And that tobacco is well worth smoking. It's pure tobacco without any rubbish in it.

I was holding the contraption that I have to speak into, a good bit away from my mouth. I think I was afraid, as I didn't know what kind of thing it was. But now, since I have heard it speaking these words, I think it is fine and beautiful. It is really beautiful.[2]

A COMMENT ON THE EDIPHONE

Séamus Ennis wrote this comment from Colm about the first recording on the Ediphone:

'Muise faraor géar cráite nár chuir muid isteach le "hammer and tongs" cainte go dtí an phutóg íochtarach ann.'[3]

'It's a terrible shame we didn't put the speech "hammer and tongs" into it, right into its heart.'

Caint bheag ó Cholm féin (cumha air ag éisteacht leis na hamhráin)[4]

Dúirt daoine go leor liomsa, tá tuairim agus sé déag nó seacht déag de bhlianta ó shin ann, go raibh cosúlacht mhór agam péin le m'athair ag gabháil fhoinn. Agus ní raibh mé cinnte ab shin í an fhírinne nó nacha ba í, nó gur chuala mé é seo ag rá mo chuid amhrán amach aríst ar ais dom; agus bhí mé tabhairt chun suime ansin go mba í an fhírinne í. Mar is éard a bhí ag m'athair, glór breá, binn ná raibh scréachta nuair a bhí sé ag rá amhrán.

A short piece from Colm (lonesome when listening to the songs)

Many people told me, about sixteen or seventeen years ago, that I was very like my father singing and I wasn't sure whether it was true or not until I heard the machine singing my songs back to me, and then I thought that it must be true. Because my father had a fine, melodious voice that wasn't too exaggerated and loud when he was singing.

Mar tharla na hamhráin ag Colm do Shéamus Ennis[5]

Nuair a bhí mise i m'fhear óg agus mé ag éirí suas in éindí le m'athair, ní raibh i gceist agam ach amhráin agus poirt. Agus bhínn dhá rá agus eisean do mo threorú le rudaí ar bith a mbínn ag gabháil amú iontub. Bhíodh siad ag taitneachtáil go han-mhór liom. Ach ansin, nuair a tháinig gnaithí an tsaoil agus go leor rudaí eile ag rith thrí mo chloigeann, bhí na hamhráin a brath ar imeacht. Ach nuair a tháinig Séamus go dtí mé, thug mé cúpla ceann dó an chéad oíche, agus cheap mé ná raibh ceann ar bith sách maith le thabhairt dó. Is mar sin féin, na cinn ab fhearr a bhí agam, thug mé dhó iad agus nuair a chonaic mé go raibh muid féin ag taitneachtáil le chéile go han-mhaith, is é an chaoi a mbínn ag breathnú ar an mbóthar le súil, le faitíos nach mbeadh Séamus ag tíocht anocht. Agus de léir mar bhí Séamus is mé féin in éineacht, is é chaoi a raibh muid féin ag gabháil i ngrá dhá chéile. Ach is é an chaoi bhfuil an-trioblóid anois orm, faoi iad a thabhairt dó uilig as a chéile, an méid a bhí agam gan iad a spáráil le haghaidh é choinneáil ag tíocht an bóthar i gcónaí, agus sin é an fáth go deimhin. Marach sin, bheadh na hamhráin uilig imithe uaimse – ní raibh agam ach cúpla ceann, bhíodar imithe as mo chuimhne. Ach nuair a bhínn ag inseacht ceann anocht dhó, bhínn ag cuimhneamh ar cheann eile lena aghaidh amáireach. Agus dhúisigh mé suas aríst ar bhealach eicínt iad, ach go bhfuil cuid acub nach bhfuil mé an-siúráilte, is go bhfuil cuid acub a bhfuil mé siúráilte fúthub.

How Colm came to have songs for Séamus Ennis

When I was a young man growing up alongside my father, all I wanted were songs and tunes. And I would sing them, and he would guide me wherever I was going astray. I liked them a lot, but then, when life became demanding and many other things were on my mind, I had almost forgotten the songs. When Séamus came, I gave him a few the first night and I thought that none of them were good enough, but nevertheless I gave him my finest. When I saw that we were getting on so well together, I used to watch the road because I was afraid that Séamus mightn't come of an evening. When Séamus and I had been together a good deal, we became very fond of one another. And now I am very upset about giving all the songs to him at one go, all that I had, not to spare them, so as to keep him coming back to see me, and that is truly the reason. If it weren't for that, all my songs would be lost. Only a few remained. I had forgotten them. Then, as I was singing one for him one night, I was thinking of another one for the next day. And I revived them again, somehow, but I'm not very sure of some of them and I'm sure of others.

Beirt amhránaí Ghlinsce[6]

Chuala mise m'athair ag rá gurb é an faisean a bhí anseo fadó i mBaile Ghlinsce, go raibh beirt ann agus ná raibh aon ríochan[7] *leo ag gabháil fhoinn – mar bhí a athair féin agus fear de mhuintir Uaithnín a raibh Tomás Ó Uaithnín air. Nuair a theagaidís isteach in san oíche léis a lá oibre, shínidís siar sa teallach agus bhainidís dhíob a mbróga agus thosaídís ag téidheamh a gcosaí leis an teine. Agus nuair a bhídís sách te leis an teine, thagadh fonn foinn orthub. Agus d'abraíodh fear acub amhrán agus bhíodh an fear eile ag fanacht nó go mbeadh sé réidh leis an amhrán le go dtosódh sé féin ceann eile. Agus bhí na dá theach a rabhadar iontub, bhíodar trí scór coisméagachaí ó chéile, agus bhídís féin ag faire a chéile go mbíodh an t-amhrán ráite ag an bhfear seo le go dtosaíodh an fear eile, agus bhíodh an ealaín sin orthub nó go mbíodh sé in am codlata.*

Two singers in Glinsce

I heard my father say that here in Glinsce long ago, there were two singers and there was no equalling them in singing. These were his own father and an Ó hUaithnín, whose name was Tomás Ó Uaithnín. When they came in at night after a day's work, they stretched back at the hearth, took off their shoes and began warming their feet at the fire. And when they were sufficiently warmed by the fire, they felt like singing and one of them sang a song and the other waited until he had finished the song before starting another. Their two houses, they were sixty steps apart, and they watched each other until one of them finished his song and the other then began and they continued in this way until it was time for bed.

Tart coiscithe[8]

Bhí mise ag iascach i nGaillimh, i mbád iascach; chuaigh muid soir as Roundstone ag iascach scadán go Caoláire na Gaillimhe. Agus tháinig an aimsir an-dona agus coinníodh istigh i ndug na Gaillimhe muid agus ní raibh muid in ann a ghabháil ag iascach ar feadh seachtaine. Ach bhí slám den iasc a thóig muid an tseachtain roimhe sin; bhí sé saillltí againn dhúinn féin agus nuair a d'itheadh muid béilí fataí agus an t-iasc goirt, bhíodh an-tart orainn.

Ach bhí muid an lá seo agus bhí muid thuas insa mbaile mór, mé féin agus fear eile den chriú, agus chuala muid muintir Chuan an Fhir Mhóir agus iad istigh tigh Tom Uí Loideáin i nGaillimh ag gabháil fhoinn go hard. Agus ní aon leathghalún amháin a bhí ag roinnt pórtair ann ach dhá leathghalún; agus bhí muid féin amuigh ar an tsráid agus dúil an domhain againn insa stuif a bhí istigh, dhá bhféadfadh muid aon deoir dhe fháil. Bhí dhá phínn nó trí pínn agam péin agus d'fhiafraigh mé den fhear eile a raibh aon phínn aige féin agus dúirt sé go raibh cúpla pínn. Ach féibrí scéal é, rinne muid suas luach píonta portair – sin gloine don fhear againn agus dúirt mise leis go ngabhfadh muid isteach agus 'nuair a ghabhfas muid isteach,' a deirim péin, 'ná leig ort féin go bhfuil duine ar bith istigh ach muid féin, agus leigfidh muid orainn féin go bhfuil muid ar dearg mheisce. Agus glaofaidh mise na dá ghloine pórtair agus ná bíodh deifir ar bith dhá n-ól orainn, ag baint fad astu, ag leigean orainn féin go bhfuil muid – braon ólta againn. Ach faoi cheann scathaimh, déarfaidh tusa liomsa más é mo thoil é, cúpla ceathrú d'amhrán a rá,' agus ar ndóigh, b'fhada liomsa gur hiarradh orm é agus lom orm agus dúirt mé 'Maidin Chiúin dhár Éirigh Mé'. Agus ní raibh ráite agam ach aon cheathrú amháin de 'Mhaidin Chiúin dhár Éirigh Mé', nuair a tháinig fear anall lena leathghalún agus lena phíonta mór go dtí mé, agus dúirt sé liom: 'Á muise, grá mo chroí go deo thú! Seo, ól é seo i dtosach. Is tú tá in ann é rá. Níor chuala mise riamh níos breáichte é.' Ach is é an chaoi a raibh drochbhail ar an amhrán ar deireadh againn agus muid ag ól pórtair. Agus ní ar amhráin a bhí aird againn faoi cheann scathaimh, ach ar ól agus is é chaoi a raibh muid dallta ar deireadh ag gabháil abhaile chun an bháid dúinn agus tart an iasc ghoirt coiscithe.

A thirst quenched

I was fishing in Galway, in a fishing boat; we went herring fishing from Roundstone to Galway Bay. And the weather turned very bad and we were held up in the docks in Galway and were unable to go fishing for a week. We had salted an amount of the fish that we had caught the previous week, for ourselves, and when we ate a meal of potatoes and salted fish we were very thirsty.

We were in the city, myself and another member of the crew, and we heard the people from Cuan an Fhir Mhóir[9] and they were in Tom Ó Loideáin's pub in Galway and they were singing loudly. And it wasn't a single half gallon of porter that was being shared but two

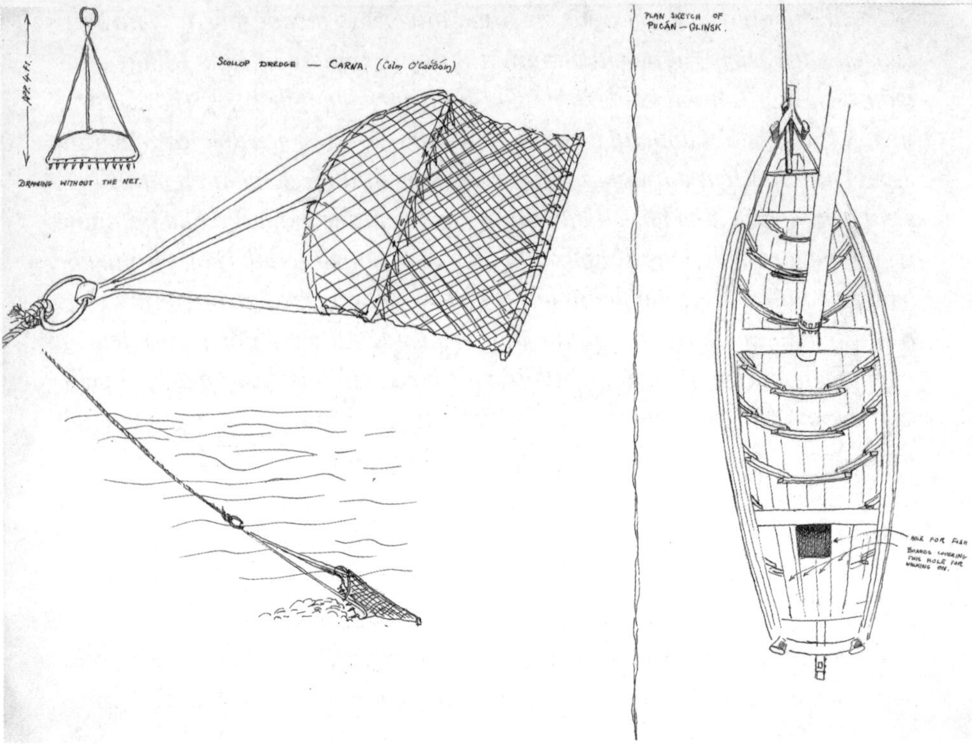

Fig. 27: Colm's scallop dredge and *púcán*. Drawn by Simon Coleman, 1959.
COURTESY NFC

half gallons; but we were on the street outside and we were longing for some of the drink inside if there was any way we could get a drop of it. I had two or three pence and I asked my mate if he had a penny and he said he had a few pence. At any rate, we put the price of a pint of porter together – that was a glass each – and I said we would go in. And 'When we go in,' I said, 'let on there is no one else here other than ourselves and we will pretend to be blind drunk. And I will order the two glasses of porter and we won't be in any hurry to drink them and we will take a long time drinking them, pretending that we have a drop taken. But after a while, tell me please to sing a few verses of a song.' Of course, I couldn't wait to be asked and I started up and I sang '*Maidin Chiúin dhár Éirigh Mé*' ['One Quiet Morning that I Got Up'] and I had only sung a verse when a man came over to me with his half gallon and his large pint and he said to me: 'Oh, my good man! Here, drink this first. You are a great singer. I never heard it sung better.' But we drank so much porter, that in the end we made a bad job of the song. After a while our attention wasn't on the songs but on drink. In the end, we were drunk going back to the boat but the thirst from the salted fish was quenched.

Comhairle faoin amhránaíocht[10]

Comhairle a thugadh a athair do Cholm fadó faoi amhránaíocht: 'Tosaigh an t-amhrán go réidh agus ardaigh de léir a chéile é, ní baol ansin go mbrisfidh do ghuth.'

Advice about singing

His father gave advice to Colm long ago about singing: 'Start the song gently and raise it slowly, there is no fear then that your voice will break.'

Fiacail an cheoil[11]

Tá mise ag fulaingt ón bpian anois le [seacht] lá na seachtaine, le dathachaí fiacal agus tá mé ag imeacht romham le pian iontub. Ní raibh a fhios agam beirthe ná beo agus gan mórán truaighe dhom. Is é an chaoi mbíodh daoiní ag gáirí fúm an t-am is measa mbínn le pian, is ní raibh rud ar bith ag cur fearg chríochnaithe orm ach nuair d'fheicinn daoine ag gairí – ní raibh a fhios agam cé mb'fhearr dom 'jumpáil' isteach ina bputógaí nó éisteacht leob. Ach mar sin féin, fuair mé an fhiacail tarraingthe agus go deimhin ní bréag tá mé a dhéanamh, mar bhí sí chomh mór ar chaoi ar bith le bosca Shéamuis (an Ediphone).

Ach nuair a bhí mé ag tíocht abhaile ansin, measann tú, nár chuimhnigh mé go mb'fhéidir gurbh í an fhiacail a raibh an ceol inti í, mar chloisinn seandaoine a rá riamh, a dtuigeann tú, i dtaobh fiacail a mbeadh ceol inti. Agus scanraigh mé go mb'fhéidir go mba í an fhiacail a raibh an ceol inti í. Ní raibh cnocán, ná claí, ná ardán ar bith dhá raibh timcheall ar an teach ná raibh mé ag seasamh suas air, féachaint a raibh Séamus ag tíocht tráthnóna. Agus b'fhaide liom go raibh se ag tíocht le go dtriálfainn mé féin ar a ghléas ceoil, go bhfeicinn an í an fhiacail a raibh an ceol inti a bhí caillte agam nó nacha ba í. Ach 'bydad', nuair a thriáil mé mé féin, míle buíochas le Dia, níor chaill mé an fhiacail a raibh an ceol inti fós.

The music tooth

I have been suffering and in pain for seven days this week from a toothache and I am going around in terrible pain. I had no idea why, and no-one took pity on me. The more I was in pain, the more people laughed at me and nothing made me more angry than seeing people laughing. I didn't know if I should have a go at them or leave them be. Nonetheless, I had the tooth pulled and it is no lie when I say that it was as big as Séamus' box (the Ediphone).

But when I was coming home then, didn't I think that maybe that was the tooth that had the music in it, because I used to hear the old people talking, do you know, about a tooth that had music in it. And I was afraid that maybe that was the music tooth. I stood on every hill, wall and height around the house to see if Séamus was coming in the evening. And I couldn't wait to see him coming to test myself on his musical instrument, to see if I had lost the tooth that had the music in it or not. But, bydad, when I tested myself, a thousand thanks to God, I hadn't lost the tooth that had the music in it yet.

Tobar a thaoscadh[12]

Na toibreachaí beannaithe seo a bhíodh leagthaí amach do na Naoimh – Tobar Cholmcille agus araile – bhí sé creistithe ag seandaoiní dhá mba mhaith leat mioscas nó díoltas imirt ar aon duine, ná raibh agat ach tobar acub seo a thaoscadh amach tirim nuair bheadh an duine seo ar an bhfarraige nó in áit mar sin ó bhaile, agus nach dtiocfadh sé slán.

Bhí siad ag ceapadh ansin go mba uafásach dona an rud é le dhéanamh, agus go dtiocfadh taispeánadh mór de chineál eicínt mar dhíoltas air sin – seal fada doininne agus droch-aimsire, b'fhéidir, nó aicíde eicínt, nó cogadh.

Draining a well

These holy wells that were dedicated to the Saints – Colmcille's Well and so on – people believed that if you wanted to do something bad to someone or exact revenge, all you had to do was to empty one of these wells dry, when this person was at sea or in some place like that, away from home, and that he would not return safely.

They thought then that it was a terrible thing to do and that some dreadful event would occur in revenge for it, a long spell of stormy or bad weather, perhaps, or some plague or a war.

Déanamh poitín[13]

Chuala mé seandaoine ag rá go minic, áit a mbíonn poitín dhá dhéanamh ann, go mbíonn na daoiní maithe timcheall ar theach na stileach ag súil le brabach i bhfuisce – le braon dhe lena ól. Nuair a bhíodh tuairim is cárt den fuisce tarraingthe, ansin leagaidís 'jug' dhe ar chúla an chocáin le haghaidh na ndaoiní maithe. Chuala mé na seandaoiní a rá gur minic fear ag leagan 'jug' amach dhób agus nuair a thagadh sé i gcoinne an 'jug' arís, bhíodh an 'jug' tirim.

Making *poitín*[14]

I often heard the old people say that a place where *poitín* is being made, the good people are there, by the stillhouse, hoping for a good supply of *poitín* to drink a drop of it. When about a quart of the *poitín* was drawn, they would place a jug of it behind the pot for the good people. I heard the old people say that a person would often leave a jug of it out for them and when they came to fetch it again the jug was empty.

Iascach ronnach[15]

Well, tháinig duine uasal go dtí mise, an Búrcach, Frainc, ag iarraidh scéalta. Agus chomh tráthúil agus chonaic tú ariamh, cén lá a dtiocfadh sé go dtí mé ach an lá a raibh mé socraithe a gabháil amach ag iascach ronnach, mar bhíodar tagthaí thiar sa mBeirtreach Bhuí breá tréan. Well, tháinig sé isteach agus leag sé Ediphone anuas ar an mbord chugam go dtosaínn ag inseacht scéalta dhó.

'Ara, téirigh i mullach an diabhail,' a dúirt mise, 'thú féin agus é féin, nach amach ag iarraidh ronnach atá mise a gabháil. Má thograíonn tú a thíocht, tearaigh.'

'Mh'anam go bhfuil mé sásta,' a deir sé.

Bhuail muid amach. Bhí an oiread gaoithe ann agus gur cheangail muid péire cúrsaí agus chuaigh muid siar. Bhí muid ag seoladh siar ón gCarraig Léith anois ag déanamh ar Ghob an Tamhain. Agus nuair a bhí muid siar ag an gCarraig Léith ní raibh muid ag aireachtáil tada go fóilleach. Agus chonaic muid cluiche breá éanachaí thiar ag Gob an Tanaí.

'Fan anois go fóilleach,' a deir an Búrcach, 'cuirfidh mé punt leat gur gearr go maraí muid iad.'

Ar ndóigh, b'fhíor dhó. Chomh luath agus chuaigh muid isteach ins na héanachaí, thosaigh muid ag tarraingt ronnach chomh tréan agus d'fhéad muid é. Ní ar scéalta a bhí aird againn go deimhin, ach ar tharraingt. Ach an bhfuil a fhios agat cén chaoi a raibh an scéal, marach go raibh cuma bháistí ag tíocht ar an tráthnóna, diabhal Búrcach ná Colm a thiocfadh isteach go mbeadh sé b'fhéidir maidneachan lae lá arna mhárach.

Well, anois na snúdaí a bheidheas agat caithfidh siad a bheith deas caol, gan aon toirt a bheith sa bhfarraige acub ná aon ghabháil uisce. Agus béarfaidh tú ar mheall mór luaidhe agus béarfaidh tú ar fhód móna nó ar scraith mhaith thirim agus gearrfaidh tú pictiúir na luaidhe síos ann. Imeoidh tú leat ansin agus gheobhaidh tú seanphota nó sean 'tin can' nó seanrud eicín agus caithfidh tú meall luaidhe síos ann go leagha tú ar an teine é go mbeidh sé bog. Agus doirtfidh tú síos insan umar seo é le haghaidh pictiúir na luaidhe a dhéanamh. Cuirfidh tú poll le gimléad insa chaon cheann dhó le haghaidh stíorópaí a chuir ann le haghaidh dorú a chur i bhfastó i gceann dó agus snúda sa gceann eile. Tá snúda siar ansin, rud atá sa siopa le ceannacht, a dtugann siad 'gut' air. Gheobhaidh tú 'gut' le haghaidh snúda. Agus rud eile 'spinner' a bhfuil taobh geal agus taobh dearg air agus tá trí cinn de dhuáin air. Well, anois nuair a bheidheas tú ag tarraingt na ronnach sin an-tréan mar gheall ar na trí cinn de dhuáin sin, cuireann siad an easonóir go deo ort, mar tá gach aon cheann acub lán le iasc. Agus is mór an jab é nuair a bheidheas tú ag iarraidh 'spinner' a thabhairt amach ansin astub agus tá sé ag coinneáil deireadh mór ort. Ní fhaca tú aon spraoi ariamh ach a bheith ag tarraingt ronnach nuair atá siad tréan le tarraingt.

Tá mise amháin in ann inseacht duit faoi iascach ó bhí mise in mo pháiste go dtí inniu. Agus tá mé sé bliana agus trí fichid d'aois. Agus nuair a bhí mé in mo pháiste, bhí mé ag imeacht in éindí le m'athair agus le m'athair mór. Agus níl aon áit ó Cheann Léime aniar nár threabh mé, maidhmeannaí agus tanaí, tanaí na mbád, Carraig Muirbh, Carraig Chollta, Maidhm an Urláir, Habrá, Carraige Míle, Tanaí Thuathail, Tanaí Mac Bán, Tanaí Uachtair, Sceirde liom isteach na bealaigh sin a marú mangach. Is iomú lá a chuaigh muid amach agus ní dhéanadh muid mórán marú. Ach laethanta eile mharaíodh muid an t-an-chuimse acub. Ní raibh rud ar bith ar an talamh a bhí a cuir aon trioblóid ormsa i gcónaí ní ba mhó nuair a bhí mé óg ná fanacht go dtagadh an chéad lá de Mhárta i gcónaí. Ba shin é nuair a thosaíodh séasúr na mangach. Agus bhíodh muid ag marú mangach agus dhá ndíol. Ach an bhliain seo anois atá ann, bliain í nach bhfuil aon mhaith léithi ar farraige, b'fhéidir go mbeadh sí ar an mhaidin is breáichte a chonaic tú ariamh a gabháil amach dhuit. Ach níor mhór dhuit thú féin fhaire go maith. Ní túisce mar seo é nó mar siúd. Tá an aimsir an-taomannach ar an bhfarraige i mbliana seachas bliain ar bith a chonaic mise fós.

Fig. 28: Colm's boat *The Lovely Anne* at the Claddagh, Galway. Good Friday, 19 April 2019. COURTESY MARGARET CLOHERTY

Mackerel fishing

Well, a gentleman came to me, Frank Bourke,[16] looking for stories. And as luck would have it, he came the very day I had decided to go mackerel fishing because the mackerel had arrived quickly to Beirtreach Bhuí.[17] Well, he came in and he placed an Ediphone machine on the table in front of me for me to start telling him stories.

'Damn it!' I said, 'yourself and itself. I'm off to fish mackerel. If you'd like to come along, do so.'

'I am happy to come along,' he said.

We set off. There was enough wind for us to take in two reefs and we headed west. We were sailing west from An Charraig Léith,[18] heading for Gob an Tamhain.[19] And when we were at An Charraig Léith we felt nothing yet. And we saw a fine flock of birds west at Gob an Tanaí.[20]

'Wait a while now,' said de Búrca, 'I'll bet you a pound that we'll catch them shortly.'

It was true for him. As soon as we went where the birds were, we began to haul in mackerel as fast as we could. Our attention wasn't on stories, but on hauling. Do you know that if it hadn't looked like turning into a wet evening, neither de Búrca nor Colm would come in until perhaps dawn the following day.

Well now, the snoods[21] that you have, they must be quite narrow, they must be small and compact in the sea and not let in any water. And you'll get hold of a large piece of lead and a sod of turf or a fine dry scraw,[22] that you will use as a mould. You cut the shape that you want the lead to take into your turf. You'll go off then and get an old pot or an old tin can or some old thing and you'll put a lump of lead into it until it melts on the fire and has softened. And you'll pour it into this container to make the shape of the lead. You'll put a hole in each end of it with a gimlet[23] to make stirrups to fasten the fishing line in one end of it and a snood in the other. There is a snood there, something you can buy in a shop, that is called 'gut'. You can get 'gut'[24] for a snood. And another thing, a 'spinner',[25] that has one bright side and the other side is red and it has three fish hooks. Well now, when you are pulling in those mackerel very quickly because of those three hooks, they make you forever indignant because each one is full of fish and it's a big job when you are trying to remove a spinner from them, and it delays you a great deal. Nothing is more fun than pulling in mackerel when they are very plentiful.

I am the only one able to tell you about fishing from the time I was a child until now. And I am sixty-six years of age. And when I was a child, I accompanied my father and my grandfather. And there isn't a place eastwards from Slyne Head that I didn't plough both wave and shoal, the shoal of the boats, Carraig Muirbh,[26] Carraig Choll-ta,[27] Maidhm an Urláir,[28] Habrá,[29] Carraige Míle,[30] Tanaí Thuathail,[31] Tanaí Mac Bán,[32] Tanaí Uachtair,[33] Sceirde,[34] all those routes catching pollock. There was many a day I went out and we didn't catch a great deal. But other days we caught a lot of them. Nothing on earth bothered me more when I was young than waiting for the first day of March to arrive. That's when the pollock season began. And we would catch pollock and sell them. But this is a year that is not good at sea. It might be the finest morning you ever saw when you set out. But you would want to watch out for yourself. It changes very quickly. The weather at sea is very hard to predict this year above any year that I have experienced.

Marú mór mangach[35]

Well, anois tá an t-am seo atá mé a gabháil inseacht daoibh, ar chaoi ar bith is éard atá sé tuairim is le deich mbliana agus dá fhichead ó shin ó tharla an cás seo. Agus bhí mise in mo 'lad' óg ins an am sin, agus ní raibh aon bhád dhúinn féin againn. Ach cheannaigh muid bád agus rinne muid suas í agus chuir muid seoltaí uirthi. Ach tá mé ag rá leat an méid seo, cébí céard a ghabhfainnse a dhéanamh i gcúrsaí obair tí ná garrantaí, ná raibh aon aird agam ar thada insan am sin ach ar an mbád. Níl lá ar bith nach dtéinn faoi dhó nó trí huaire chun an chalaidh ag breathnú uirthi le spóirt aisti. Ní raibh mé féin in m'eolaí thar cionn amach faoin bhfarraige an t-am sin chor ar bith, ach ní raibh m'athair mar sin. Bhí eolas aige. Fuair muid doruithe, gléas iascach agus chuaigh muid amach go Carraige Míle. Bhíodh muid bunáite gach uile lá amuigh ann. Ba lá gaoithe aduaidh a bhí insa lá seo anois. Agus ní raibh cor ariamh i bhfarraige ach nós mar bheifeá ar an loch. Agus os cionn Na Coirthíní Charraige Míle taobh thiar de Charraige Míle, tá áit ann a dtugann siad An Coirthín air, Leac Rúlach, Leac Sheáin Mhic Pádraig agus An Mullán Cor, An Charraig Mhór agus An Charraig Scoiltithe. Well, taobh thiar de Charraige Míle tá stopógaí tanaí ann ach go mbeifeá gar don charraig istigh. Agus ní raibh aon chur síos le a raibh de mhangaigh ann. Bhí muid ag tarraingt mangach anois i gcaitheamh an lae ann agus bhí slám mór mangach insan mbád againn, agus bhí an lá an-te. Agus nuair atá aimsir mhaith i gcónaí seasta ann, feicfidh tú an ghaoth thoir ar maidin agus leanann sí an ghrian go mbeidh sí ina gaoithe aduaidh arís tráthnóna. Agus is é an rud céanna a rinne an ghaoth an lá sin. Agus bhí an lá an-te i gcaitheamh an lae, ach nuair a chuaigh an ghaoth ó thuaidh tráthnóna bhí sé roinnt fuar mar bhí sé roinnt crua. Bhí an ghrian i bhfoisceacht fad maide rámha de bheith a gabháil insa bhfarraige an t-am sin.

'Tá sé chomh maith dhúinn,' a deir sé, 'a bheith a gabháil abhaile.'

'Mh'anam go bhfuil sé thar am againn,' a deirimse, 'go bhfuil muid píosa maith den lá anseo agus go bhfuil an-chuimse éisc marbh againn. Céard a ghlanfas iad nó céard a shailfeas iad nó céard a dhéanfas muid leob?'

'Ó gheobhaidh muid gnaithe dhíobh,' a deir sé. Bhí sé a gabháil a leanacht an bháid le scód anois síos faoin gcarraig.

'Á, ná leag í,' a deirimse, 'síos faoin gcarraig. Má leagann tú síos faoin gcarraig í ní bhéarfaidh tú ar Chruach na Caoile isteach. Ach tharla go bhfuil tú taobh thiar den charraig, déan bord beag siar na farraige anseo, tharla an oíche go breá agus tiocfadh tú thimpeall isteach ansin.'

'Mh'anam gur fíor dhuit é,' a deir sé, 'ceart go leor.'

Well anois, seo faisean atá ag iascairí a bhfuil géireadas iontu: nuair a tharraingíónn siad isteach an dorú agus an luaidhe, má fhágann siad an snúda i ndiaidh an bháid, leagfaidh siad an luaidhe trasna ar bhealach eicínt le dhá n-éireodh aon bhreac ar an snúda go mbeadh cead ag an luaidhe a ghabháil amach. Nó má tá an luaidhe taobh istigh de thada agus go dtiocfaidh aon bhreac ar an mbaoite amuigh, coinneoidh an luaidhe uirthi agus tá an snúda le bheith briste. Leag mise mo luaidhe féin thuas i gceann an bháid trasna ar bhord an bháid le go mbeadh, dá dtagadh tada ar an mbaoite amuigh, go mbeadh cead ag an luaidhe a ghabháil amach. Ach níor chuimhnigh seisean go deo ná go brách go dtiocfadh aon bhlas ar a dhorú féin. Is éard a rinne sé an luaidhe a chaitheamh taobh isteach den mhaide a bhí thiar ag an stiúir. Sheol muid siar chun na farraige agus bhí an taoille siar, agus creidim nár airigh muid an bád ag sciorradh siar níos faide ná bhí sí. Agus chuala mé féin an torann abhus agus chroch mé mo chloigeann. Well, chonaic mé go leor Éirinn rudaí agus spraoi agus greann agus báire.

Ní fhaca mé ariamh aon cheo ba tréine ná bhí mangaigh thimpeall ar an mbád ag pléascadh i mbarr farraige agus ag pléascadh na heasconnaí. Agus bhí an oiread acub ann agus go raibh sé cinntithe ar cheachtar acub breith ar an eascann, mar bheadh 'lad' ann a bheadh ag rith i ndiaidh liathróide. Ach ar deireadh chuaigh mé féin suas chomh tréan agus d'fhéad mé agus bhí mo luaidhe tugthaí amach ag ceann. Tharraing seisean isteach a dhorú féin agus ní raibh aon bhlas aige ach aon dorú amháin den tsnúda ag an luaidhe. Bhí an duán agus gach uile shórt eile imithe. Bhí pota teine leagtha ar an mballasta le haghaidh tae dhúinn.

Thosaigh mé féin ag tarraingt. Níorbh fhearr liom punt ná dá bhfághadh an luaidhe cead a ghabháil go tóin an phoill, mar bhí mé leigthe amach ar iascach an t-am sin, ar thanaí agus ar mhaidhmeannaí agus dhá bhfághadh an luaidhe cead a ghabháil go tóin an phoill go bhfeicfinn cén domhain a bhí ann. Ach nuair a bhíodh an luaidhe a gabháil síos i gcónaí leanadh ceann acub seo é agus bheireadh sé air agus ní leigeadh sé síos í. Ach faoi dheireadh chuaigh an luaidhe síos agus thomhais mé é. Agus ocht bhfeá ar domhain a bhí sé leis an tarraingt a bhí mise a dhéanamh agus iad san an-mhéid agus níor thada na cinn a bhí marbh i gcaitheamh an lae roimhe sin againn thosaíodar ag oibriú a gcuid rubaille ar an mballasta agus chuireadar pota na teine in aer gur chuireadar an teine isteach idir dhá mhaide sa mbád agus thosaigh boladh an teara agus an bád ag lasadh.

'Cuir as an teine,' a deirimse.

Níor cheap mé ó bhí a ghléas iascach briste go mbeadh sé in ann aon chaoi a chuir air agus é deireanach seans a thabhairt dom féin a bhí ag tarraingt.

'Ó cuir féin as í,' a deir sé.

Creidim go raibh deifir aige féin chucu. Mé féin ab éigin an teine a chuir as, bíodh a fhios agat. Well, thóig mé marcannaí air. Dún na Faoileann atá amach ó Sceirde Mór míle a thabhairt ar shean-'lighthouse' Árainn. Carraig Mhór Míle a thabhairt ar Chruach na Cara, agus Cnoc an Chaisil a thabhairt scathamh beag taobh thiar de Chruach na Caoile. Bhí mé an-bhródúil ansin ar son na marcannaí a bheith agam. Agus sheol muid isteach abhaile. Bhí lucht an bháid againn.

'Á, nach é an feall,' a deir sé, 'nár casadh ar maidin linn iad.'

'Á ar ndóigh,' a deirimse, 'ní raibh a fhios againn a raibh an áit ann.'

Maidin lá arna mhárach ó mhoiche dhár éirigh an ghrian, is moiche a d'éirigh mise. Agus bhí mé ag imeacht le cladaigh, gach uile áit ar fud chladaigh Ghlinsce ag tóraíocht eascannaí, maidir le baoití dearga ná tada eile ní raibh aon chaint orthu ins an am sin, ach eascannaí cladaigh le haghaidh baoití. Agus líon mé suas sáspan le eascannaí mar bhíodar agus tháinig mé abhaile agus ní raibh sé ina shuí. Á, thosaigh mé sórt gleo faoi ná raibh muid amuigh lá chomh breá leis.

'Á, tóig d'am, a bhuachaill,' a deir sé, 'tiocfaidh an aois ort féin fós.'

Nuair a bhí seisean réidh, sheol muid siar an cuan. Agus nuair a bhí muid siar an cuan bhí muid síos le Inis Leacan.[36] *Bhí scoil in Inis Leacan an t-am sin agus gasúir agus máistir scoile. Agus bhí na gasúir amuigh ag a gcuid spraoi nuair a bhí muid a gabháil síos le Inis Leacan. Ní raibh mórán gaoithe ann, 'breeze-ín' beag. Ba mhaith liomsa dá mbeadh tuilleadh ann ar chuma ar bith a dheifreodh amach muid. Bhí muid amach ag Carraig an Ghabhair, amach thríd Maidhm an Urláir agus amach faoi Bhealach na nOileán. Nuair a bhí muid amach faoi Bhealach na nOileán, leag mé féin uaim an maide rámha a raibh mé ag iomramh leis agus chuir mé na heascannaí suas ar na doruithe arís. Bhí muid a gabháil amach Poll Chrúcha, amach na Leacrachaí Dearga, amach Tanaí Mac Bán, amach Na Cóirthíní agus Na Leacrachaí Ruála. Níor éirigh aon mhangach mór ar na heascannaí agus iad i ndiaidh an bháid go dtáinig muid isteach ar na marcannaí céanna a raibh muid inné roimhe sin. Agus nuair a tháinig muid isteach ar na marcannaí céanna a raibh muid an lá roimhe sin air, aníos leis An gCoill aríst lá arna mhárach timpeall orainn bhí muid ag tarraingt. Thagadh míle agus céad aníos i ndiaidh na cinn a bhíodh muid a tharraingt.*

'Ara,' a deirimse leisean, 'dá mbeinnse taobh thiar dhíotsa agus an geaf agam bheadh ceathair nó cúig de cheanna caite isteach i gcónaí agam nuair a bheidís do do leanúint aníos.'

'M'anam muise sílim go mbeadh,' a deir sé.

Chaith mise mo dhorú féin ag ceapadh go ndéanfainn níos fearr agus fuair mé an geaf agus chuaigh mé taobh siar dhe-san. Ach bhí an ghrian ag scaladh ard, ard os a gcionn. Nuair a chuirinnse amach an geaf, creidim go raibh an geaf ag déanamh scáile dhóib. Ach an ceann féin níor bhain mé astub leis an ngeaf. Agus b'éigin dom a ghabháil suas arís ag tarraingt le mo dhorú. Well, luchtaigh muid síos an lá sin í go mb'éigin dhúinn ballasta a chuir aisti. Tháinig mé abhaile san oíche ar íochtar An Roisín Dóite. Bhí sé ina iarthrá. Cheap mé ná raibh sé in Éirinn ariamh mórán fear in mo thoirt a bhí ina fhear chomh maith liom. Thosaigh mé ag cur na mangach móra ar rópa mar bheifeá ag líonadh rópa féir gur chuir mé an oiread seo air. Bhrúigh m'athair amach é orm ar bhord an bháid, beannacht Dé lena anam.

Shíl mé go n-iompóinn an bád agus a raibh inti. Ach breathnaigh, ní raibh mé ach píosa beag den chladach nuair a chuaigh mé a leigean scíth. Nuair a chuaigh mé a leigean scíth an bhfuil a fhios agat céard a rinne na mangaigh, mangach a ghabháil an taobh seo agus mangach a ghabháil an taobh sin agus i mbarr an chladaigh. Níor thuig mise iad.

A good catch of pollock[37]

It's about fifty years ago since this event, now that I'm going to tell you about, happened. I was a young lad at the time and we didn't have a boat of our own. But we bought a boat and we did it up and we put sails in her. I'm telling you that whatever I did in relation to housework or in the fields, I had no time for anything but the boat. There wasn't a day that I didn't go twice or three times to the harbour to see her, she was so lovely. I wasn't very knowledgeable about the sea at that time at all, but my father wasn't like that. He had knowledge. We got fishing lines and fishing gear and we went out to Carraige Míle.[38] We were out there nearly every day. This particular day, there was a northerly wind. And there wasn't a stir in the sea but just as you would see on a lake. And above the Coirthíní[39] of Carraige Míle, behind Carraige Míle, there is a place called An Coirthín, a flat rock, Leac Sheáin Mhic Pádraig,[40] and An Mullán Cor,[41] An Charraig Mhór,[42] and An Charraig Scoiltithe.[43] Well, west of Carraige Míle there are narrow parts[44] as you go in near the rock. And there was no end to the amount of pollock there. We were pulling in pollock all day there and we had a large quantity of pollock in the boat, and the day was very warm. And when there is a spell of fine weather, you'll see the east wind in the morning, and it follows the sun until it becomes a northerly wind again in the evening. The wind did the same thing that day. It was very warm all day, and when the wind changed to the north in the evening it became cold because it was a harsh wind. The sun was within an oar's length of setting in the sea at that point.

'We may as well be going home,' my father said.

'Indeed, it is past the time for us,' I said, 'we've spent a good part of the day here and we have caught a great number of fish. How will they be cleaned, salted or what will we do with them?'

'Oh, we'll find a use for them,' he said. He was going to follow the boat with the jib down past the rock.

'Oh, don't leave it down past the rock,' I said. 'If you leave it below the rock you won't reach Cruach na Caoile. But as you are behind the rock, do a little tacking towards the west as the night is fine and you will come around into the harbour then.'

'Indeed, it is true for you,' he said. 'Very well.'

It is a practice that keen-minded fisherman have, when they draw in the fishing line and the lead, if they leave the snood behind the boat, they will lay the lead across in some way so that if any fish rose to the snood the lead could find its way out. If the lead is inside anything and any fish comes to the bait that is outside, the lead will keep going and the snood will break. I placed my own lead at the head of the boat, across the leeside, so that if anything came to the bait outside, the lead could make its way out. But my father never thought that anything would happen to the actual fishing line. He threw the lead inside the tiller behind the helm. We sailed west and it was low tide and I believe we didn't feel the boat drifting. I heard a noise and lowered my head. Well, I have seen a great deal of amusing, funny, awkward things but I have never seen anything like the number of pollock around the boat bursting on top of the sea and splitting eels [bait]. There were so many pollock and yet none of them could capture the eels. They were like lads going after a ball. But at last I put all my strength into it and one of them had taken my lead out. My father pulled in his own fishing line and he only had one leader[45] of the snood with the lead. The fishing hook and everything else was gone. A pot of fire was laid on the ballast for our tea.

I began pulling. Nothing would have pleased me more than if the lead had been let go to the bottom, because I was totally immersed in fishing at that point, on a shoal or in the waves, and the lead might be allowed to sink to the bottom so I could see how deep it was. But when the lead was constantly sinking, one of them followed it and would catch it and wouldn't let it go down. But in the end the lead sank and I measured it. And it was eight fathoms deep according to my pulling on it and they were enormous and the ones that we had caught earlier in the day were nothing by comparison. And they began to apply their tails to the ballast and they upset the pot for the fire and set the fire inside two sticks in the boat and the smell of tar arose and the boat began to smoke.

'Put out the fire!' I said.

I didn't think, as his fishing gear was broken, that he would be able to repair it and it was too late for me to have a go as I was engaged in pulling.

'Oh, put it out yourself,' he said.

I think he was in a hurry to get to them himself. I will have you know that it was I who had to put the fire out. Well, I remembered to position Dún na Faoileann[46] that is beyond Sceirde Mór[47] by the old lighthouse in Aran; to position Carraig Mhór Míle by Cruach na Cara, and position Cnoc an Chaisil a little bit west of Cruach na Caoile. I was very proud of having these markers. And we sailed back home. We were carrying cargo in the boat.

'Oh, isn't it a pity,' he said, 'that we didn't find these this morning.'

'Oh, of course,' I said, 'we didn't know the place was there.'

The following morning, however early the sun rose, I rose earlier than it. And I was going along by the shore, everywhere along the shores in Glinsce, in search of eels, because that time there was no talk of red bait or anything else, only shore eels as bait. And I filled up a saucepan with eels just as they were, and I came home, and he wasn't up. Oh, I started a bit of a racket about the fact that we weren't out at sea on such a fine day.

'Oh, take your time, lad,' he said, 'you'll grow old in time.'

When he was ready, we sailed westwards in the harbour. And when we were in the west, we were near Inis Leacan. There was a school in Inis Leacan at that time and children and a schoolmaster. And the children were out playing as we were passing down by Inis Leacan. There wasn't much wind, just a small breeze. I would have liked if there were more that would speed us out. We were out at Carraig an Ghabhair,[48] Maidhm an Urláir,[49] and out by Bealach na nOileán.[50] When we were out by Bealach na nOileán I put aside the oar with which I was rowing, and I put the eels up on the fishing lines again. We were going out by Poll Chrúcha,[51] out by Na Leacrachaí Dearga,[52] out by Tanaí Mac Bán,[53] out by Na Coirthíní and Na Leacrachaí Ruála.[54] No big pollock rose to the eels as they followed the boat until we came to the same markers we had the previous day.

And when we arrived at the same markers where we had been the previous day, up by An Choill[55] again the following day, we were pulling all around us. A thousand and a hundred rose up following those that we were pulling.

'Oh,' I said to him, 'if I were behind you now and had the gaff[56] I would have thrown four or five in all the time as the pollock were following you.'

'Indeed, I think you would have,' he said.

I threw in my own fishing line thinking that I would do better, and I got the gaff and went behind him. But the sun was shining very high above. Whenever I put the gaff out, I think the gaff was creating a shadow. I didn't get even a single one with the gaff. And I had to go up again pulling with my fishing line. Well, we loaded her down that day so that we had to get rid of ballast. I came home at night below An Roisín Dóite.[57] It was past low tide. I thought there weren't many men in Ireland ever of my size who were as good as I was. I began putting the large pollock on a rope just as you would fill a rope of hay[58] and I put a fair number on it. My father pushed it out for me on board the boat, God rest his soul. I thought I would overturn the boat and everything in it. But, look, I had only gone a short distance along the shore when I went to take a rest. When I went to take a rest do you know what the pollock did? One went this way and one went the other way and I couldn't understand it.

> There is much that could be examined and explored in these examples of Colm's lore. They demonstrate his joy in being part of the collecting process itself, as well as recounting his adventures on land and sea.

CHAPTER 4

'There Was a Man Long Ago'

A SELECTION OF TALES AND RHYMES

Colm told stories, anecdotes, legends, riddles and rhymes of many different kinds to a number of collectors. Within the broader realm of folk narrative, he told stories that are part of the international canon of folktales. He had tales of origin, historical lore, comical tales, religious tales, fairylore, stories with an otherworldly dimension as well as games for children and adults. The following pages present a short selection of these narratives.

The earliest item collected from Colm was transcribed by Mairéad Ní Chathasaigh, An Aird Thoir, Carna, on 8 February 1937.[1] It is uncertain as to how Mairéad came to know Colm or how she came to be associated with the Irish Folklore Commission. She and Bairbre, her sister, worked as part-time collectors for a brief period in the 1930s and were reimbursed for their contributions, a fact which emerges in the correspondence of the commission. Mairéad wrote some 500 pages of material and Bairbre wrote around 300 pages, which now form part of the National Folklore Collection. The tale '*Tadhg Mac Craith*' or 'Thady McGrath' combines two international tale types.[2] The collector Liam Mac Coisdeala also recorded a version of the tale from Colm in 1944.[3]

Collected by Mairéad Ní Chathasaigh:

Tadhg Mac Craith

Fear a bhí sa tír seo fadó agus bhí cailín óg as aon áit leis nach raibh aon duine lena fáil, ach fear d'fhulaingeodh na trí báis ar a son. Dúirt Tadhg leis féin go dtriáilfeadh sé féin an bhean fháil. Bhuail leis go dtáinig sé go dtí teach na mná óige. Chaitheadar an lá sin, trian le fiannaíocht, agus trian le scéalaíocht nó gur thit an oíche. Bhí triúr deartháir ag an mbean óg agus is éard a bhí iontu triúr daoine dubha. Bhídís amuigh ag fiach agus ag fíonscaradh gach uile lá nó go dtitfeadh an oíche.

An tráthnóna seo nuair a d'airigh an bhean óg ag teacht iad, chuir sí suas don tseomra é. Tháinig na triúr deartháir isteach agus d'itheadar a suipéar. Nuair a bhí sin déanta acu tharraingíodar chucu paca cártaí agus dúirt siad go mba bhocht an ní nach mbeadh fear eile acu go ngabhfaidís ag páirtíocht. Dúirt fear acu go raibh fear eile thiar sa seomra agus a dhul siar agus é thabhairt aniar. Tugadh aniar Tadhg agus caitheadh chúig chárta chuige. Ní imreodh Tadhg aon chárta, agus nuair nach ndéanfadh, caitheadar síos i bpota mór uisce é bhí fiuchadh ar an teine.

Ar maidin, chomh luath is bhí a mbeilí caite ag an triúr deartháir, chuadar ag fiach agus ag fíonscaradh. Phioc an bhean óg aníos na cnámhannaí as an bpota is chuimil sí an poitín íocshláinte dhíob is rinne sí é chomh maith is bhí sé ariamh.

Chaitheadar an lá go spóirtiúil go dtí gur thit an oíche. Chuir sí suas don tseomra é. Tháinig an triúr deartháir isteach is nuair a bhí a mbéilí caite arís acu, tharraingíodar chucu paca cártaí.

'Is bocht an ní é,' a deir fear acu, 'nach mbeadh fear againn d'imreodh chúig chárta i bpáirt linn.'

'Nach bhfuil fear sa seomra,' a dúirt fear eile acu, 'is imreodh sé linn.' Tugadh aniar Tadhg arís agus caitheadh chúig chárta chuige, ach má caitheadh féin, ní imreodh sé aon chárta. Chrochadar den mhatal ansin é is ligeadar a chloigeann síos sa teine. D'fhágadar mar sin é gur cailleadh é.

Chomh luath is bhí a mbéilí caite acu maidin lá arna mháireach, chuadar ag fiach agus ag fíonscaradh. Chuaigh an bhean óg arís agus bhí sí cartadh na luaithe gur phioc sí a chuid cnámhannaí chomh maith is d'fhéad sí. Chuimil sí an poitín íocshláinte agus rinne sí é chomh maith is bhí sé ariamh. 'Sin dhá bhás fulaingthe agat ar mo shonsa,' a deir sí, 'is iontach an fear thú.'

Tháinig an triúr deartháir aríst an tráthnóna céanna agus chuir an bhean óg Tadhg suas sa seomra i bhfolach. Nuair a bhí a suipéar ite ag na triúr deartháir an oíche sin, tharraingíodar chucu paca cártaí agus dúirt fear acu go mba mhór an truaigh nach raibh páirtí acu. Dúirt fear eile acu céard faoin bhfear a bhí sa seomra. Ní dhearna sé ach a ghabháil suas don tseomra agus Tadhg a strachaillt leis anuas as. Caitheadh chúig cinn de chártaí amach chuige ach ní imreodh sé aon chárta. Chaitheadar tamall fada ag iarraidh air imirt ach ní dhéanfadh, is nuair nach ndéanfadh, caitheadh síos ins an bpota uisce fiuchta aríst é. Fágadh ansin é nó go dtí go raibh a mbricfeasta ite ag na triúr deartháir. Agus iad imithe leo, phioc an bhean óg a chuid cnámhannaí ina chéile is chuimil sí an tslaitín draíochta is an poitín íocshláinte dhe nó go ndearna sí chomh maith é is bhí sé ariamh.

'Tá mé agat anois inniu,' a deir sí, 'ach caithfidh tú ghabháil chun an aonaigh anois amáireach dhom,' a deir sí, 'agus an cóiste is deise gheobhfas tú ann a thabhairt leat, agus na trí cinn de chaiple a bheidheas faoi, bheith ar aon dath agus an buachaill is deise ar an aonach le muid a thiomáint don Domhan Soir ar maidin, mar tá turas le tabhairt agamsa ann sul má bpósfaidh mé.'

Chuaigh sé chun an aonaigh ar maidin go moch agus fuair sé gach ar theastaigh uaithi. Tháinig sé abhaile agus chomh luath is gheal an lá maidin lá arna mháireach aríst, d'imigh an bheirt acu sa gcóiste le ghabháil don Domhan Soir. Bhí an bhean óg agus Tadhg sa gcóiste agus an buachaill ar an gcapall deiridh. Díreach nuair a bhíodar gabháil thar theach a máthair mhóir, chuir sí a láimh ina póca agus fuair sí chúig phunt ann.

Dúirt sí leis an mbuachaill, 'Tabharfaidh mé chúig phunt duit,' a deir sí, 'má éiríonn leat an lá chuir as don fheur seo.'

Ach ní raibh an Tadhg ag éisteacht léi. 'Cén chaoi gcuirfidh mise as dó é, a chailleach?' a deir an buachaill.

'Seo biorán dhuit,' a deir sí, 'agus nuair a chónóidh muid ag an tobar, caith an biorán leis.'

'Cén chaoi mbeinnse in ann an biorán a chuir ann a chailleach?' a deir an buachaill.

'Caith an biorán,' a deir an bhean óg, 'agus déanfaidh mise an chuid eile.' Chaith an buachailll an biorán nuair a bhíodar ag an tobar agus thit Tadhg ina chodladh gan mórán achair. Tháinig an bhean óg agus an buachaill abhaile agus d'fhágadar Tadhg ina chodladh chois an tobair. Ach tháinig sé abhaile roimh thitim na hoíche.

'Céard a tharla dhuit?' dúirt an bhean óg leis.

'Á, níl a fhios agam,' deir sé, 'ach ní tharlóidh sé amáireach dhom.'

Maidin lá arna mháireach aríst nuair a bhíodar ag gabháil go dtí an Domhan Soir, díreach agus iad gabháil thar theach na caillí, dúirt an bhean óg leis an mbuachaill, an lá chuir as don fhear óg.

'Cén chaoi ndéanfaidh mise sin?' a deir an buachaill.

'Caith an biorán seo leis mar rinne tú inné agus tá chúig phunt ar íochtar mo phóca agus tabharfaidh mé dhuit é.'

Rinne an buachaill mar hordaíodh dhó agus thug an bhean óg na chúig phunt dhó.

Tháinigeadar abhaile í féin is an buachaill is d'fhágadar Tadhg ina chodladh chois an tobair. Ach tháinig sé abhaile aríst shul má bhí oíche titithe.

Maidin an tríú lae d'imíodar soir leo le ghabháil go dtí an Domhan Soir. Nuair a bhíodar gabháil thar dhoras na caillí an tríú lá, dúirt an bhean óg leis an mbuachaill, 'Tá chúig phunt anseo agam agus tabharfaidh mé dhuit é má ghníonn tú an obair chéanna rinne tú an dá lá seo caite.'

Rinne an buachaill amhlaidh is nuair a bhí Tadhg ina chodladh, thug an bhean óg fáinne don bhuachaill is dúirt sí leis fanacht ansin nó go n-éireodh Tadhg as an suan agus an fáinne thabhairt dhó is inseacht dhó freisin an bealach a ndeachaigh sí féin.

Chomh luath is d'éirigh Tadhg, d'inis an buachaill dhó an chaoi a bhí leis is an bealach a ndeachaigh an bhean óg agus thug sé an fáinne dhó freisin. Thug sé aghaidh ar an mbealach a dtug an bhean óg í féin, is bhí sé ag siúl is ag síor-imeacht agus an gearrán bán gabháil ar scáth na copóige, ach ba diúin [?] í an chopóig dá seasfadh sí leis go raibh diúin agus deireadh an lae teannadh leis agus go bhfaca sé solaisín beag i bhfad uaidh is ní i ngar dhó. Tháinig sé isteach sa teach.

'Céad míle fáilte romhat, a Thaidhg Mhic Craith,' a deir seanfhear a bhí istigh sa teach. 'Is mise uncail na mná óige sin tá tusa chuartú agus ar fhulaing tú na trí báis ar a son, ach creidim a dhuine bhoicht,' a deir sé, 'go mba bheag an mhaith dhuit é.'

Chaitheadar an oíche sin, trian le scéalaíocht, trian le fiannaíocht, togha gach dí is rogha gach bídh, blas na meala ar gach greim is gan greim ar bith tor. 'Níl aon tuairisc agamsa le d'aghaidh,' a deir an seanfhear ar maidin nuair a bhí Tadhg fáil faoi réir le n-imeacht, 'ach beidh tú ag deartháir dhomsa san oíche anocht.'

Thug an seanfhear – uncail na mná óige – capall marcaíochta do Thadhg is dúirt sé leis ghabháil ag marcaíocht uirthi agus chuaigh. D'éirigh an capall is chuaigh sí leath bealaigh go dtí an ghrian is bhuail sí a ceithre cosa fúithi sa tsráid aríst is bhí Tadhg ar a droim i gcónaí.

'Dar brí an leabhair is ait an fear thú,' dúirt an seanfhear leis, 'shíl mé nach raibh tú do mharcaigh chomh maith sin. Dall é mo dheartháir-sa ach mar sin féin níor lig sé aon duine ariamh bhfoisceacht céad míle d'aon taobh dhe nach maródh sé. Ach seo cáca dhuit,' a deir an seanfhear, 'agus nuair a fheicfeas tú tíocht do do mharú é, caith an cáca leis, agus aithneoidh sé lorg láimhe a dhearthára is ansin ní dhéanfaidh sé aon bhlas ort.'

D'fhág Tadhg slán is beannacht ag an seanfhear agus níor stad sé ná níor mhórchónaigh sé go dtáinig sé i ngar do theach an dall. Thug sé an cáca don dall.

'Céad míle fáilte romhat, a Thaidhg Mhic Craith, aithním thú, seo é cáca mo dhearthára a raibh tú in aon teach leis aréir.'

Chaitheadar an oíche, an trian le fiannaíocht, trian le scéalaíocht, blas na meala ar gach greim is gan greim ar bith tor.

Ar maidin, nuair a bhí Tadhg réidh le n-imeacht, dúirt an dall, 'Mise an máistir ar éanachaí an domhain uilig agus mara bhfuil aon tuairisc ag aon cheann acu ar an mbean óg seo atá tusa thóraíocht creidim nach bhfuil sí le fáil.'

Ansin dúirt an dall le Tadhg a ghabháil taobh thuas den teach. Chuaigh.

'Bhfeiceann tú aon chloich mhór thuas ansin?' a deir an dall.

'Feicim,' a deir Tadhg.

'Iompaigh suas í,' deir an dall leis.

'Á, ní iompódh ar bhain dom ariamh í,' deir Tadhg, 'tá sí chomh mór sin.'

'Féach, mar sin, an ndéanfá poll isteach a mbeinn in ann mo mhéarachaí féin chuir isteach fúithi.'

Rinne Tadhg amhlaidh.

'Cuir mo mhéarachaí isteach fúithi,' dúirt an dall.

Nuair a fuair sé a chuid méarachaí istigh ann, chaith sé an chloich seacht n-iomaire agus seacht n-acra uaidh.

'Bhfeiceann tú tada fúithi sin?' dúirt an dall.

'Feicim,' a deir Tadhg, 'tua, feadóg, scian, ord agus mála.'

'Cuir an fheadóg sin in mo bhéal anois,' deir an dall.

Chuir, agus shéid an dall an fheadóig go tréan is faoi cheann scathaimh d'fhiafraigh sé de Thadhg bhfaca sé aon duibheachan san aer ó thuaidh.

'Feicim,' a deir Tadhg, 'múr mór millteach a tíocht.'

Is gearr eile nuair nach raibh aon éan sa domhan nach raibh cruinnithe thart orthu faoi cheann nóiméide, ach amháin aon éan amháin. D'fhiafraigh sé de gach uile éan acu a raibh aon tuairisc acu ar an mbean óg agus dúradar nach raibh. Shéid sé an fheadóg aríst agus faoi cheann scathaimh d'fhiafraigh sé de Thadhg bhfaca sé tada tíocht agus dúirt Tadhg go bhfaca sé duibheachan beag tíocht ar an spéir ó thuaidh. Is gearr go dtáinig éan mór dubh.

'Is mór atá curtha agaibh as domsa,' deir sí, 'bhí mé ar bhanais insan Domhan Thiar. Bhí banais naoi n-oíche agus naoi lá ag an lánúin óg sul má bpósfaidís agus bhí féasta breá acu is bhí an-am agamsa ann.'

'Caithfidh tú fanacht,' a deir an seanfhear dall leis an éan, 'go dtuga tú siar an fear seo leat.'

Bhí cnoc capall, cnoc caorach, is cnoc beithíoch ag an dall. 'Téirigh a marú anois,' deir an dall le Tadhg.

Chuaigh. Faoi cheann scathaimh, d'fhiafraigh an dall de Thadhg an raibh mórán maraithe fós aige.

'Níl tada maraithe agam fós,' a deir Tadhg, 'ar ndóigh níl sé i bhfad ó thosaigh mé.'

'Ó shoraidh go deo dhíot,' a deir an dall, 'tabhair dhom féin é.'

Chomh luath agus bhíodar maraithe ar aon chnoc amháin aige dúirt sé le Tadhg ghabháil ag feannadh. D'fheannadar iad is chuireadar a chuile bhlas de na trí cnoc isteach sa mála. Ansin chuir an dall faoi mhuineál an éin é le rópa agus chuir sé Tadhg ar a dhroim.

'Seo duit slaitín draíochta anois,' a deir an dall, 'is nuair a chaithfeas an t-éan seo uaidh thú, an chéad chloich a dtiocfaidh tú suas leis, buail trí laisc uirthi is tiocfaidh cóiste amach as an gcloich chugat a thabharfas an chuid eile den bhealach thú. Agus freisin,' a deir sé, 'ná tabhair cead don éan breathnú an tríú huair ort gan ruainne den fheoil a chaitheamh chuige.'

D'imigh le Tadhg is é marcaíocht ar dhroim an éin agus bhí sé dá bheathú nó go raibh an fheoil caite. Nuair nach raibh níos mó feola ag Tadhg le tabhairt don éan, chaith an t-éan uaidh é agus tháinig leath dhe sa bhfarraige is leath dhe ar an talamh sa Domhan Thiar. Shiúil leis is chonaic sé cloich mhór. Bhuail sé trí bhuille ar an gcloich den tslaitín draíochta agus tháinig an cóiste is breátha chonaic sé ariamh amach as an gcloich. Bhí sé ag imeacht leis nó go raibh diúin is deireadh an lae a teannadh leis, ach is gearr go ndeachaigh sé thar theach na mná óige. Bhí an bhean óg go dtína leath amach thar an bhfuinneog is chaith na caiple iad féin ar a ndá nglúin agus d'umhlaigh siad dhi. Chaith Tadhg é féin ar a dhá ghlúin freisin is d'umhlaigh sé dhi é féin.

Rith an bhean óg anuas na staighre agus dúirt sí leis na daoine go ndeachaigh cóiste thart ansin anois agus nach bhfaca sí aon chóiste ariamh ba bhreátha ná é. 'Ba mhaith liom,' a deir sí lena fear, 'an fear a bhí ann istigh a thabhairt chun na bainise.'

Chuaigh giolla is gearrán amach ina dhiaidh is tugadh chun na bainise Tadhg. Chaitheadh gach uile dhuine dá raibh ag an mbainis scéal inseacht. 'Más é do thoil é,' dúirt Tadhg leis an mbean óg, 'an dtabharfá deoch an uisce dhomsa?'

Thug sí dhó é is nuair a bhí a leath ólta aige chaith sé fáinne síos sa ngloine is thug sé don bhean óg é is dúirt léi an chuid eile dhe a ól. Nuair a chonaic sí an fáinne: 'Céad fáilte romhat a Thadhg Mhic Craith,' a deir sí, 'is tú d'fhulaing na trí báis ar mo shon. Tá sé chomh maith duit,' a deir sí leis an bhfear eile, 'ní tusa a fuair aon anró uaimse.'

Chuireadar banais eile ar siúl ansin. Nuair a bhí an bhanais sin thart chuaigh Tadhg agus an bhean óg amach le píosa den áit fheiceáil sa gcóiste. Nuair a bhíodar ag imeacht dúirt an Rí leo ar a bhfaca siad ariamh, gan a ghabháil thar theorainn an fhathaigh mhóir na gcúig gceann, na gcúig meall is na gcúig muiníl. Bhíodar ag imeacht leo is níor airigh siad ariamh go rabhadar imithe thar theorainn an fhathaigh. Is gearr go dtáinig an fathach agus ní dhearna sé ach breith ar Thadhg is é chaitheamh amach as an gcóiste, is chuaigh sé féin isteach sa gcóiste in éineacht leis an mbean óg. Ní raibh ag Tadhg bocht ansin ach imeacht leis. Chuaigh sé thar áit a raibh caora caillte, is bhí cú, leamhan, seabhac, is damhan alla ag troid le chéile faoin gcaora.

'Well,' a deir ceann acu leis an gceann eile, 'íosfaidh muid féin a chéile fúithi agus nach fearr dhúinn duine eicínt a fháil roinnfeas go cneasta eadrainn í.'

'Ní achar fada,' deir an seabhac, 'ó chuaigh fear thart ansin is is fearr dhúinn fios a chur air lena roinnt.'

Cuireadh fios ar Thadhg is tháinig sé. Roinn sé an chaora eatarthu. Chuir sé an cloigeann agus an craiceann ar thaobh, na putógaí ar thaobh eile, na cnámhannaí ar thaobh eile, agus an fheoil ar thaobh eile.

'Seo,' a deir sé leis an leamhan, 'dhuitse an fheoil.'

'Seo dhuitse na putógaí,' deir sé leis an seabhac.

'Seo dhuitse na cnámhannaí,' deir sé leis an gcú.

'Agus seo,' deir sé leis an damhan alla, 'an craiceann agus an cloigeann.

Bí ag fiodhchán ar an gcraiceann an lá breá is téirigh isteach sa gcloigeann an drochlá.'

Nuair a bhí an chaora roinnte aige d'imigh leis ina bhealach féin aríst.

Dúirt na hainmhithe le chéile go mba mhór an náire dhóibh an té roinn an chaora eatarthu gan comaoin eicínt a chuir air. 'Well,' deir an seabhac, 'is éard mise teachtaire maith is ní bheidh mé i bhfad dul ina choinne sin aríst.' Chuaigh sé i gcoinne Thaidhg agus thug sé ar ais é. Bhí faitíos ar Thadhg gurb é an chaoi roinn sé an chaora contráilte is gurb é an chaoi marófaí é.

'Tá muid an-bhuíoch díot,' dúirt na hainmhithe leis nuair a tháinig sé ar ais, 'faoin gcaoi ar roinn tú an chaora eadrainn.'

'Mar is é an chaoi maródh muid féin a chéile fúithi agus lá ar bith,' deir an leamhan, 'iarrfas tú bheith i do leamhan uasal na coille léithe, beidh tú amhlaidh.'

'Lá ar bith iarrfas tú bheith do chú uasal na coille léithe,' deir an cú, 'beidh tú amhlaidh.'

'Lá ar bith,' deir an seabhac, 'iarrfas tú bheith do sheabhac uasal na coille léithe, beidh tú amhlaidh.'

'Lá ar bith,' deir an damhan alla, 'iarrfas tú bheith i do dhamhan alla uasal na coille léithe, beidh tú mar sin.

D'fhág sé slán acu go buíoch beannachtach agus d'imigh leis. Is gearr gur chuimhnigh sé air féin. 'Ó,' deir sé, 'dá mbeinn in mo sheabhac uasal na coille léithe anois, ghabhfainn go dtí simléar an fhathaigh bhfuil mo bhean aige.'

Ní túisce chuimhnigh sé air, ná bhí sé ina sheabhac agus d'imigh leis go dtáinig sé [go] barr simléir an fhathaigh.

'Dá mbeinn mo dhamhan alla na coille léithe anois,' deir sé ina intinn féin, 'ghabhfainn síos thrí pholl na deataí.' Ní túisce bhí sé sin cuimhnithe aige, ná mar bhí sé ina dhamhan alla. Chuaigh sé síos agus isteach leis i bpoll chois na tine. Bhreathnaigh sé amach as an bpoll is chonaic sé nach raibh istigh ach a bhean.

'Dá mbeinn i m'fhear anois,' a deir sé, 'mar bhí mé cheana, bheinn ceart go leor agus ghabhfainn chun cainte léi.' Ní túisce chuimhnigh sé air, ná bhí sé ina Thadhg Mac Craith aríst. Tháinig an-iontas is áthas ar an mbean óg, ach d'inis sé thríd thíos is thríd suas mar bhí an scéal aige féin. Bhí sé ina thráthnóna faoi seo. D'airíodar an fathach a tíocht agus rinne Tadhg damhan alla dhe féin aríst is chuaigh sé isteach ina scailp.

Nuair a tháinig an fathach isteach: 'Fú, fá, féasóg!' a deir sé, 'fághaim boladh an Éireannaigh bhréagaigh, bhradaigh.'

'Bíodh ciall agat,' a deir a bhean leis, 'is é mo chuid éadaigh a thug mé as Éirinn liom a bhí scartha amuigh inniu agam agus sin é an boladh fhághanns tú.'

'B'fhéidir gur fíor dhuit é,' deir sé.

Nuair a bhí a bhéilí ite aige shuigh sé féin is an bhean síos chois na teine ag comhrá.

'Ach cá bhfuil d'anam,' a deir an bhean leis, 'mar feicthear dhom go raibh tú ag rá ansin an lá cheana nach ionat féin a bhí d'anam chor ar bith.'

'Is fíor dhuit,' a deir sé, 'ní ionam féin atá m'anam chor ar bith.'

'Ach cá bhfuil sé mar sin?' deir sí.

Ó,' deir sé, 'tá oileán ansin thiar, an ceann is mó atá ann is tá muc ann a bhfuil lacha istigh inti agus tá ubh istigh sa lacha agus istigh ansin tá m'anam. Nó go mbuailtear an ubh sin ar an mball dobhráin ormsa, ní marófar choidhchin mé. Is ar ndóigh tá an oiread oibriú sa bhfarraige is nach féidir a ghabháil isteach ann fiú amháin an lá is breátha sa mbliain.'

Bhí Tadhg ag éisteacht le gach uile fhocal dá raibh an fathach a rá. Chuaigh sé suas thríd an deatach aríst is rinne sé seabhac dhe féin. Chuaigh sé go dtí an oileán a raibh an mhuc ann. Bhí sé leis an muc go deo, nó gur stróic sé ó chéile í. D'éirigh an lacha amach is chuaigh suas san aer ach lean Tadhg í agus nuair a bhí an crua ar an lacha chaith sí uaithi an ubh.

Rug Tadhg ar an ubh sul má tháinig sé chun na talún. Bhí cruinniú mór daoine ag teach an fhathaigh an oíche sin. Tháinig Tadhg ar ais agus rinne sé fear dhe féin aríst. Chuaigh sé isteach i dteach an fhathaigh thríd na daoine. Bhí an fathach osclaithe amach aige féin le brothall de bharr damhsa. Nuair a fuair Tadhg an deis, bhuail sé an ubh ar an mball dobhráin ar an bhfathach agus thit sé sin mín, marbh.

Thug sé leis abhaile a bhean ansin go hÉirinn is bhí banais naoi n-oíche agus naoi lá eile ansin acu. Ní raibh agamsa dá mbarr ach bróga páipéir is péire stocaí bainne ramhar.

Tadhg Mac Craith

Long ago, there was a man in this country and there was a young girl from the same place that no man could win except a man who would suffer death three times for her sake. Tadhg said to himself he would try to win the woman. He set off until he came to the young woman's house. They spent that day, a third telling tales of Na Fianna[4] and a third storytelling until nightfall. The woman had three brothers and they were three dark men. They used to be out hunting and rounding up game every day until nightfall.

One evening, when the young woman heard them coming, she sent Tadhg to hide in a room. The three brothers came in and ate their supper. When they had finished, they took out a pack of cards and said it was a poor state of affairs not to have another man who could play with them. One of them said there was another man in the room and to go and fetch him. Tadhg was brought in and was given five cards. Tadhg wouldn't play any card and, when he refused, they threw him into a large pot of water that was boiling on the fire.

In the morning, as soon as the three brothers had eaten, they went hunting and rounding up game. The young woman picked the bones out of the pot and rubbed them with the healing balm of *poitín* and made him as well as he had ever been.

They spent the day sporting until nightfall. She sent him to the room. The three brothers came in and, once again, when they had finished their meal, they took out a pack of cards.

'It's a sad state of affairs,' one of them said, 'that there isn't a man in the room who would play five cards with us.'

'Isn't there a man in the room?' said another one of them, 'and he will play with us.'

Tadhg was brought out of the room again and five cards were thrown to him, but if they were, he wouldn't play any cards. They hung him from the mantlepiece then and let his head down into the fire. They left him like that until he died.

As soon as they had finished their meal the following morning, they went out hunting and rounding up game. The young woman went once again and cleared out the ashes until she picked out his bones as best she could. She rubbed the healing *poitín* on them and made him as well as ever.

'Those are two deaths you have suffered,' she said, 'for my sake,' she said. 'You are a wonderful man.'

The three brothers came again the same evening and the young woman sent Tadhg to hide in the room. When the three brothers had eaten their supper that night, they took out a pack of cards and one of them said it was a shame they didn't have a partner. Another one of the men said, 'What about the man in the room?' He simply went up to the room and dragged Tadhg down. Five cards were thrown to him but he wouldn't play any card. They spent a long time trying to persuade him to play but he wouldn't and, when he refused, he was thrown into a pot of boiling water again. He was left there until the three brothers had finished their breakfast. When they had left, the young woman picked out his bones and put them together and she drew the magic wand and the healing *poitín* over him until she made him as good as new.

'You have me now today,' she said, 'but you must go to the fair tomorrow for me,' she said 'and bring away the best coach you can find there and the three horses pulling it that will be of the same colour, and the finest boy at the fair to drive us to the World of the East in the morning, because I must undertake a journey there before I marry.'

He went to the fair early in the morning and he found everything that she wanted. He came home and as soon as daybreak came again the following day, the two set off in the coach to go to the World of the East. The young woman and Tadhg were in the coach and the servant boy was on the horse behind. Just as they were passing her grandmother's house, she put her hand in her pocket and found five pounds there.

She said to the boy, 'I will give you five pounds,' she said, 'if you ruin this man's day.' But Tadhg wasn't listening to her.

'How can I upset his day, woman?' said the boy.

'Here is a pin,' she said, 'and when we stop at the well, throw the pin at him.'

'How would I be able to put the pin in him, woman?' said the boy.

'Throw the pin,' said the young woman, 'and I will do the rest.' The boy threw the pin when they were at the well and Tadhg fell asleep shortly afterwards. The young woman and the boy came home and they left Tadhg asleep at the well. But he came home before nightfall.

'What happened to you?' said the young woman to him.

'Oh, I don't know,' he said, 'but it won't happen to me tomorrow.'

The following morning again, as they were going to the World of the East, just as they were passing the old woman's house the young woman said to the boy to ruin the young man's day.

'How will I do that?' said the boy.

'Throw this pin at him as you did yesterday and I have five pounds in the bottom of my pocket and I will give it to you.'

The boy did as he was told and the young woman gave him the five pounds. They came home, she and the boy, and they left Tadhg sleeping by the well. But he came home again before nightfall.

The morning of the third day, they set off for the World of the East. When they were passing the woman's door the third day, the young woman said to the boy, 'I have five pounds here and I will give them to you if you do the same thing you did the last two days.'

The boy did so and when Tadhg was asleep, the young woman gave the boy a ring and told him to stay there until Tadhg would wake and to give him the ring and also tell him where she had gone.

As soon as Tadhg got up, the boy told him the story and where the young woman had gone and he gave him the ring as well.

He set off along the way where the young woman had gone and he was walking along and the white horse was sheltering by the shade of the dock leaves but the dock was as if she stayed by it until the evening. The end of the day approached and he saw a little light far away, not near him. He came into the house.

'A hundred thousand welcomes, Tadhg Mac Craith,' said an old man who was in the house. 'I am the young woman's uncle. I am the uncle of the young woman you are seeking and for whom you suffered three deaths, but I believe, my poor fellow, that it didn't do you much good.'

They spent that night, a third with storytelling, a third with tales of Na Fianna, the finest of drink and the best of food, every morsel tasting of honey and no morsel dry.

'I have nothing to report to you,' said the old man in the morning when Tadhg was preparing to leave, 'but you will come to my brother tonight.'

The old man – the young woman's uncle – gave Tadhg a horse to ride and told him to ride it and he set off. The horse got up and went halfway to the sun and set her four legs down again on the road and Tadhg was still sitting on her back.

'Indeed, you are a strange man,' the old man said to him, 'I did not think you were such a good horseman. My brother is blind but at the same time, he never let anyone within a hundred miles from him that he didn't kill, but here is a cake for you,' said the old man, 'and when you see him coming towards you to kill you, throw the cake at him, and he will recognise his brother's hand and then he will not harm you.'

Tadhg said goodbye to the old man and did not stop or pause until he came to the blind man's house.

'A hundred thousand welcomes, Tadhg Mac Craith. I recognise you, this is my brother's cake in whose house you stayed last night.'

They spent the night, a third telling tales of Na Fianna, a third storytelling, every morsel tasting of honey and no morsel dry.

In the morning when Tadhg was ready to leave, the blind man said, 'I am the master of all the birds in the world and if none of them have news of this young woman that you seek, I believe she is not to be found.'

Then the blind man said to Tadhg to continue up past the house. He did so. 'Do you see any big stone up there?'

'I do,' said Tadhg.

'Turn it over,' said the blind man to him.

'Oh, there is no way I can turn it over,' said Tadhg, 'it is too large.'

'See, then, if you make a hole in it where I could put my fingers in under it.' Tadhg did so.

'Put my fingers in under it,' said the blind man.

When his fingers were in under it, he threw the stone seven ridges and seven acres away from him. 'Do you see anything under it?' said the blind man.

'I see,' said Tadhg, 'an axe, a whistle, a knife, a hammer and a bag.'

'Put that whistle in my mouth now,' said the blind man. He did so, and the blind man blew the whistle loudly and in a while he asked Tadhg if he saw anything dark in the sky to the north.

'I see,' said Tadhg, 'a great dark mass coming.'

In another short while, there wasn't a bird in the world that hadn't gathered around them within a minute, except for one bird. He asked every single bird if they had any news of the young woman and they said they did not. He blew the whistle again and in a while, he asked Tadhg if he saw anything approaching and Tadhg said he saw a small dark object coming into view in the sky to the north.

It wasn't long before a big black bird arrived. 'You have upset me a great deal,' she said. 'I was at a wedding in the World of the West. The young couple had a wedding feast for nine nights and nine days before the marriage and they had a great feast and I had a great time there.'

'You'll have to wait,' said the blind old man to the bird, 'until you bring this man west with you.'

The blind old man had a hill of horses, a hill of sheep and a hill of cattle. 'Go and kill now,' said the blind man to Tadhg. He did. In a while, the blind man asked Tadhg if he had killed many so far.

'I have killed none yet,' said Tadhg. 'Of course, it isn't long since I started.'

'Oh, hurry up,' said the blind man, 'give it to me.'

As soon as he had killed them on one hill, he told Tadhg to begin skinning. They skinned them and they took everything from the three hills into the bag, then the blind man put it under the bird's neck with a rope and he put the rope and Tadhg on his back.

'Here is a magic wand now,' said the blind man, 'and when this bird throws you away, the first stone you meet, hit it three times and a coach will come out of the stone that will bring you the rest of the way. And also,' he said, 'don't allow the bird to look at you a third time without throwing it a morsel of the meat.'

Tadhg headed off riding on the bird's back and he was feeding it until the meat was gone. When Tadhg had no more meat left to give to the bird, the bird threw him off and half of him fell into the sea and half fell on land in the World of the West. He walked on and saw a big stone. He hit the stone three times with the little magic stick and the finest coach he ever saw came out of the stone. He kept going until the day was coming to an end but he passed the young woman's house shortly afterwards. The young woman was halfway out the window and the horses went down on their two knees and paid homage to her. Tadhg went on his knees as well and also paid homage to her. The young woman ran downstairs and said to the people that a coach had passed by just then and that she had never seen a finer coach.

'I would like,' she said to her man, 'to bring the man who was in it to the wedding.'

A servant and a horse went after him and Tadhg was brought to the wedding. Everyone at the wedding had to tell a story.

'Please,' said Tadhg to the young woman 'would you give me a drink of the water?'[5]

She gave it to him and when he had drunk half of it he threw a ring into the glass and gave it to the young woman and told her to drink the rest of it. When she saw the ring: 'A hundred welcomes, Tadhg Mac Craith,' she said, 'you suffered three deaths for my sake. You may as well [leave],' she said to the other man, 'you did not get any trouble from me.'

They organised another wedding then. When that wedding was over, Tadhg and the young woman went out to look around a little in the coach. As they were leaving, the king said to them on no account to cross the boundary of the great giant of the five heads, the five bulges and the five necks. They were going along and they didn't notice anything until they had crossed the giant's boundary. The giant appeared shortly and he simply grabbed hold of Tadhg and threw him out of the coach and he went into the coach with the young woman. All Tadhg could do then was to head away. He passed a place where there was a dead sheep, and a hound, a moth, a hawk and a spider were fighting over the sheep.

'Well,' said one of them to the other. We will eat one another about it and wouldn't we be better off finding someone who would divide it correctly between us?'

'It's not long,' said the hawk, 'since a man passed by and we should send for him to divide it.'

Tadhg was sent for and he came. He divided the sheep among them. He put the head and skin to one side, the innards to another side, and the meat to another.

'Here,' he said to the moth, 'is the meat for you.'

'Here are the innards for you,' he said to the hawk.

'Here are the bones for you,' he said to the hound.

'And here,' he said to the spider, 'are the skin and head for you. You can weave from the skin on a fine day and go into the head on a bad day.'

When he had divided the sheep, he went off on his way again.

The animals told one another that they should be ashamed they did not give any reward to the person who had divided the sheep among them.

'Well,' said the hawk, 'I am a good messenger and I won't be long fetching him again.

Tadhg was afraid he had divided the sheep badly and that he would be killed.

'We are very grateful to you,' the animals said to him when he returned, 'for the way you divided the sheep among us because we would have killed each other over it.'

'And any time,' said the moth, 'that you ask to be a noble moth of the grey wood, you will be so.'

'Any day you ask to be a noble hound of the grey wood,' said the hound, 'you will be so.'

'Any day,' said the hawk, 'you ask to be a noble hawk of the grey wood, you will be so.'

'Any day,' said the spider, 'you ask to be a noble spider of the grey wood, you will be thus.'

He bade them farewell and gave them his grateful blessing and set off.

Shortly afterwards he had a thought. 'Oh,' he said, 'if I were a noble hawk of the grey wood now, I would go to the chimney of the giant who has my wife.' He no sooner thought of this than he became a hawk and he travelled until he arrived at the top of the giant's chimney.

'If I were a spider of the grey wood now,' he said in his own mind, 'I would go down through the smoke hole.' He had no sooner thought of that than he was a spider. He went down and into a hole beside the fire. He looked out the hole and saw there was no one in apart from his wife.

'If I were a man now,' he said, 'as I was once, I would be alright and I would go and speak with her.' He no sooner thought of that than he was Tadhg Mac Craith again. The young woman was very surprised and delighted and he told her his story from start to finish. By then it was evening. They heard the giant coming and Tadhg changed himself into a spider again and went into his shelter.

When the giant came in: 'Fee, foh, fum!' he said, 'I smell the lying, thieving, Irishman.'

'Have sense,' the woman said to him, 'that's from my clothes that I brought with me from Ireland that I spread out today and that's the smell you get.'

'You may be right,' he said.

When he had eaten his meal he and the woman sat by the fire talking.

'But where is your soul,' said the woman to him, 'because it seems to me that you were saying the other day that your soul did not live inside you at all.'

'True for you,' he said, 'my soul is not in me at all.'

'But where is it then?' she said.

'Oh,' he said, 'there is an island to the west, the largest one there, and there is a pig there that has a duck inside it and there is an egg inside the duck and my soul is inside that. Until that egg strikes me three times on my mole, I will never be killed. And the sea is so agitated of course that you can't go in even on the finest day in the year.'

Tadhg was listening to every word the giant spoke. He went up through the smoke again and he changed himself into a hawk. He went to the island where the pig was. He stayed with the pig until he tore it asunder. The duck came out and went up in the air, but Tadhg followed it and as the duck tired it threw the egg out of herself. Tadhg caught the egg before it landed on the ground.

There was a great gathering of people at the giant's house that night. Tadhg returned and made himself a man again. He went into the giant's house among the people. The giant had taken off some of his clothes as he was warm from dancing. When Tadhg got the chance he struck the giant's mole three times with the egg and he fell down, dead.

He brought his wife home to Ireland then, where they had another wedding feast for nine nights and nine days. All I got from them were shoes of paper and a pair of socks of thick milk.

Collected by Liam Mac Coisdeala:

Fig. 29: Folklore Collector Liam Mac Coisdeala. COURTESY NFC

An Fear a Leig Air Féin Go Raibh Fios Aige[6]

Siod boc mór a bhí fadó ann agus bhí sé dhá bhochtú anuas go han-mhór. Agus bhí an fear seo ag gabháil thart – bhíodh sé ag iarraidh déirce i gcónaí – agus uair ar bith castaí thart é, d'fhághadh sé culaith éadaigh agus go leor rudaí maithe ón mboc mór seo. Ach d'iarr sé déirc an lá seo air agus dúirt an boc mór leis:

'Bhí mé lá,' a deir sé, 'agus bhí mé in ann déirc a thabhairt duit, ach níl mé in ann aon déirc a thabhairt anois dhuit – tá mé bochtaithe.'

'Á, muise, céard tá tagtha ort chor ar bith,' a deir sé, 'ó chonaic mé cheana thú? Bhí tú an-tréan.'

'Tá mé bochtaithe anuas go han-mhór,' a deir sé.

'Well, dhá bhfágtá mise istigh go maidin,' a deir sé, 'b'fhéidir go ndéanfainn maith dhuit. Leigfinn orm péin go bhfuil fios agam agus ní bheadh fhios agat cén mhaith a dhéanfainn: seomra thabhairt dhom péin go maidin agus mo shuipéar.'

'Tabharfad,' a dúirt an boc mór.

'Well, má thugair is go dtabharfair,' a deir sé, 'cuirfidh tú siar trí bhuidéal óil chugam, agus cuirfidh tú do bhuachaill siar le ceann acu ins an oíche agus cuirfidh tú siar do chailín leis an gceann eile, is cuirfidh tú an mháistreás siar leis an gceann deiridh.'

Well, nuair a tháinig an t-am, agus a shuipéar ite aige, chuaigh an buachaill siar le ceann de na buidéil agus leag sé ar an mbord é. Agus bhreathnaigh sé seo suas i gclár an éadain air. Agus dúirt sé:

'That's one of them,' a deir sé.

Agus nuair a tháinig an buachaill aniar: 'Céard dúirt sé?' a deir an mháistreás agus an cailín.

'Ó, m'anam péin gur cuma céard dúirt sé nó nár dhúirt sé ach go bhfuil mé cheapadh gur diabhal corportha atá ann,' a dúirt an buachaill.

Chuaigh an cailín siar leis an darna buidéal.

'That's two of them,' a deir sí, agus bhreathnaigh sé suas i gclár an éadain uirthi.

Nuair a tháinig sí aniar: 'Céard dúirt sé?' a dúirt an mháistreás.

'Ó, mh'anam go bhfuil an fios aige go cinnte,' a dúirt an mháistreás.

Chuaigh an mháistreás siar leis an tríú buidéal.

'That's the last of them,' a deir sé.

'Ó, ná habair aon bhlas anois,' a deir an mháistreás, 'faoi thada, agus ná hinsigh aon bhlas don bhoc mór faoi rud ar bith. Inseoidh mise dhuit cá bhfuil an t-airgead agus cá bhfuil an t-ór agus cá bhfuil na rudaí uilig curtha agam agus tabharfaidh mé saibhreas maith dhuit féin freisin, ach ná hinsigh tada.'

Ach ar maidin, d'insigh sé seo don bhoc mór gach uile shórt agus leigheas sé a chás agus chroch sé suas ar ais aríst é go maith.

Agus chuaigh an boc mór anonn go Sasana ansin faoi cheann scathaimh agus bhí sé ag caint le fear a raibh eolas aige thall air. Agus bhí an fear thall é féin, bhí sé bochtaithe go mór ó chonaic an fear abhus go deireanach é.

'Muise, m'anam go bhfuil fear in Éirinn agamsa,' a deir an boc mór seo, 'agus go leigheasfadh sé do chás, a bhfuil fios aige.'

'Maise, m'anam nach gcreidim é,' a dúirt an fear thall.

Ach fébí cén scéal é, chuireadar geall mór le chéile go raibh, agus chuir a fhear féin fios ar an bhfear bocht anall – ar an bhfear feasa. Agus dúirt an fear feasa nuair a fuair sé an scéal:

'Á, muise,' a deir sé, 'is bocht an ceann agamsa é seo, ag ceapadh go bhfuil fios agamsa is gan agam ach tráthúlacht chainte.'

Mar sin féin, chuaigh sé anonn. Agus fébí cé bhfuair an fear thall sionnach, fuair sé sionnach agus bhruith sé i bpota é, agus rinne sé trí leith den sionnach agus chuir sé ar thrí cinn de mhiasa é agus mias eile anuas os a gcionn le haghaidh nach mbeadh a fhios ag fear ar bith sa domhan céard a bhí ar an mias. Agus dúirt sé leis an mboc mór seo:

'Anois,' a deir sé, 'tabhair d'fhear feasa aníos don tseomra chugamsa agus insíodh an fear feasa dhomsa cén sort feola atá ar na plátaí sin – ar na miasaí sin.'

Tháinig an fear bocht, chuaigh sé siar don tseomra. Agus nuair a bhí a fhios aige go maith ná raibh fhios aige cén sórt feola a bhí ann, chuir sé a láimh suas agus thosaigh sé ag tochas a mhullaigh ag déanamh dobróin.

'Á, well,' a deir sé, 'dhá chríonna dhá mbíonn an sionnach féin, beirtear uair eicínt air!'

Ní dhearnadar seo ach a mbosa a bhualadh faoi chéile agus thosaigh ag gáirí. Agus ag gáirí go tréan le áthas a bhí an fear seo as ucht go raibh a chúis buachtaithe aige. Agus ní raibh a fhios ag an bhfear bocht san am sin chor ar bith, ach go mba tráthúlacht cainte é.

The Man Who Pretended He Had Knowledge[7]

Long ago, there was a rich man who had become greatly impoverished. And this man was going around – he was always begging – and anytime he came by, he got a suit of clothes and a lot more besides from the rich man. But he asked for alms this particular day and the rich man said to him:

'There was a time,' he said, 'and I was able to give you alms, but I cannot give you any alms now – I am impoverished.'

'Oh, indeed what has happened to you, at all,' he said, 'since I last saw you? You were very powerful.'

'I have become very impoverished,' he said.

'Well, if you let me stay until the morning,' he said, 'perhaps I would do you some good. I would pretend that I have special knowledge and you wouldn't know what good I might do: if you give me a room until the morning and my supper.'

'I will,' said the rich man.

'Well, if you do give these to me,' he said, 'you'll send three bottles of drink to me to my room, and you'll send your servant boy with one of them in the night. You'll send your servant girl with the other one, and the mistress of the house with the last one.'

Well, when the time came, and he had eaten his supper, the servant boy went to him with one of the bottles and he put it on the table. And the fellow looked him directly in the face and said:

'That's one of them,'[8] he said.

And when the boy returned, 'What did he say?' asked the mistress of the house and the girl.

'Oh, I believe it doesn't matter what he said or didn't say but I think we have a supernatural being[9] with us,' said the boy.

The girl went to the room with the second bottle.

'That's the second of them,'[10] she said, and he looked her straight in the face.

When she returned: 'What did he say?' asked the mistress of the house.

'Oh, I'm sure he has special knowledge without a doubt,' said the mistress of the house.[11]

The mistress of the house went along with the third bottle.

'That's the last of them,'[12] he said.

'Oh, don't say a word now,' said the mistress of the house, 'about anything, and don't tell the rich man anything about anything. I will tell you where the silver is and where the gold is and where I have put everything and I will give you riches for yourself, but do not say anything.'

But in the morning, he said all of this to the rich man and he settled his lot and he created a better situation for him again.

And the rich man went over to England, then after a while over there he was talking to a man of whom he had heard. And the man in England had become very impoverished since the other man had last seen him.

'I know a man in Ireland,' said this rich man, 'who has special knowledge and he could solve your problem.'

'I don't believe it,' said the man.

In any case, they placed a large bet with one another that there was such a man and this man sent for the poor man to come over – sent for the man with the special knowledge. And the man with the special knowledge said when he got word:

'Oh,' he said, 'this is a difficult one for me when people think that I have special knowledge when all I have is aptness of speech.'

Nonetheless, he travelled over. And wherever the man beyond got a fox, he got a fox and boiled it in a pot, and he made three parts of the fox and put them in three dishes and placed another dish on the three dishes and another dish over them so that no one on this earth could guess what was in the dish. And he said to this rich man:

'Now,' he said, 'bring your man with the special knowledge here to this room and let this man tell me what kind of meat is on those plates – in those dishes.'

The poor man, he went to the room, and when he fully realised that he didn't know what kind of meat it was, he put his hand up and began scratching his head in sorrow.

'Oh, well,' he said, 'however wise the fox is he will be caught out at some point.'

The others simply clapped their hands and began laughing. And this man was laughing loudly for joy as he had won the day. And the poor man didn't know at that time at all, that it was merely aptness of speech.

An Bhean a d'Iompar Mac Dé [13]

Fadó, nuair a bhí an Mhaighdean Mhuire ag siúl ar an talamh seo agus í ag iompar a hAonmhic, bhí sí roinnt tuirseach, agus casadh bean di agus d'iarr sí cúnamh uirthi le haghaidh an páiste a iompar píosa den bhóthar. Agus d'eitigh an bhean an páiste a iompar a chúnamh dhi píosa den bhóthar. Agus is gearr a bhí siúlta aici nuair a casadh bean eile dhi, agus d'iarr sí cúnamh uirthi an páiste a iompar píosa den bhóthar agus thug an bhean eile cúnamh dhi agus d'iompar sí an páiste a chúnamh dhi.

'Muise, a Mhic,' a deir an Mhaighdean Mhuire, 'céard tá tú a ghabháil a thabhairt don bhean a d'iompar thú a chúnamh dhom?'

'Tá mé ag gabháil a tabhairt dháréag clainne dhi,' a deir sé, 'agus gan aon nduine acu a bheith i láthair a báis aici.'

'Muise, céard a thabharfas tú don bhean nár iompar thú?' a deir sí.

'Tabharfaidh mé dháréag eile dhi agus a gach uile dhuine acu a bheith i láthair a báis aici.'

'Á, céard?' a deir sí, 'is iontach an rud é sin, tú ag fágáil na clainne ag an mbean a d'eitigh thú a iompar agus an bhean a d'iompar thú ag baint na clainne dhi.'

'Á,' a deir sé, 'is fearr dhi solas roimpi ná dhá sholas ina diaidh.'

The Woman Who Carried the Son of God

Long ago, when the Virgin Mary was walking on this earth and she was carrying her only Son, she was rather tired and she met a woman and asked her for help to carry the child part of the road. And the woman refused to help carry the child along the road. She had walked only a short distance when she met another woman and she asked her to help carry the child part of the road and the other woman helped her and carried the child.

'Oh, my son,' said the Virgin Mary, 'what are you going to give to the woman who carried you in order to help me?'

'I'm going to give her a family of twelve,' he said, 'and not one of them present at her death.'

'Oh, what will you give the woman who did not carry you?' she said.

'I will give her another twelve and every one of them present at her death.'

'Oh, what's this?' she said, 'it's a wonder that you are leaving her family to the woman who refused to carry you and that you are taking her family away from the woman who carried you.'

'Oh,' he said, 'she is better off having a light ahead of her than two lights after her.'[14]

An Fear a Thug Blaosc as an Teampall[15]

Bhí bádóirí as an mBeirtreach Bhuí cheana, bhíodar i gContae an Chláir thall agus bhí cruinniú acu in éineacht i dteach an ósta. Agus creidim nuair a theangmhaigh an t-ól leob go rabhadar ag caint ar rudaí. Ach dúirt fear acu go mba mhaith an misneach ag an té thabharfadh blaoisc duine mhairbh as teampall na Ceathrún – as teampall na Ceathrún anseo. Agus dúirt fear eile ná raibh aon fhear in ann é dhéanamh ná de mhisneach aige. Agus chuir ceann de mhuintir Chonamara – chuireadar geall as Pádraig Mac Craith go ndéanfadh sé féin é. Ach le leisce an geall a ligean ar fhear abhus, chuaigh Pádraig ag seasamh dhóibh agus chuaigh sé amach agus tháinig sé taobh amuigh den doras. Chaisric sé é féin in ainm an Athar, an Mhic agus an Spiorad Naomh agus thug sé aghaidh ar an teampall. Agus tháinig sé isteach sa teampall. Agus i gContae an Chláir ins an am sin – níl a fhios agamsa cén chaoi bhfuil sé anois – nuair a curtaí na cnámhannaí aníos as an bhfuaigh in aimsire duine eile a chur, ní curtaí síos ar ais iad. Agus bhí na blaoscannaí leagthaí ar íochtar na fuinneoige. Rug sé ar cheann de na blaoscannaí.

'Leag ansin í sin,' a deir an fear istigh.

Leag sé uaidh é agus rug sé ar cheann eile.

'Leag ansin í sin,' a deir an fear eile.

Agus rug sé ar an tríú ceann.

'Leag ansin í sin,' a deir sé.

'Ó hanam ón diabhal!' a deir sé, 'ní leat uilig iad.'

Thug sé leis í seo agus thug sé isteach insan teach í a rabhadar ag ól ann. Ach tá sé cloistithe agam nach ngabhfadh sé ar ais leis an mblaoisc ar bhás an domhain.

The Man Who Took the Skull from the Church

There were boatmen from Beirtreach Bhuí over in County Clare and they met up at the public house. And I believe after a few drinks they began discussing things. But one of them said it would be a brave deed for a man who would take the skull of a dead person from the church of An Cheathrú[16] there. And another man said that no one could, or would, be brave enough to do that. And one of the people from Conamara made a bet that Pádraig Mac Craith would do it. But rather than let the bet go to one of the others, Pádraig took it on on their behalf and he went out and was outside the door. He blessed himself in the name of the Father, the Son and the Holy Ghost and went into the graveyard. And in County Clare at that time – I don't know how it is today – when the bones were taken up from the grave while another person was being buried, they were not buried again. And the skulls were placed below the window. He took hold of one of the skulls.

'Put that one there,' said the man inside.

He put it down and took up another one.

'Put that one there,' said the other man.

And he took hold of the third one.

'Put that one there,' he said.

'Oh, to hell!' he said, 'they are not all yours.'

He took this one with him and he brought it to the house where they were drinking. But I heard that he would not on pain of death return with the skull.

An Sagart a Chaith an tÉadach Dhe[17]

Bhí sagart fadó ann agus d'éirigh sé an-mhoch ar maidin – ba é a ghnaithe é – le haghaidh ghabháil ag léamh aifrinn agus mainistir. Agus bhí sé ag breathnú amach thríd an bhfuinneoig bairr – bhí sé uachtarach ins an mbaile mór a raibh sé ann – bhí sé sa teach bairr agus bhí feiceál mór aige amach thríd an bhfuinneoig. Ach chonaic sé fear ag tíocht anuas an tsráid – an bhaile mhóir – agus chonaic sé búistéara ag éirí amach as a theach féin agus ráipéar agus scian aige agus ag marú an fhir agus ag gabháil isteach ar ais arís. Agus is gearr an t-achar ina dhiaidh gur shiúil fear eile anuas an tsráid agus nuair a chonaic sé an fear marbh sheas sé suas ag déanamh iontas den fhear maraithe, nó cén fáth é bheith marbh nó céard a mharaigh é. Agus cén fear a crochfaí leis an bfear a bhí marbh ach an fear a sheas suas ag déanamh iontas de.

Agus mar gheall ar go bhfaca an sagart gach uile shórt, dúirt sé … rugthas ansin ar an bhfear a sheas suas ag déanamh iontas den fhear marbh, agus dúirt an sagart nach ndéanfaí tada air mar gheall ar go raibh a fhios aige nach é a mharaigh é. Bhí sé ag gabháil ó sheisiún go seisiún agus d'abraíodh an sagart i gcónaí nach ndéanfaí tada air. Ach bhí sé ag gabháil ar deireadh chuig an seisiún a raibh sé le tligeadh ann, agus crochadh é. Agus ní dhearna an sagart ach an t-éadach a chaitheamh dhe – an chulaith a bhí air a chaitheamh dhe – agus dúirt sé nach ndéanfadh sé níos mó i seirbhís Dé, ná raibh aon bhuachtáil insa gcás, in áit a raibh círín air mar gheall ar gur crochadh, cheap sé, go neamhchiontach é nuair nach é mharaigh é. Ní dhearna sé ach an t-éadach a chaitheamh de agus siúl amach agus dúirt sé go ngabhfadh sé ag obair ar nós gach uile fhear.

Agus ní raibh mórán achair siúlta aige, agus culaith phlánáilte fir air, nuair a casadh fear dhó agus d'insigh sé gur ag iarraidh obair a bhí sé. Agus dúirt an fear gur maith mar tharla, a deir sé, 'Teastaíonn fear uaimse agus tá sé chomh maith dhuit ghabháil ag obair dhom.' Ach thug sé láí dhó agus dúirt sé leis a ghabháil isteach in íochtar na páirce sin thíos, 'agus bí dhá spréamh sin,' a deir sé, 'nó go dtaga mé chugat le do bhéilí.' Chuaigh sé ag spréamh agus ní raibh mórán spréite aige ach tuairim is trí spreab, nuair a lig sé fear marbh leis. Agus rinne sé – tháinig an-eagla air agus ní raibh sé ag gabháil a déanamh níos mó spréamh go dtagadh an máistir. Agus nuair a tháinig an máistir:

'Bydad,' a deir sé, 'níl mórán déanta agat ó scar mé leat.'

'Níl tada,' a deir sé, 'déanta agam; cúpla spreab a bhí bainte agam nuair a lig mé fear marbh leis agus níor mhaith liom níos mó a dhéanamh go dtagtása.'

'Bhreathnaigh sé an-iontach dhuit,' a deir sé, 'nuair a lig tú an fear leis.'

'Bhreathnaigh,' a deir sé.

'Well,' a deir sé, 'an fear,' a deir sé, 'a sheas suas ag déanamh iontas den fhear a mharaigh an búistéara, ba shin é an fear a mharaigh an fear sin a lig tusa leis, agus chaithfeadh an roth a bheith ag gabháil timpeall le go dtagadh sé anuas le go n-íocfadh sé é. Agus mar gheall ar an bhfear lig tusa leis, a crochadh é sin. Agus tá a chúis féin roimh an mbúistéara fós. Gabh thusa abhaile anois agus cuir ort an chulaith chéanna arís a bhí cheana ort. Teachtaire ó Dhia mise.'

The Priest Who Cast His Clothes[18]

There was a priest long ago and he got up very early in the morning – as was his wont – to go and read mass and pray. He was looking out the highest window – it was the highest in the town where he was – he was in the highest house and had a great view out the window.

He saw a man coming down the street – in the town – and he saw a butcher coming out of his house with a rapier and a knife and he killed the man and went back indoors. Shortly afterwards, another man walked down the street and when he saw the dead man, he stood in wonder at the dead man, as to how he came to be dead or what caused his death. And who was to hang because of it, but the man who had stood in wonder at it.

And because the priest had seen everything, he said … then the man who had stood in wonder at the dead man was taken away and the priest said nothing would be done to him because he knew that man had not killed him. It was going from session to session and the priest always said that nothing would be done to the man. But in the end it was due at the session where the verdict was to be given and he was hanged. And the priest simply took off his clothes – threw off the suit he was wearing – and he said he would no longer work in God's service, that there was no winning the case, as he was so angry as he was hanged, he thought, although he was innocent, as it was not he who had killed him. He simply took the clothes off and walked out and he said he would go to work like everyone else.

And he had not walked far wearing a man's plain suit, when he met a man and he told him he was looking for work. And the man said it was opportune, he said, 'I need a man and you may as well go to work for me.' And he handed him a spade and told him to go to the bottom of the field below: 'and dig it,' he said, 'until I bring your meal to you.' He set about digging and he hadn't dug a great deal, only about three spadefuls, when he uncovered a dead man.[19] And he did – he became very fearful and he wasn't going to do any more digging until the master would come. And when the master came:

'Bydad,' he said, 'you haven't done much since I left you.'

'I've done nothing,' he said. 'I had only dug a few spadefuls when I uncovered a dead man and I didn't want to do any more until you would come.'

'You must have been amazed,' he said, 'when you uncovered the dead man.'

'I was,' he said.

'Well,' he said, 'the man who stood in wonder at the man that the butcher killed, he was the man who killed the man you uncovered.

The wheel must turn and were he responsible, he will pay the price. And it was because of the man you uncovered that he was hanged. And the butcher still has a charge to face. Go home now and put on the same suit you wore earlier. I am a messenger from God.'

Comhairle an Fhir Sí don Chailín[20]

Well, chuala mise mo mháthair mhór féin dá inseacht dom go bhfaca sí féin lena dhá súil an cás seo. Marach gurb í bhí dá inseacht dom, ní chreidfinn é. Bhí sí i gciumhais cnoic, agus gan aon teach gar dóib ach iad féin. Agus idir Féile Bríde agus Nollaig, tháinig fear isteach acu nach bhfaca siad ariamh agus ná raibh a fhios acu cé mba as é. Agus ní raibh bróg ná stoca air, agus is éard a bhí air treabhsar córd. Agus bhí mála – dhá mhála – ag tíocht aige, mála a raibh min bhuí ann agus mála a raibh fataí ann. Agus fébí am san oíche a n-éireoidís, bhíodh bruthnóg insan tine aige agus é ag bruith fataí. Agus an pota a gcuireadh sé an mhin bhuí dá bruith ann, caithfí bheith dá sciúradh go mbeadh sé chomh sciúrtha le a bhfaca tú ariamh le faitíos nach mbeadh sé sách glan: bhí sé chomh glan leis an bhfíoruisce. Agus nuair a thagadh fonn ábhars[21] *air, thosaíodh sé ag filleadh – bhíodh an treabhsar crapaithe suas go dtína ghlúna – agus nuair a thosaíodh sé, fonn ábhars air, thosaíodh sé ag scaoileadh síos na bhfillteachaí seo bhíodh sa treabhsar. Agus ní raibh filleadh ar bith dá raibh sa treabhsar ná raibh 'row sovereigns' thart timpeall ann. Agus bhí a fhios acu go maith nár dhuine ceart a bhí ann faoi cheann scathaimh.*

Ach nuair a thagadh sé gearr i gcónaí insan mbeatha, théadh sé taobh siar i ngleann a bhí ann. Agus níorbh fhada – théidís sin ag imeacht féachaint an ag imeacht a bhíodh sé – agus níorbh fhada bhíodh sé thiar insan ngleann nuair a thagadh sé aniar aríst agus an oiread céanna aige. Agus chaitheadh sise bheith ag 'tendáil' i gcónaí air, fébí am a mbeadh sé ag ithe.

Agus bhí seanfhear muintearthach léi insan mbaile, in íochtar an bhaile, agus dúirt sé lena máthair: 'Sin é do chuide-sa don chailín beag,' a deir sé, 'nó go n-imí sé sin. Tabharfaidh sé leis í siúráilte.' Agus bhí sí dearfa go dtabharfadh. Ach mar sin féin nuair a bhí an t-am thuas aige seo le imeacht, thosaigh sé ag tabhairt comhairleachaí don chailín beag.

'Ná téirigh a chodladh choidhche,' a deir sé, 'gan uisce glan a fhágáil istigh. Agus ná téirigh a chodladh choidhche gan do theach a scuabadh gan aon

bhlas salachair fhágáil ann. Agus ná coigil an tine choidhche gan aghaidh bheag fhágáil uirthi. Sin comhairle anois,' a deir sé, 'atá mise thabhairt duit.'

The Fairy Man's Advice to the Girl

Well, I heard my own grandmother say to me that she saw this with her own two eyes. If it weren't that it was she who told it to me, I wouldn't believe it. She was in a recess in a hill, and there was no house near to theirs. Between St Bridget's Day and Christmas, a man called into them that they had never seen before and that they didn't know where he came from. And he wore neither shoes nor stockings, but he was wearing corduroy trousers. And he had a bag – he had two bags – one bag contained yellow meal and the other contained potatoes. And whatever time of night they got up, he had a batch of potatoes in the fire cooking them. And the pot in which he placed the yellow meal to cook it, it had to be scoured until it was perfectly scoured in case it might not be sufficiently clean; it was as clear as spring water. And when he wanted to have some fun, he began to fold – his trousers were turned up to his knees – and when he began, when he wanted some fun, he began to let down the folds of the trousers. And there wasn't a fold in the trousers that didn't have a row of sovereigns around in it. And they knew well, after a while, that he wasn't a mortal being.

But when his supply was reduced, he always went to a valley towards the west. And it wasn't long – they went to see where he was going – and he wasn't long in the valley when he would return again with the same amount. And she [the grandmother] always had to tend to him, whenever he would eat.

There was an old man, a relation of hers there, at the end of the village, and he said to her mother: 'That's your part for that little girl,' he said, 'until he goes away. He will take her with him for sure.' And she was sure that he would. But nonetheless when his time came to leave, he began giving pieces of advice to the little girl.

'Never go to sleep,' he said, 'without having clean water indoors. And never go to sleep without brushing your house and don't leave a scrap of dirt in it. And don't ever rake the fire without leaving a little glow of it there. That is the advice,' he said, 'that I am giving you.'

Baiste Páistí Neamhdhlisteanacha[22]

Tháinig an t-easpag go Roundstone 'trip', ach ní mar gheall ar an gcúis seo tháinig sé; is é chaoi dtáinig sé ag cur daoine faoi láimh easpaig, an bhfuil a fhios agat. Agus bhí sagairt mar tá a fhios agat, cruinnithe as gach uile áit air; na paráistí ba gaire bhí na sagairt uilig cruinn air. Ach bhí an sagart seo ann. Agus bhlaoigh sé air ina ainm a baisteadh air agus níor thug sé aon aird air. Agus bhlaoigh sé aríst air agus níor thug sé aon aird air. Agus bhlaoigh sé an tríú huair air agus thug sé 'Athair' air agus d'fhreagair sé ansin é. Agus tháinig sé go dtí é.

'Creidim,' a deir an t-easpag, a deir sé, 'go bhfuil tusa ag baiste páistí atá beirthe neamhdhlisteanach, taobh amuigh den dlí, in aghaidh dlí Dé.'

'Ó, táim,' a deir an sagart, a deir sé, 'nuair a déanadh sagart díom, ba é a cuireadh de dhiútaí orm agus d'iallach orm nuair thiocadh páiste go dtí mé, aingeal a dhéanamh dhe.'

'Ó, níl aon locht air sin,' a deir an t-easpag, 'aingeal a dhéanamh dhe, ach cén fáth dhuit a bheith ag coisreacan na máthar?'

'Ó, a thiarna easpag,' a deir sé, 'cé chaoi gcuirfinn an t-aingeal ag diúl ar an diabhal?'

The Baptism of Children Born out of Wedlock

The bishop came to Roundstone once, but he didn't come because of this matter. He came to confirm people, do you know. And there were priests gathered from everywhere there; the neighbouring parishes, all the priests had gathered. But there was this priest. And the bishop called him by his baptismal name, and he paid him no heed. And he called him again and he did not heed him. And he called him the third time and he called him 'Father' and he answered him then. And he came to him.

'I believe,' said the bishop, he said, 'that you are baptising children who are born out of wedlock, outside the law, outside the law of God.'

'Oh, I am,' said the priest, he said, 'when I was ordained a priest, my duty and obligation was if a child came to me, to make an angel of the child.'

'Oh, there is nothing wrong with that,' said the bishop, he said, 'to make an angel of him but why do you bless the mother?'

'Oh, my lord bishop,' he said, 'how could I make an angel suckle the devil?'

Collected by Séamus Ennis:

Cé hÉ Siúd Thuas Os Cionn Mo Thí-Sa?[23]

Ráiméis eile le haghaidh bréagadh gasúr:

'Cé hé siúd thuas os cionn mo thí-sa?'
'Mise an fhíneog charnach.'
'Céard é sin agat ann?'
'Luimpín mín bán.'[24]
'dTabharfaidh tú aon bhlas domsa dhe?'
'Mh'anam péin nach dtabharfad.'
'Tuige sin?'
'Mar tiocfaidh cúis mhór orm péin anocht.'
'Céard é sin?'
'Sionachó-Biorachó mo bheirt pháistí,
I mbroc Pháidín,
Agus an préachán liath.'

Sionachó-Biorachó
Is éard é an t-údar atá leis an bhfocal cainte seo – le 'Sionachó-Biorachó' – bhí sé ag seandaoine, tá cúpla líne daoine ó shin ann, coitianta insan áit seo. Dhá mbeadh fear ann nach mbeadh siad in ann a thrust leis an rud a dhéanamh, agus nach mbeadh aon bharúil acub go mbeadh sé in ann an rud a dhéanamh ceart agus go dtiocfadh sé isteach insan oíche agus go ndéarfadh sé go ndearna sé a leithéide seo de rud (bád a fheistiú nó beithigh a chur isteach) – go ndéarfadh an seanfhear 'Sionachó-Biorachó' – sin ag ceapadh amach ná raibh aon déanamh ar an rud sin.

Who Is That Above My House?

Another nonsense piece to entice children:

'Who is that above my house?'
'I am the mite of heaps.'
'What have you there?'
'A small smooth white lump.'
'Will you give me any bit of it?'
'Indeed, I will not.'

'Why so?'
'Because a heavy charge falls on me tonight.'
'What is that?'
'Sionachó-Biorachó my two children,
In Páidín's mess,[25]
And the grey crow.'

Sionachó-Biorachó
The reason for the word in this piece – 'Sionachó-Biorachó' – the old people had it a few generations ago. It was common here. If there was a man they couldn't depend upon to do something and they had no idea if he was able to do it right; and that he came in at night and said that he had done such a thing – rig a boat or put the cattle in – the old man would say 'Sionachó-Biorachó' – that was because he thought there was no proper structure to what he had done.

D'éirigh Sodar agus d'Ith Sé Sochar-bhoinn[26]

D'éirigh sodar agus d'ith sé sochar-bhoinn,
D'éirigh cabhair agus dhóirt sí an mheag (meadhg?= whey) ar fud do ríochta;
Sháigh súmas a thóin sa nglóire,
Is mara bhfuil neart den iomardú istigh agat, beidh do ríocht dóite.

Sodar = gadhar; sochar-bhoinn = bróga (iad bealáilte le him);
Cabhair = bó; meag = bainne?(meadhg=whey) i mbarraillí;
Ríocht = teach; Súmas = cat (tuí ag dó, ceangailte dá dhrioball);
Glóire = tine; iomadra = uisce;
Seanduine agus filí – cainteoir maith, agus é leigean air ná raibh fios tada aige agus bhí sé ag fiafraí den fhear eile.

Sodar Got Up and Ate Sochar-Bhoinn[27]

Sodar got up and ate *sochar-bhoinn,*
Help got up and poured the whey all over your kingdom;
Súmas stuck his bottom in the glory,
And if you don't have a lot of water in store,
Your kingdom will be burned.

Sodar = dog; *sochar-bhoinn* = shoes (greased with butter);
Help = cow; whey = milk in barrels;
Kingdom = house; *Súmas* = cat (burning hay, tied to his tail);
Glory = fire; *iomardú* = water;
An old man and a poet – a good speaker, and he pretended that he knew nothing and he was questioning the other man.

An Mhaighdean Mhara[28]

Dhá mbeifeá ar an bhfarraige agus maighdean mhara do d'fheiceáil gan tusa dá feiceáil an chéad uair, bhí tú le bheith tugthaí as an mbád i bhfarraige aici.

Bhí fear ar Thrá an Ghoirtín cheana, agus chonaic sé maighdean mhara ina suí ar leic agus a ceann-chochall caite dhi aici lena hais. Agus bhí sé in ann í bheith tugthaí as an draíocht aige ach ní raibh sé de mhisneach aige. Agus chonaic sise é shula dtáinig sé comh fada leis an gceann-chochall agus d'éalaigh sí uaidh.

Chreid seandaoine gur mná saolta iad a bhí faoi dhraíocht agus dhá n-éiríodh le duine an ceann-chochall a bhaint dhíobh, bheidís fuasclaithe.

The Mermaid

If you were at sea and a mermaid saw you and you didn't see her first, she would take you out of the boat into the sea with her.

There was a man once in Trá an Ghoirtín[29] and he saw a mermaid sitting on a rock and she had taken off her cloak and put it beside her, and he could have broken the spell that she was under, but he lacked the courage. And she saw him before he came as far as the cloak and she escaped from him.

The old people believed that they were mortal women who are under a spell and if a person succeeded in taking the cloak from them, the spell would be broken.

Lúrabóg, Lárabóg[30]

Cluiche le gasúir (ó chois go cois)

Lúrabóg, lárabóg,
Buí ó Néill,
Néill an preabán,
Preabán súileach,
Súileach seicneach,
Seicne mulláin,
Ladhróg lathaí,
Buille beag,
Ar barr do shlaite,
Agus crap isteach an phéachóg.

(Ag cur na coise go leataobh)

Lúrabóg, Lárabóg[31]

A game for children (from leg to leg)

Lúrabóg, lárabóg,
Buí ó Néill,
Néill the patch,
A muslin patch,
Eyed, with a covering,
A covering of a hillock,
A claw of mud,
A small blow,
On top of your stick,
And draw in the peacock.[32]

(Putting a leg to one side)

Sceál na nAilleadóirí[33]

Bhí fear as na cnoic ar an mbaile seo agus nuair tháinig na bádóirí as Árainn anseo, bhíodar ag inseacht dó cén chaoi mbíodh na héanlaith dhá marú insna hailltreachaí ag na hailleadóirí, 'agus ansin bhailigh siad síos i gcliabh a raibh dhá iris ann', a dúirt na bádóirí leis agus rópa mór fada as, agus nuair a bheadh sé thíos ansin ghabhadh sé amach ar an gcliabh agus thosódh sé ag imeacht ar fud na scailpí ag marú na n-éanlaith agus nuair a bhíodh na héanlaith marbh ansin aige dhéanadh sé 'sign', é féin a thabhairt suas.

Well, bhí sé dhá tharraingt aníos ansin go raibh sé leath-bealaigh agus bhris dual insa rópa.'

'Ó,' a deir fear na gcnoc.

'Bhí sé ag tarraingt aníos, ag tarraingt aníos, go raibh sé dhá chuid bealaigh agus nuair a bhí sé dhá chuid bealaigh bhris an dual eile ar a rópa.'

'Ó, tháinig faitíos agus eagla níos mó ná sin ar fhear na gcnoc – bhí fuar-allas ag tíocht air le faitíos.'

'Bhí sé ag tarraingt aníos, ag tarraingt aníos ariamh,' a deir sé, gur shíl sé – gur shíl sé breith ar an bhfear lena láimh agus nuair a shíl sé breith air, bhris an dual eile agus thit sé síos.' (agus rug sé de láimh ar fhear na gcnoc agus titeann fear na gcnoc i lagar. Is é an chaoi a raibh sé in aon turas ag iarraidh é scanrú agus bhí a shliocht air – scanraigh sé é!)

The Story of the Cliffclimbers

There was a man from the hills here and when the boatmen from Aran came, they were telling him how the cliffclimbers would kill the birds in the cliffs and would gather them then in a basket that had two straps, the boatmen said to him, and he had a long rope tied to him. When he was down then, he would go out in the basket and go around the crevices killing the birds. And when he had killed the birds, he would make a sign to bring him up.

'Well, he was being pulled up then until he was halfway up and a strand in the rope broke.'

'Oh!' said the man from the hills.

'He was pulling upwards, pulling upwards, until he was two thirds of the way up and when he was two thirds of the way up, the other strand in the rope broke.'

The man from the hills became even more fearful then – he was in a cold sweat from fear.

He was pulling up, continuing to pull up, he said, until he thought he could catch hold of the man with his hand, and when he thought to catch hold of him, the other strand broke and he fell down.' (And he caught the man from the hills by the hand and the man from the hills fainted. He was, in fact, deliberately trying to frighten him and so it was – he scared him!)

Collected by Proinnsias de Búrca:

Fig. 30: Collector Proinnsias de Búrca. COURTESY NFC

Scéal Sidhiúil[34]

Sin scéalta a chuala mise anois ag mo mhuintir féin, agus creidim rud ar bith a chloisfeas tú ag do mhuintir féin go gcaithfidh muid é a chreisteachtáil. Ach níl mé a gabháil anonn ná anall leis ach an rud a d'éirigh dhom péin, tá mé fíor shiúráilte dhe. Bhí m'athair-sa ag bádóireacht idir Cloch na Rón agus Gaillimh agus as Cloch na Rón a d'fhághadh muid an plúr anseo, an tae agus an tobac agus gach uile shórt an t-am sin. Bhíodh na báid a gabháil siar i gcónaí, uair sa tseachtain i gcoinne chuile shórt a d'fheilfeadh don teach. Ní raibh siopaí ar bith thart insan am sin san áit seo, níos gaire abhaile ná Carna ná An Caiseal nó Cloch na Rón. Ach go Cloch na Rón a bhíodh muide a gabháil.

Ach chonaic mé féin an bád an lá seo a gabháil aníos. Húcaera a thugadh siad ar na báid trí seolta agus dúirt mé gurb é m'athair a bhí a tíocht. Bhí mé óg croíúil agus mo dheartháir in eindí liom. Agus mo léan, ní raibh ag teastáil uaim ach leithscéal le ghabháil chun seoil. Lá breá gaoithe aduaidh. Ní dhearna mé ach ardú ar an mbád agus tosaí ag tornáil go Cloch na Rón. Nuair a tháinig mé go Cloch na Rón, ní hé m'athair a bhí ann ach bád a bhí ag an 'mBoard' a bhí ag tráchtáil idir Cathair na Mart, An Cloigeann, Boifinn, Árainn, gach uile áit ag tarraingt adhmaid agus rudaí a bhain do thithe. Dúirt fear an bháid liom, fear as Gaillimh, d'fhiafraigh sé dhíom a raibh aithne agam ar a leithéide seo d'fhear. Dúirt mise go raibh.

'A dtabharfá adhmad chuige,' a deir sé, 'atá anseo agam le haghaidh caoi a chuir ar theach?'

'Á, tabharfad agus míle fáilte,' a deirimse, 'tuige nach dtabharfainn?'

'Tá d'athair i gCasla,' a deir sé, 'agus beidh sé anseo amárach. Go raibh maith agat,' a deir sé, 'faoin adhmad.'

Chuir sé isteach an t-adhmad chugam péin. Oíche spéirghealaí a bhí ann agus tháinig muid aniar. Chuir muid amach an t-adhmad as an mbád. Agus chuir an fear seo a dtáinig an t-adhmad chuige, chuir sé a dhearthá́ir aniar in éindí liom chuig mo chaladh féin gur fheistigh muid an bád. Agus dúirt sé mise a thabhairt siar nuair a bheadh an bád feistithe. Chuaigh mise siar agus tháinig mo dhearthá́ir abhaile. Agus thug an fear isteach 'jar-ín' fuisce agus thosaigh muid dhá ól. Well, níor leag mise aon tsuntas ar an méid a bhí ólta agam péin, ach chaith muid an oíche. Creidim go raibh an stuif go maith. Bhí muid ag ól go raibh sé tuairim an dó a chlog san oíche. Agus nuair a cheap muid go raibh sé in am againn a ghabháil abhaile, chuaigh mise amach go dtáinig mé anuas ar an mbóthar. Bhí an oíche go hálainn. Bhí gach uile theach ina chodladh. Bhí mé ag siúl liom aniar. Mar gheall ar an ól a bheith déanta agam, ba chuma liom beo. Bhí mé ag imeacht liom go dtáinig mé abhaile. Agus is é an faisean a bhíodh an t-am sin ins na tithe dá mbeadh duine amuigh ag cuartaíocht, mara mbeadh sé tagthaí isteach is éard a níodh na seandaoine cathaoir a leagan taobh istigh leis an gcomhla, a choinneodh an chomhla dúinte amach go dtagadh an duine. Agus nuair a thiocfadh sé ansin ní raibh air ach an chomhla a bhrú agus d'imeodh an chathaoir isteach.

Tháinig mise chuig an doras agus bhrúigh mé isteach an chomhla agus d'imigh an chomhla isteach. Agus nuair a dhún mise an chomhla amach aríst chuir mé an bolta ar an doras mar bhí a fhios agam nach raibh níos mó le tíocht isteach. Ní raibh mé aon bhlas ach abhus ag an teallach nós mar bheadh slat mhór shailigh, nuair a buaileadh an doras trí huaire. Buaileadh chomh tréan é agus gur croitheadh an chomhla agus an moirtéal agus na hursaineachaí. Agus dúirt a raibh istigh agus amuigh, chuireadar béic astub, céard é seo. Níor leag mise suntas ar bith air mar gheall ar an ól a bheith déanta agam go dtí lá arna mhárach.

A Fairy Story

These are stories I heard, now, from my own people, and I believe, anything you hear from your own people, we have to believe it. I'm not going to go back and forth with it, but I'm absolutely certain of anything that happened to myself. My father was boating between Roundstone and Galway and we used to get the flour from Roundstone, along with the tea and the tobacco and everything else at that time. The boats were always going westwards, once a week to fetch all kinds of supplies for the house. There were no shops around here at that time nearer than Carna, An Caiseal or Roundstone and we used to go to Roundstone. I saw the boat one day as it approached. They called the boat with three sails a Galway Hooker and I said it was my father who was coming. I was young and spirited and my brother was with me. And indeed, all I needed was an excuse to set sail. It was a fine day with a northerly wind. I went up into the boat and began tacking to Roundstone. When I came to Roundstone it wasn't my father but a boat belonging to the Board[35] trading between Westport, Cleggan, Inishbofin, Aran, everywhere, carrying wood and building supplies.[36] The boatman, from Galway, asked me if I knew such a man. I said I did.

'Would you bring wood to him,' he said, 'that I have here for repairing a house?'

'Oh, I will, with pleasure,' I said, 'why wouldn't I?'

'Your father is in Casla,' he said, 'and he will be here tomorrow. Thank you,' he said, 'for the wood.'

He transferred the wood to my boat. It was a bright night and we came home. We lifted the wood out of the boat. And this man to whom the wood was sent, he sent his brother over with me to my own harbour and we rigged the boat. And he said to bring me over when the boat was rigged. I went over and my brother came home. And the man brought in a little jar of whiskey and we started drinking. Well, I took no notice of how much I had drunk, but we passed the night. I believe it was good stuff. We were drinking away until it was two o'clock at night. And when we thought it was time to go home, I went out until I arrived at the road. It was a beautiful night. Every house was asleep and I was walking along. As I had drink taken I was heedless. I continued on until I arrived home. And it was the custom at that time in the houses, that if a person were out visiting, if he hadn't come home, the old people would place a chair inside the half-door which would keep the door closed until the person would come back. And when he came then, he only needed to push the door and the chair would go in.

I came to the door and I pushed it in and the door went in. And when I closed out the door again, I bolted it because I knew there was no one else to come. I had only got as far as the hearth like a big sally rod, when the door was knocked three times. It was struck so hard that the door and the mortar and the door jambs shook. Everyone who was inside and outside let out a roar, wondering what this was. I didn't pay any attention to it until the following day because of the drink I had taken.

Cnoga Caorthainn[37]

Well, aimsir na gcnúdán seo anois, bhí gach uile bhád á marú, beag is mór. Agus bhí báid á marú nach ngabhfadh mórán achair chun farraige chor ar bith anois iontub. Ach an bhfuil fhios agat, bhíodar timpeall Árainn an fhad agus ná raibh Árainn le feiceáil acub, agus céard a shéidfeadh ach stoirm gaoth anoir aduaidh.

Bhí 'a Mhuire mhuirneach' ag gach uile dhuine ar maidin go raibh na báid scuabthaí agus ar ndóigh scuabadh cuid mhaith acub an oíche chéanna. Ach bhí seanfhear ar a leaba i gCill Chiaráin agus gan é in ann a leaba fhágáil. Agus nuair a dúradh leis go raibh na báid uilig caillte agus curtha chun farraige agus nach bhfeicfí aon amharc go deo orthub, 'Ach feicim aon bhád amháin a gabháil aníos ag Ceann Gólaim,' a deir sé, 'ach sin é a bhfeicim.'

'Well, sin í mo bhádsa,' a deir an fear a bhí sa leaba.

'Cén chaoi a ndeir tú gurb í do bhád í,' a deir seisean, 'thar bhád ar bith eile?'

'Tá mé cinnte gurb í.'

'Cén fáth gurb í agus cén chreisteachtáil a bhí aige?'

Ach san am a raibh sé ag ardú crann ar an mbád sa gcaladh chuir sé an chroch chéasta caorthainn faoin gcrann.

Sin é anois an – an maide atá thíos ar thóin an bháid a bhfuil boltaí tugthaí dhó le haghaidh an crann a choinneáil daingnithe. Agus chuir sé an chroich chéasta de chrann caorthainn faoin gcrann. Agus sin é a raibh de chreideamh aige as, mar tá sé ráite ag seanúdair ná raibh aon cheo in do bhád ariamh chomh beannaithe, chomh siúráilte le cnoga caorthainn, nach bhfuil aon chall imní dhuit má tá cnoga caorthainn inti. Sin é dlí an tsean-bhuachaill a bhí fadó ann.

Rowan Thole Pins

Well, the time of these gurnards now, almost every boat, big and small, was fishing them. And there were boats fishing them that wouldn't go any distance at sea at all. But do you know they were around Aran, and they weren't able to see Aran, and a north-east wind and storm arose.

Everyone thought in the morning that the boats were lost and of course a lot of them were lost that same night. But there was an old man in Cill Chiaráin who was bedridden. And when he was told that all the boats were lost and had put to sea and that they would never be seen again: 'But I see one boat going along at Ceann Gólaim,' he said, 'but that's all I see.'

'Well, that is my boat,' said the man who was in bed.

'How can you say it is your boat,' another said, 'rather than any other boat?'

'I am sure of it.'

'Why is it so and how could he be believed?'

But when he was raising the mast on the boat in the harbour he put the sacred rowan[38] under the mast.

That is it now – the timber on the floor of the boat that has bolts made in it to hold the mast steady. And he put the sacred rowan timber under the mast. And that was his faith, because old wise people have said that there was nothing as blessed, as safe in your boat, as a thole pin of rowan timber, that you need not worry if there is a thole pin of rowan timber in it. That was the accepted rule of action of the old boy who lived long ago.

The foregoing items of narrative from Colm, given to different collectors, are examples of the breadth of his repertoire and of his narrative style. Chapters 3 and 4 serve to illustrate the broad variety of items documented from Colm's vast store of popular lore.

APPENDIX 1

CD Track Listing

(song and tune titles are in italics)

1. *The Mountain Top*
2. *Bean Pháidín* [*Páidín's Wife*]
3. *Bríd Thomáis Mhurchadha*
4. *Soldier, Soldier, Will You Marry Me Now?*
5. Oileán Mhic Dara [St MacDara's Island]
6. *The Keel Row*
7. *Port na Giobóige [The Unfortunate Widow's Tune]*
8. *An Sceilpín Draighneach [The Thorny Little Rock]*
9. *An Súisín Bán [The Little White Blanket]*
10. *Ceann gan Arann [An Unfeeling Suitor]*
11. *Neainsín Bhán [Fair Neainsín]*
12. *Sail Óg Rua [Red-Haired Sail Óg]*
13. *The Rocks of Bawn*
14. *Colm's Welcome to Séamus Ennis*
15. *Séamus Ennis' Collecting*
16. A Competition Between Two Singers
17. *Séamus Ennis*
18. *Ciste Mhic Uí Cheallaigh [Mac Uí Cheallaigh's Treasure]*
19. *An Bhó Bhán [The White Cow]*
20. *Hóbhá, a Dhiarmuidín [Howa, Diarmuidín]*
21. Micheál Mhac Suibhne
22. *Murchadh Ó Maoláin*
23. *Johnny Seoighe*
24. *P Stands for Paddy I Suppose*
25. *Wild Rover*
26. Finnbheara
27. Bráth Thír Locha [Lakeside Waste]
28. An Mharthain Phádraig [St Patrick's Sustaining Prayer]
29. *Barr an tSléibhe [The Top of the Mountain]*
30. *Captain Wedderburn's Courtship*
31. Oíche Shamhna [Hallowe'en]
32. *Cúirt an tSrutháin Bhuí [The Court of the Yellow Stream]*
33. *Miss McLeod's Reel*

APPENDIX 2
The Recordings

Context, re-mastering, transcription and editing

There are many remarkable aspects to the recordings published here and we are indeed extremely fortunate to experience them in the twenty-first century. They exist due to the dedication of the field collectors with the Irish Folklore Commission (IFC), Radio Éireann (RÉ) and the British Broadcasting Corporation (BBC), in addition to the far-sighted ethos of these institutions. They are all 'one-off' recordings. It is amazing that they survived in such good condition over so many decades. The original recordings were placed under a microscope in the re-mastering process and this highlighted the high standard that was achieved.

The editorial policy in this book is based on the desire to disseminate the rich repertoire of Colm Ó Caodháin to as wide an audience as possible. The content reflects the dynamic, vibrant and fluid nature of tradition. Audio recordings are the core primary source; in total, some ninety-six items were recorded from Colm in audio format. They span the period from the mid-1940s to the 1970s and include a number of formats, including Ediphone wax cylinder, acetate disc and reel-to-reel magnetic tape. As far as can be ascertained, the recordings were all made in Colm's home in Glinsce, County Galway, and a limited amount of editing has been put in place to ensure complete versions. The recording quality of all original versions from acetate disc to reel-to-reel tape is consistent and there is little difference between the results of the various recording sessions. However, differences in sound quality arise in some of the tracks where Colm is a certain distance from the microphone, while in others he is closer.

The standard system for sound recording with immediate playback, from the early 1920s through to the 1950s, was the 'acetate' disc (cellulous nitrate was the chemical mix used for the recording surface), normally revolving at a speed of 78 rpm. Blank discs of 10, 12 and 16 inches in diameter were manufactured to give various recording durations. This is the system that was used by record companies, radio stations and sound recording institutions, and, although a high standard of sound fidelity was achieved with acetate discs, the system had a major limitation: the possible length of time that could be recorded. As a normal rule, the 12-inch disc had a recording limit in the region of five minutes.

As many of the songs in Colm's repertoire exceeded this available time, it was only possible to record edited versions of his long songs. When a song exceeded the five-minute limit, the collectors would have to agree with Colm, before a recording was made, what the key verses of each song were and then only record those. Attempting to record additional verses on a subsequent disc led to the problem, especially for an unaccompanied singer, of maintaining continuity of pitch.

This time limitation ceased to be an issue once the newly developed reel-to-reel recorder using magnetic tape was introduced in the 1950s, from which time tape gradually replaced disc recording.

At times, the incidental sounds arising in field recordings can be heard, as is the case, for example, in '*Sail Óg Rua*' (track 12), where the voices of children can be heard in the background.

The running order selected for the CD aims to present the material in a consistent, flowing fashion, with tracks arranged based on how they best work together as a whole. The recordings vary in terms of content, sound quality and collecting ambience, and in the case of numerous recordings of a particular item, as a general rule priority has been given to sound quality. The exception to this is '*Port na Giobóige*' (track 7), where part of the earliest known recording of Colm on Ediphone cylinder has been included, followed by the BBC recording representing an earlier and later recording of the same item. Visual and audio recordings relating to Ó Caodháin have been consulted: these include *Miles and Miles of Music* (1975), *Hand Me Down* (1981), audio recordings by Éamon de Buitléar (1970s), Raidió na Gaeltachta programmes and some private recordings.

In this publication, transcriptions have been made by the editor directly from the sound recordings. These do not necessarily parallel the handwritten transcriptions Séamus Ennis provided during his time with the Irish Folklore Commission (1942–7), as it would be impossible to identify the particular performance and/or recording Ennis used when transcribing text and music. If Ennis transcribed material from audio recordings, the recordings in question were most likely those of the Irish Folklore Commission. Ennis' field notes have also contributed to the transcriptions in this publication. The close working relationship between the commission and Radio Éireann is evident. This was in no small measure due to the expertise, contacts and a certain shared interest in what was being recorded. Radio Éireann established their Mobile Broadcasting Unit in 1947. As Maurice Gorham has written in his *Forty Years of Irish Broadcasting*, an 'important addition' to Radio Éireann's resources was the appointment of two outside broadcasting officers and the provision of mobile recording equipment. These officers were intended primarily to go to the Irish-speaking areas of Ireland and bring back recordings of speech and music that could occasionally be broadcast from the studios. The first two such appointees were Seán Mac Réamoinn and Séamus Mac Aonghusa (Séamus Ennis). Both soon made their mark.[1] As Anne O'Connor has written of them: '... they were directly and deliberately employing the collecting methods of the IFC, as well as those of the BBC. This parallel process and similarity of approach between the broadcast and folklore collectors, especially with regard to the collecting of folklore, folk music and song, continue down to the present day.'[2] Ennis left Radio Éireann in 1951,[3] and the challenge to the station of finding a replacement was significant: '... no successor had been found who had his gift of extracting traditional music from amateurs all over the country and weaving it into radio programmes'.[4] He began working with the BBC, and once again his previous contacts were to prove invaluable to him and to his new colleagues, among whom were Brian George, Alan Lomax and Peter Kennedy.

The BBC and RÉ material consists of audio recordings. The National Folklore Collection has a number of formats, including manuscript, photographic, music transcription and audio. Where an audio recording is from the NFC, the reference indicates the format, such as disc (D) or tape (T).

It is essential to bear in mind, and it is central to the concept of ethnographic fieldwork, that any recording or transcription is a reproduction of a single performance given at a particular time by one performer. The transcription of the music and words of traditional song poses particular challenges. Séamus Ennis described his methodology:

> The words of the first verse would be dictated to you. You'd write them under the staff line, the staff notes, the stave. And then, sing the verse, and you'd get the first line down and the third line down and sing the verse again and you'd get the second line down and the fourth line down and then sing it again and you could check on what you had done maybe over and over to get intricacies and ornamentations correctly down.[5]

Transcriptions in this publication are in normalised Irish orthography, giving recognition to dialect forms. This approach makes the material accessible to a wide readership. A written transcription, however, creates a formality and a visual structure that was not part of the spoken vernacular as reproduced by Ennis and other collectors in their written material. The re-mastered sound recordings, the transcriptions and additional text bring together the available sources and information.

Séamus Ennis wrote some 180 items of song and tunes with staff notation, from Colm, and also wrote several hundred pages of narrative, much of which was written and rewritten by Ennis from field notes. We can imagine the number of hours he spent working with Colm. The physical surroundings and atmosphere of where recordings were made in Colm's house were described by Máire, Colm's daughter,[6] who explained that Colm and Ennis would sit at the kitchen table while Colm sang, lilted and narrated and Ennis wrote from him. The kitchen table was where the Ó Caodháin family had their meals. The kitchen was in the centre of the house and when you came in the front door you came straight into the kitchen, with its concrete floor. There was an open fire, and a dresser that Colm had made himself, just as he made all the furniture in the room. The mugs and cups hung on the dresser and it had two drawers, and a press below for loaves of bread and tea, for example. On the wall there was a big clock that he got in An Aird Mhóir. It would strike on the hour and on the half-hour. There was a picture of the 'Sacred Heart'[7] on the wall, and Colm's rosary beads[8] were hanging beside it, because he said the rosary every night.

When his wife and children had gone to bed, Colm and Ennis would chat, probably deciding what Ennis would write that evening.

It might be nine or half past nine in wintertime, and the light was poor, just a paraffin oil lamp. And they would write until two or three in the morning. The table was at the window. In the summer, on the odd occasion they would sit outside at the gable end of the house. The house was white, all coated in lime inside and out. The front door was painted red.

The sound recordings bring the listener as close as possible to Colm's live performance. The following list of recording sessions demonstrates the span of years during which the recordings took place, in addition to illustrating Colm's rich repertoire.

Recording sessions

In order to frame the timespan appropriately, recording sessions are presented in chronological order where information is available. Each item is a song, verse or tune unless otherwise indicated. Titles might vary, as a title may have been provided, for example, by Colm, by a collector, by a cataloguer or a broadcaster, and a number of recordings of most items, or versions of items, were made. Some items are in English [E]. Disc numbers are given in parentheses.

Abbreviations:

AL	Alan Lomax
BBC	British Broadcasting Corporation
BG	Brian George
CB	Ciarán Bairéad
COD	Caoimhín Ó Danachair
LC	Leo Corduff
LMacCI	Liam Mac Con Iomaire
NFC	National Folklore Collection
RÉ	Radio Éireann
RTÉ	Raidió Teilifís Éireann
SE	Séamus Ennis

1945

SE/COD (?) (NFC) (120)
Port na Giobóige (The Unfortunate Widow's Tune) [NFC first transfer probably by Caoimhín Ó Danachair from Ediphone cylinder on 7 November 1945] [includes speech].

1947[9]

SE/COD (NFC)
Barr an tSléibhe [The Top of the Mountain] (353); *Bríd Thomáis Mhurchadha* (354); *Johnny Seoighe* (355a); *Sadhbh Thomáis* (one verse) (355b); Soldier, Soldier [E] (356a); *A Pheige na gCarad* [Peige, My Dear] (356b); *Bean Pháidín* [Páidín's Wife] (357a); *An Spailpín Fánach* [The Migrant Worker] (357b); *Caint ar dhéanamh na bplátaí* [Talk on making discs] [speech] (358); *Neainsín Bhán* [Fair Neainsín] (359); *Éirigh i do Shuí a Bhean an Leanna* [Rise Up, Woman of the Alehouse] (360); *An Sceilpín Draighneach* [The Thorny Little Rock] (361); *Sail Óg Rua* [Red-Haired Sail Óg] (362); *An Súisín Bán (Casadh an tSúgáin)* [The Little White Blanket (The Twisting of the Straw Rope)] (363a); Soldier, Soldier [E] (363b); *Baile Uí Laoigh* (364a); Blank (364b); *Cúirt an tSrutháin Bhuí* [The Court of the Yellow Stream] (365); *Ceann gan Arann* [An Unfeeling Person] (366a); *Goirim Féin Micil is Máire* [I Acclaim Micil and Máire] (366b); *Is é D'Uan Féin é* [It is Your Own Lamb] (366c).

20 August 1947 SE/BG (BBC discs)
Bean Pháidín [Páidín's Wife] (899a); The Tune of the Old Hag [*Port na Giobóige*] [includes speech] (899b); Bridget Thomas Murt [*Bríd Thomáis Mhurchadha*] (900); Soldier, Soldier [E] (901); *Goirim Féin Micil agus Máire* [I Acclaim Micil and Máire] (925); MacDara's Island (1089).
[Items 899a and 899b were included in *Tiachóg Ceoil as Éirinn*, published by the Cultural Relations Committee of Ireland. A collection of folk songs and melodies from Ireland. Selected by Brian George from the library of the BBC. Edited and annotated by Séamus Ennis. They were dubbed from two LPs.]

1948

26 October 1948. SE/RÉ (Tape A 1602) (NFC copy to disc M1130)
Oíche Shamhna – eachtra a bhain dá mháthair mhór [Hallowe'en – an experience his grandmother had] [speech].

27 October 1948. SE/RÉ (Tape A 1602)
Sean-nósanna Shamhna (Caint le Séamus Ennis) [Old Hallowe'en customs (Talking with Séamus Ennis)] [speech].

30 October 1948. SE/RÉ (Tape BBC 12925 (124/72) 7" tape, 7½ ips twin track)
Fionnbheara agus an fómhar [Fionnbheara and the harvest season] [speech]; *An Gorta, Máire agus Neile Línse* [The Famine, Máire and Neile Línse] [speech]; *An Gorta, bia, fataí i ngarraithe* [The Famine, food, potatoes in fields] [speech]; *An Gorta* [The Famine] [speech]; *Eachtra faoin min bhuí i nGaillimh* [An incident about yellow meal in Galway] [speech]; Man from Inis Ní buries plague victim [speech]; *Johnny Seoighe* [3 verses] [includes speech] (this item repeated on Tape AA 14442, transmitted on *Airneán*, 7 June 1987); *Micheál Mhac Suibhne agus an sagart* [Micheál Mhac Suibhne and the priest] [speech with song fragment].

30 October 1948 SE/RÉ (RÉ acetate)
Johnny Seoighe [3 verses] [includes speech].

31 October 1948 RÉ (Tape AA 13708)
Eileanór na Rún [My Dear Eileanór]

2 November 1948 RÉ (Tape AA 13708)
Scéal faoi thaibhse [A ghost story] [speech].

1948 RÉ (Tape AA 13707)
Scéal faoi Mhicil Eoin Uí Chadhain [A story about Micil Eoin Ó Cadhain] [speech]; *Scéal faoi thaibhse ag feistiú báid* [A story about a ghost mooring a boat] [speech].

1948 SE (NFC) (7″ tape T67, 3¾ ips half-track; T68 [side 2 of T67]) *Fionnbheara* [speech] (T67h); *Scéal sidhiúil* [A story of the Otherworld] [speech] (T67i); *Peigí Ní Fhlathartaigh* (T67j); *Barr an tSléibhe* [The Top of the Mountain] (T67k); *Filí agus amhráin* [Poets and songs] [*Johnny Seoighe*] [includes speech] (T67h); *Murchadh Beag Ó Maoláin* [includes speech] (T67m); *Is Trua gan Mé is Mo Stóirín* [It is a Pity My Darling and I] (T67n); *Port Béil* [Lilting] [The Mountain Top] (T67p); *Páidín agus Brídín* [Páidín and Brídín] [speech] (T67q / T68a).

SE (NFC discs @ 33 ⅓;, playing from the centre towards the outer rim of the disc (recorded in 1948 and transferred from RÉ recordings by LC in 1959)
Fear a bochtaíodh [A man who became impoverished] [speech] (T67c original tape 1089, 1844, 1846–9) (1844a); *Conchúr an dá chaorach 1* [Conchúr of the two sheep] [speech](1844b); *Conchúr an dá chaorach 2* [speech] (1846); *Conchúr an dá chaorach 3* [speech] (1847); *Fear a chuir a mhac chun na scoile* [A man who sent his son to school] [speech] (1848); Baile Uí Laoigh (1849).

SE (NFC) (7″ tape, T68 [side 2 of T67]) (recorded in 1948 and transferred from RÉ recordings to magnetic tape by LC in 1959)
Miss McCleod's Reel (melodeon) (T68a); The Keel Row (melodeon), (T68c); Thady McGrath (T68d) [speech].

SE / RÉ (NFC 16″ discs @ 33 ⅓; marked 'dubbed RÉ Discs')
Filí Chonamara [radio programme with inserts by Colm] [The poets of Conamara] [speech] (M1123 / M1124); *Micheál Mharcais agus a bheirt mhac* [Micheál Mharcais and his two sons] [speech] (M1123a); *De réir mo thuairim is tú Seán Ó Guairim* [I believe you are Seán Ó Guairim] [speech] (M1123b); *Micheál Mhac Suibhne agus an hata* [Micheál Mhac Suibhne and the hat] [speech] (M1123c); *An bháisteach anuas* [The rain coming down] [includes speech] (M1123d); *Muilleoir Tréitheach an Átha Leacrach* [The Talented Miller from the Ford of the Flagstones] [includes speech] (M1124); *Tomás Shiúnach* (M1124) [includes speech]; *An Gorta*[10] *i gConamara* [The Famine in Conamara] [speech]; [Fragment *Johnny Seoighe*] (M1125 / M1126); Poet Micheál Mhac Suibhne and priest journeying to Galway [includes speech] (M1129a); *Rachad go*

Ceannúir [I will go to Ceannúir] [includes speech] (M 1129b); *Neile agus Máire Línse* [Neile and Máire Línse] [speech] (M1129c); *Scéal?* [Story?] [Marked 'Reject'] [speech] (M1129d); *An Gorta* [The Famine] [speech] (M 1129e); *Oíche Shamhna* [Hallowe'en] [speech] (M1130).

RÉ (Tape AA 15559)
Clár: Filí Chonamara – inserts by Colm [Programme: The poets of Conamara] [speech and song fragments] [Presented by SE].
(Tape AA 15560)
Clár: An Gorta i gConamara [transmitted 21 February 1949] [Programme: The Famine in Conamara] [speech and song fragments] [Presented by SE].

1951

January 1951. AL (BBC 2271)
A Pheige na gCarad [Peige, My Dear].

January 1951. Columbia LP AKL 4941, AL, SE and Robin Roberts
Bean Pháidín [Páidín's Wife]; Soldier, Soldier [E].

1952

June 1952. BBC (5363)
Murchadh Beag Ó Maoláin; Cúirt an tSrutháin Bhuí [The Court of the Yellow Stream].

1953

December 1953. BBC (5287)
Amhrán na Bó Báine [The Song of the White Cow]; *Hóbhá a Dhiarmuidín* [Howa, Diarmuidín] [includes speech]; Baby in the *buaile* [Baby in the hut] [speech] [E]; *An Mharthain Phádraig* [St Patrick's Sustaining Prayer]; *Brá thír locha* [Lakeside waste] [speech].
Fear siúil agus sovereigns [A travelling man and sovereigns] [speech] (5288).

1954

July 1954. BBC.
I went out on a May morning (P Stands for Paddy) (5433) [E]; The Kerry Recruit (5433) [E]; The Wild Rover (5433) [E]; *Cúirt an tSrutháin Bhuí* [The Court of the Yellow Stream] [includes speech] (5434); Grandfather singing [speech] (5434) [E]; The Rocks of Bawn (5434) [E]; Colm welcomes Séamus Ennis [transmitted 18 August 1985 RTÉ, *Lest They Perish*]; Welcome continues [E] (5127); *Seán Ó Duibhir an Ghleanna* [Seán Ó Duibhir of the Glen] [includes speech [E]] (5434).

BBC (5129)
Soldier, Soldier [E].

July 1954. BBC (5398)
Captain Wedderburn's Courtship [E] [includes discussion with SE]; The rich man and the beggar [speech] [E].

BBC (5297)
Oileán Mhic Dara [St MacDara's Island] [speech]; *Bean Pháidín* [Páidín's Wife]; *Bríd Thomáis Mhurchadha.*

1973

26 July 1973 (NFC) (CB T125 & C0981)
A Pheaitsín is Tú mo Thrua [Peaitsín, I Pity You] [includes speech]; *Loch na Ní; Ar chuala sibhse a bhuachaillí a fheabhas is a chruthuigh Féilim* [Boys, did you hear how well Féilim turned out] [recited verse and speech]; *Abhainn Mhór* [recited fragment]; *Nach mór an t-údar báis dhom mo chlann a bheith ró-dheas* [Isn't it a great reason of death for me, my family are too close] [includes speech]; *A shaol* [Colm's life] [speech]; *Loch na Ní* [speech and recited fragment]; *Amhrán an Tae* [The Song of the Tea] [speech and recited verses]; *Cúirt an tSrutháin Bhuí* [The Court of the Yellow Stream] [includes speech]; *Souphouse Mhaírois (níor mhaith le Colm labhairt faoi)* [Maíros Soup-House (Colm did not wish to speak about it)]; *Bhí Mise is Mo Shláimín Adhmaid …* [I and My Small Amount of Wood Were …] [one verse]; *An Bhó Bhán* [The White Cow] [includes speech]; *Bád an Chaisil agus caint faoi*

Nuala an Chnoic – údar [The An Caiseal Boat; and talk about Nuala an Chnoic – composition] [includes speech]; *Maitias Ó Guairim, déantóir bád* [Maitias Ó Guairim, boatwright] [speech]; *An Dingle – bád a bhfuil baint aige leis an Oileán Máisean* [The Dingle – a boat connected to An tOileán Máisean] [includes speech]; *Rachad go Ceannúir (ní raibh Colm in ann cuimhneamh air)* [I will go to Ceannúir (Colm was unable to recall it)] [speech and fragment]; *Bád Shéamuis Éamoinn* [Séamus Éamoinn's Boat] [speech]; *A Stiofáin Bhuí Shalach* [O, Sallow, Wretched Stiofán]; *An Traiseach* [The Traiseach] [fragment and speech]; *Céad Míle Slán Duit a Leitir a hArd* [A Hundred Thousand Farewells to You Leitir a hArd] [fragment and speech]; *Johnny Seoighe* [speech and fragment]; *Iascaireacht agus déanamh bád* [Fishing and building boats] [speech].

27 September 1973 CB (NFC) (CB T130)
Seanchas, cur síos ar a shaol féin [Lore, an account of his life] [speech]; *Na tithe a thóg sé* [The houses he built] [speech]; Séamus Ennis [speech]; *Deisiú bád* [Repairing boats] [speech]; *Tús agus deireadh an duine* [Beginning and end of life] [speech]; *Feamainneacha* [Types of seaweed] [speech]; *Seán Mac Séamais* (scéal) [story] [speech]; *Seán Ó Guairim agus amhrán a chum sé* [Seán Ó Guairim and a song he composed] [speech]; *Cúirt an tSrutháin Bhuí* [The Court of the Yellow Stream] [includes speech]; *Amhrán faoi bháisteach ag teacht anuas ar an altóir lá stáisiúin* (Inis Ní) [A song about rain coming down on the altar one day when stations were taking place (Inis Ní)] [includes speech].

APPENDIX 3
The Documented Repertoire According to Type

Material collected from Colm Ó Caodháin

This list presents details of material collected from Colm Ó Caodháin according to type. It conveys the breadth of the repertoire and it is evident that song is the dominant feature. Song and tune titles are not translated and are listed in alphabetical order. Some rhymes and verses cannot be clearly identified as 'song'. If it is stated that a particular item was not sung it is not included as 'song'. The song '*Gugannaí Gú*' is an example of this, where a number of attempts have been made to transcribe the accompanying music.[1] Irish titles of tales, lore and other material have been translated. Unless otherwise stated, the material is in the NFC and was collected by Séamus Ennis.[2] Manuscript references, for example 1281:191–2, refer to NFC volume number followed by the page numbers.

Abbreviations

AL Alan Lomax (1915–2002)

ATU H.J. Uther, *The Types of International Folktales: A classification and bibliography. Based on the system of Antti Aarne and Stith Thompson* (FFC 284) (Helsinki: Finnish Academy of Science and Arts, 2004); and Seán Ó Súilleabháin and Reidar Th. Christiansen, *The Types of the Irish Folktale* (FFC 188) (Helsinki: Finnish Academy of Science and Arts, 1963)

BBC The British Broadcasting Corporation

CB Ciarán Bairéad (1905–76), full-time collector with the Irish Folklore Commission

COD Caoimhín Ó Danachair (1913–2002), ethnologist with the Irish Folklore Commission, and with University College Dublin

NFC National Folklore Collection, University College Dublin

LC Leo Corduff (1929–92), collector and sound recording officer with the Irish Folklore Commission, and with University College Dublin

LMacC Liam Mac Coisdeala (1906–96), full-time collector with the Irish Folklore Commission and afterwards a part-time collector

MM Music Manuscript NFC: music transcribed by Séamus Ennis

PdeB Proinnsias de Búrca (1904–96) was a collector with the Irish Folklore Commission from 1935 until 1944, and again from 1953 until 1964

RTÉ Sound Archive, Raidió Teilifís Éireann

Songs, verse and their lore

A Fheilipe Dhílis 1281:191–2, 218–19; MM 19.075

(*Ag*) *Gabháil Siar le Ceann Boirne Níor Mhór do Chuid Feochain* (air: *Caithfidh mé Fairnis*)[3] 1281:405

(Ag) Gabháil Soir Thrí Bhéal an Daingin Dom, 1281:399; MM 18.031, 19.056, 124

A gCuala Sibh Tuairisc ar Lorcán? 1281:79; MM 019.062

A Labhcáis, Mo Ghrá Thú 1281:65; MM 19.005

A Labhráis an Dreabhláis 1281:83; MM 19.001

A Mhaoil, Tabhair do Mholadh Leat 1281:97–9; MM 19.095

Amhrán an Choiligh 1281:411–13

Amhrán an Ediphone 1 (air: *An Dingle*) 1281:381

Amhrán an Ediphone 2 1281:382–3

Amhrán an Phoitín 1280:711–12; MM 18.041

Amhrán an Phríosúin 1281:315–16; MM 19.103

Amhrán an Tae CB 1863:31–3; Tape CB 0125.2

Amhrán an Tairbh (*Seán Mac Guidhir*) 1281:226–8

Amhrán Bréagach, An tA- 1281:342–342a; MM 19.115

Amhrán na Bó Báine, see *An Bhó Bhán*

Amhrán na Buinní 1280:752; MM 18.061

Amhrán na hEascainne see *Tá Mé Tinn Fó Mo Chroí*

Amhrán na nGaibhne 1281:78–9 (air: *An tSailchuach*)

Amhrán na Speile (*Amhrán An Speal*) 1281:343

Amhrán na Trá Báine 1281:347–8; MM 19.116

Amhrán Ros an Mhíl MM 19.04

Amhrán Shéamuis Uí Chonchúir as Árainn 1281:376–80

Amhrán Tom Neansa 1281:198–201, 204

A Mhuigín, Marbhfháisc Ort 1280:742–3; MM 18.060 (air: *Peigín Adley / An tIolrach Mór*)

A Pheige na gCarad 1280:749–51; MM 18.044; Disc 356b; BBC 2271

A Stór Ó, is a Stór Eile 1281:328–9; MM 19.110

A Théagaire, ná Tréig Thusa (air: *A Labhráis an Dreabhláis*) 1281:172

Aoileann Loch na Ní, see *Loch na Ní*

A Pheadair is a Pheadair 1281:247; MM 19.015

A Pheaitsín, is Tú Mo Thrua 1281:229–30; CB 1863:23–5; MM 19.007

Argóinteacht an Bháis Leis an Muilleoir Bán 1281:96–7; MM 19.092

A Shéamuis, Tá Tú Tíocht Chugamsa ó Tháinig an Samhradh 1281:158–9

A Stiofáin Bhuí Shalach 1281:189–91; CB 1863:46; Tape CB 0125.2; MM 19.074

Bád an Chaisil 1 1280:735–7; CB 1863:39–42; Tape CB 0125.2

Bád an Chaisil 2 (air: *Amhrán na mBréag*) 1280:738

Bád Dóite Loideáin 1281:372–4

Bád Pheige Seoighe (air: *Contae Mhaigh Eo/An Bhó Bhán*) 1281:308

Bád Shéamuis Éamoinn (air: *An Coistealach Mór*) 1281:344–5; CB 1863:45; Tape CB 0125.2

Baile Uí Laoigh 1281:110–11; MM 19.022; Disc 353/364A; Tape LC 1849

Bain an Ceann Caol de 1281:156; MM 19.094

Bainfidh Mise an Caol-tSlaitín Seo 1281:354, 375; MM 19.121

Báisteach Anuas, An (*An Bhá-*) 1281:57–8; MM 18.063; Tape CB 0130.2; RTÉ 1247

Barr an tSléibhe (air: *Murchadh Beag Ó Maoláin*) 1281:73–4; Disc 353; Tape LC T67k

Bean Pháidín 1281:168–9; MM 19.067; Disc 357a; BBC 899a, 5297

Beidh Aonach Amáireach 1281:298; MM 19.043

B'fhearr Leigin Dó 1281:239–40; MM 19.008

Bhfuil Sé ina Lá, ina Lá? 1281:337; MM 19.113

Bhí Leathbhord i gCionn tSáile 1281:418

Bhí Mé Lá Gabháil Anoir le hInis Meáin (air: *Amhrán an Phríosúin*) 1281:352

Bhí Mé Oíche ag Gabháil Faoin gCoill Chraobhach 1281:195–6; MM 19.083

Bhí Mé Oíche Aoibhinn (*Tomás Cheannabháin*) 1281:100, 194; MM 19.077

Bhí Mise is Mo Shláimín Adhmaid 1281:368–9; 1863:37–8; Tape CB 0125.2

Bhuail Mise an Doras go Tláth, Tláth 1281:58; MM 19.003

Binsín Luachra, An 1281:360–1; MM 19.105

Bó Bhán, An Bhó Bh- (*Amhrán na Bó Báine*) 1281:174–5, 219; CB 1863:38–9; MM 19.069; Tape CB 0125.2; BBC 5287 SE

Bocaí í Hó 1281:102–3; MM 19.019

Boisín Aoilinn, Boisín Álainn (for children) 1281:153

Bóithrí Ros an Mhíl 1281:259–60; MM 19.034

Buinneán Buí, An 1280:739–41

Briathra Chríost ag an Suipéar Deireanach, see *Brisimse an tArán Seo*

Bríd Ní Ghaora 1280:617, 616; 1281:255–6; MM 18.040

Bríd Thomáis Mhurchadha 1281:85–6; MM 19.053; Disc 354; BBC 900, 5297

Brisimse an tArán Seo (*Briathra Chríosta ag an Suipéar Deireanach*) 1281:113; MM 18.047, 19.023

Bródach Uí Ghaora 1281:154; MM 19.064

Bromach, An 1281:75–7; MM 19.060

Bruach na Carrtha Léith 1281:126–7

Buachaill an Chúil Doinn 1281:303; MM 19.045

Cáibín Dhónaill Póil 1281:145–6; MM 19.078

Cáilín, Cáilín (*A Cháilín, a Cháilín*) 1281:264

Cailín Deas Crúite na mBó 1281:244–6; MM 19.014

Cailín Fearúil Fionn, An 1281:86–7; MM 19.088

Cailíní Chontae an Chláir 1281:372; MM 19.122

Caipín Thomáis Shiúnach (air: *An Spailpín Fánach*) 1281:391

Caisleán Rí Néill 1281:208–9; MM 19.102

Caithfidh Mé Fáirnis Fháilt ar Do Dhream (*Uacht Pháidín Thoirdhealbhaigh*) 1281:400; MM 19.106

Caoineachán na Maighdine 1281:133

Caol-Stailín Uasal, An (air: *Éirigh i Do Shuí Bhean an Leanna/Cailín Deas Crúite na mBó*) 1281:389, 417

Capall Sheáin 1281:124–5; MM 19.028

Captain Wedderburn's Courtship, BBC 5398, SE

Carróigín Sheáin Bhriarta 1281:169–70; MM 19.068

Casúr Sheáin Mhóir (air: *Cill Aodáin*) 1280:728–9; MM 19.101

Cat Mháirtín Uí Éiniú (air: *Baile Uí Laoigh*) 1280:721–2

Céad Míle Slán Duit a Leitir Ard (air: *An Coisdealach Mór*) 1281:185–6; Tape CB 0130.2

Ceaite na gCuach 1280:743–5; MM 18.064

Ceallachaín Fionn, An 1281:241–2; MM 19.011

Ceannabháin Bhána, Na (*Goirim Féin Micil is Máire*) 1281:112; MM 18.054; Disc 353/366b; BBC 925

Ceann gan Arann 1281:103–4; MM 18.051; Disc 366a

Draighneán Donn, An 1281:362–4; MM 19.119

Dúín, Dú, Ó Daighdil Ó 1281:74–5; MM 043

Eileanóir na Rún 1280:704–10; MM 18.046; RTÉ 124/72a

Éirigh i Do Shuí Bhean an Leanna (air: *Cailín Deas Crúite na mBó*) 1281:146–7; Disc 360

Éirigh Suas a Bhríd (air: *Óró Thaidhg, a Thaidhg*) 1281:337

Faightín, An 1281:89–90; MM 19.090

Fáilte Uí Cheallaigh 1281:127

Fáinnín Bán an Lae 1281:219–20, 269–70; MM 19.040

Faochain Bharr an tSáilín 1281:338; MM 19.112

Fear Ceoil, An 1280:713–15; MM 18.042

Fuic Fuiliúrail Aidí Am (*Fear na Féithe Móire*) 1281:69–70; MM 18.055, 19.059

Fear na Mapaí Dorais (air: *An Faightín*) 1281:317

Five American Oysters 1281:314

Forú Súgach 1281:70; MM 19.006

Frank Conaola (air: *An tSail Óg Rua*) 1281:401

Gandal Bacach, An MM 19.085

Go bhFille Mo Mhuirnín Slán, Slán 1281:193

Go Deireanach Aréir is ea Dhearc Mé an Marcach Géar 1280:741–2; MM 19.002

Goirim Féin Micil is Máire see *Ceannabháin Bhána, Na*

Grá Chailín Óig, Ó 1281:308-309; MM 19.051

Híol al al á 1281:99; MM 18.038

Hóbhá, A Dhiarmuidín 1281:203; BBC 5287

Hóbhá mo Leana 1281:304–5; MM 19.046

Hóróbhó (Óróbhó) Bhairbre 1281:196–7; MM 19.009

Hughie O'Hara (*Páidín agus Brídín*) 1281:166; Tape LC T67q/68a

Iolrach Mór, An tI- 1281:61–4; CB 1863:26–8; MM 19.055

Is é d'Uan Féin é, a *Bhródachín* 1281:313; Disc 366c

Is Trua Gan Me is Mo Stóirín Tape LC T67n

It's Happened of Late (air: *Péarla Breá Deas an tSléibhe Bháin*) 1281:419

I Went Out on a May Morning BBC 5433

I Wish I Was in Bed with You 1281:399

Johnny Seoighe 1073:52–3; 1281:182–3; CB 1863:47–9; MM 19.073; Disc 355a; Tape CB 0125.2; RTÉ 157/72; BBC 12925

Kerry Recruit, The 1281:258; MM 19.033; BBC 5433

Loch na Ní (*Aoileann Loch na Ní*) (*Tráthnóna Aréir is Mé ag Siúl Liom Péin*) 1280:730–2; CB 1863:25–6, 29–31; MM 18.050; Tape CB 0125.2

Luch a Ghearr an Snátha, An 1281:283 (see: *Fuic Fuiliúrail Aidí am*)

Mainistir na Búille 1281:339–40; MM 19.114

Máirín Flanagan (air: *Cúirt O'Loughlin*) 1281:404

Máirín Ní hIoparláin 1281:76; MM 19.061

Máirín Ní Rúnadáin 1281:157; MM 19.093

Marcas Ó Cormacáin 1281:330; MM 19.111

Meastú a Sheáin? 1281:328

Mé Féin is Tú Féin 1281:109; MM 18.056, 19.021

Mister Dooley 1281:167; MM 19.087 (air only)

Mná Bána Sheáin Uí Bhriain 1281:261–2; MM 19.035

Muilleoir Tréitheach an Átha Leacrach 1281:55–6; MM 18.062

Mullach Mór, An 1281:67–8; MM 19.058

Murchadh Beag Ó Maoláin 1281:59–61, 420; MM 19.004; Tape LC T67m; BBC 5363

Nach Dona an Díon atá sa tSail Disc M 1129a; RTÉ 157/72

(Ó's) Nach Trua gan Mé i Mo Chodladh 1281:188 (302); MM 19.044[4]

Neainsín Bhán 1281:91–2; MM 19.091; Disc 359

(Is) Ní Codladh é Mo Chodladh is Ní Suan Mo Néal (air: *Clár Bog Déil*) 1281:320

Night of the Wedding of Latchey McGrath, The MM 19.086

Níl Agam ach Sé Pingine 1281:101; MM 19.018

Níl Mé Críonna, Céad Faraor Nílim (air: *Anach Cuain*) 1281:196

Nóra Ní Chonchúir Bháin 1281:421; MM 19.084

Nuair Éirímse ar Maidin Uaigneach (air: *Tá na Páipéir Dhá Signeáil*) (*Thart Síos go Deo má Théann Tú*) 1280:733–5; MM 18.057

Nuala Ní Uaithnín and the Priest (*Nuala Ní Uaithnín agus an Sagart*) RTÉ 1247

Óra Mhíle Grá 1281:256–7; MM 19.032

Páidín agus Brídín see *Hughie O'Hara*

Peaca a Rinne Naomh Seosamh (*Éad Naomh Seosaimh*) LMacC NFC 1008:81–2; 1281:130–1

Peaitsín Mac Ceallacháin (air: *Úna Dheas Ní Nia*) 1281:149–50, 210–11

Péarla (Breá) Deas an tSléibhe Bháin 1281:177–8; MM 19.071

Peigí Ní Fhlathartaigh Tape LC T67j

Píopa Aindí Mhóir (air: *An Bhó Bhán/Contae Mhaigh Eo*) 1281:206

Pisín Rua Dheas (air: *Silthiú Fox*) 1281:385

Plúirín Álainn na mBan Donn Óg 1281:243; MM 19.013

Poets and Songs (*Filí agus Amhráin*) Tape LC T67i

Poets of Conamara (*Filí Chonamara*) Disc M 1123–4; RTÉ 79/68

Port na Giobóige 1280:702–3; 1281:394–8; MM 18.024; Disc COD 120; BBC 899b

Púcán, An (*Branley*) (air: *Marcas Ó Cormacáin*) 1281:332–5

Rachad go Ceannúr 1281:371; CB 1863:44–5; Disc M 1129b; Tape CB 0125.2 RTÉ 1247

Raicín Álainn, An 1281:271, 270; MM 19.041

Rocks of Bawn, The MM 19.127; BBC 5434

Sadhbh Ní Bhruinneallaigh (Mhoinghile) MM 18.045, 19.107

Sadhbh Thomáis 1281:413; MM 19.126; Disc 355b

Sagart Ó Dónaill, An 1281:115–16; MM 19.024

Sailchuach, An tS- 1281:402–3

Sail Óg Rua 1281:118–19; MM 19.026; Disc 362

Sceilpín Draighneach, An 1281:120–1; MM 19.016; Disc 361

Seachrán Sí 1281:341

Seaicéad Mhicil Mhóir 1281:224–6; MM 19.100

Seán Bacach Ó Guairim 1281:392–3; Tape CB 0125.2

Seanbhean Bhocht, An tS- 1281:351; MM 19.117

Seanbhean Liath, An tS- 1281:128–9; MM 19.029

Seán Mac Uidhir an Ghleanna 1281:77, 236–7, 390; MM 18.048; BBC 5434

Seán Tobarra 1281:231–3

Shoraidh Dhíotsa, a Ghrian 1281:99

Silthiú Fox 1281:77; MM 19.081

Soldier, Soldier, Will You Marry Me Now? 1281:142–4; MM 19.082; Disc 356a, 363b; BBC 901, 2271, 5129

Souphouse Mhaírois (air: *Úna Dheas Ní Nia*) 1073:53–5; 1281:183–5; CB 1863:36–7; Tape CB 0125.2

Spailpín Fánach, An 1281:265–6; MM 19.037; Disc 357b

Súisín Bán, An (*Casadh an tSúgáin*) 1281:179–81; MM 19.072; Disc 363a

Tá Bothán ag Stiofán 1281:66; MM 19.057

Tadhg an Mhargaidh (Rocky Road) 1281:353[5]

Táilliúir an Mhagaidh 1281:101

Táilliúir Mé gan Dabht 1280:745–8; MM 18.039

Tá Mé Anois Roinnt 'Beatráilte' 1281:246

Tá Mé Tinn Fó Mo Chroí 1281:358–9; MM 19.118; BBC 22829

Taobh Thiar (Thall) de Chlaí na Teorann 1281:81–2; MM 19.063

Tarraing do 'Qhueen' 1281:155; MM 19.065

Teighre Chun an Mhargaidh 1281:205; MM 19.098

Tháinig an Faoileán Mór 1281:321

Tháinig Séamus Ennis Chun Mo Thí-sa BBC 5127-SE

Thart Síos go Deo Má Théann Tú (*Nuair Éirímse ar Maidin Uaigneach*) (air: *Tá na Páipéir Dhá Signeáil*) 1280:733–5; MM 18.057

Thuas ar an Lota 1281:302

Tomás Ceannabháin, see *Bhí Mé Oíche Aoibhinn*

Tom Mullouney Is Dead 1281:172

Toomín na Gruaige Báine 1281:80–1; MM 19.048

Traiseach, An 1281:107–8; CB 1863:47; Tape CB 0125.2

Tráthnóna Aréir is Mé ag Siúl Liom Péin see *Loch na Ní* (*Aoileann Loch na Ní*)

Trua gan Mé is Mo Stóirín is Teach Mór Againn i Meiriceá 1281:122–3; MM 19.027

Trua Nach Mise Bean Pháidín see *Bean Pháidín*

Trua Sin Mise Lá le Pádraig 1281:87–8; MM 19.089

Tús agus Deireadh an Duine Tape CB 0130.2

Úna Bhán 1281:84; MM 19.052

Úna Dheas Ní Nia 1281:71–3, 212–13; MM 19.079

When Will You Return Again or When Will You Get Married? 1281:357; MM 19.049

Whiskey You're the Devil 1281:205; MM 19.050

Wild Rover, The BBC 5433

William Reilly 1281:365–7; MM 19.120

Tunes

[Boys of Ballinahinch, The] (Reel) (Six reels from Colm no. 2) (*Sé chor ó Cholm*), MM 19.132

[Boys of Ballisodare, The] (Reel) (Six reels from Colm no. 3) (*Sé chor ó Cholm*), MM 19.133

Cailín Lása Shál Roc (Slip jig), MM 18.035

Colm is Neil (Jig), MM 18.036

[Colm Ó Lonnáin's] (Air), 1281:421

Conamara Lasses (Reel), MM 18.028

Cos na Muice Duibhe (Slip jig), MM 18.058

Double Jig (Double Jig from Colm no. 1) (*Poirt dúbalta ó Cholm*), MM 19.096

Éiri' 'Pheadair, a Pheadair (Slip jig), MM 18.059

Gabháil Soir Trí Bhéal an Daingin Dom, MM 18.031, 19.124 (with lyrics)

Gleann ó Thuaidh, An (Reel), MM 19.109

[Hardiman the Fiddler] (Slip jig) (*Sean-phort*), MM 18.037; (Variant) (9/8 Jigs from Colm no. 1) (*Poirt 9/8 ó Cholm*), 19.136

Is Óra, Dheartháirín Seol do Bhó agus Cuir ar an mBogán is Fearr í (Jig), 1281:360, MM 18.034

Jolly Tinker (Reel), MM 18.029; (Variant) (Six reels from Colm no. 5) (*Sé chor ó Cholm*), MM 19.135

[Keel Row, The] (Fling), Tape LC T68c

[Kennaw's] (Reel), MM 19.129

Lasses of Bunker Hill, The, MM 18.027

Máirseáil na Fuiseoige (Double jigs from Colm no. 2) (*Poirt dúbalta ó Cholm*), MM 19.097 ((Variant), MM 18.029a)

[Mickey Rattley's Fancy] (Reel) (*Sean-ríl ó Cholm*), MM 18.032

[Miss McCleod's] (Reel) (Six reels from Colm no. 6) (*Sé chor ó Cholm*), MM 19.135a; Tape LC T68c

Mister Dooley, MM 019.087

[Mountain Top, The] (Reel), Tape LC T67p

Old Reel (*Sean-ríl ó Cholm*), MM 18.030

Páidín Ó Raifearta(igh) (Jig) 1281:242; (Lilted) (*Port Béil*) (music only), MM 19.012

Port an Phláta (Six reels from Colm no. 4) (*Sé chor ó Cholm*), MM 19.134

Port na Giobóige (Old tunes lilted by Colm no. 2) (*Sean phoirt béil ó Cholm*), MM 18.024

Port na Sióige (Jig) (Old tunes lilted by Colm no. 1) (*Sean phoirt béil ó Cholm*), MM 18.024

Port Phádraig na Corann (Reel) (Six reels from Colm no. 1) (*Sé chor ó Cholm*), MM 19.131

[Ride a Mile] (Slip jig) (9/8 jigs from Colm no. 2) (*Poirt 9/8 ó Cholm*), MM 019.136a

Robhlairín, An (Reel), MM 19.108

Ruidín Beag a D'imigh Uaim, MM 19.128

[Scatter the Mud] (Jig), MM 19.130

Seoladh na nGéabha (Jig), MM 18.033

Stoirm is a' Bháisteach, An (Jig) (Old tunes lilted by Colm no. 4) (*Sean phoirt béil ó Cholm*), MM 18.026

Tá Port ag an bPíobaire (Jig), 1281:410

Titse Miller, An, 1281:107 (Old tunes lilted by Colm no. 3) (*Sean phoirt béil ó Cholm*), MM 18.025

Narratives of Colm's life

Adventure of the storyteller, An (*Eachtra a d'éirigh don scéalaí*) LMacC 1008:121–3

Colm's account of his life (*Tuairisc air féin ó Cholm*) 1281:425–57; Tape CB 0130.1

Colm's nickname (*Tugadh Colm an Bhlácaigh air*) 1280:710

Day Colm spent singing in Galway, A (*Lá ag Colm féin i nGaillimh le amhráin*) 1281:237–9

Day Séamus Ennis spent with Colm collecting songs, A (*Lá a chaitheas le Colm Ó Caodháin ag Bailiú Amhrán*) 1281:215–28

Ediphone, The 1281:229; Colm scolds the Ediphone (*Greann ó Cholm féin ag sciollaíocht leis an Ediphone*), 233–4

Few words from Colm, A (lonesome listening to the songs) (*Caint bheag ó Cholm féin, cumha air ag éisteacht leis na hamhráin*) 1281:253

How Colm came to have songs for me [SE] (*Mar tharla na hamhráin ag Colm dhomsa*) 1281:235

List of songs 1280:621–7; 1281:271a

Making the discs (*Déanamh na bplátaí*) Disc 358

Music tooth, The (*Fiacail an Cheoil*) 1281:295–7

Sea fog (*Ceo ar an bhfarraige)* LMacC 1009:97–105

Singing, Advice about (*Comhairle faoi amhránaíocht*) 1281:127

Singing when his grandfather was alive; local singers BBC 5434-SE

Songs from Glinsce (*Amhráin Ghlinsce*) 1280:701

Two singers from Glinsce (*Beirt amhránaí Ghlinsce*) 1281:236

Historical lore, social history and folklife

Accident while fishing at sea and survival (*Tubaiste ag iascach, teacht slán*) PdeB 1553:222–8

Adventure at sea[6] (*Eachtra farraige*) PdeB 1509:255–8, 1552:272–8

Boatmen see tidal water on a street in Galway (*Feiceann bádóirí an taoille ar shráid na Gaillimhe*) LMacC 1008:108–9

Boats carrying turf (*Báid ag tarraingt mhóna*) PdeB 1553:56–8

Boats going to Westport (*Báid ag gabháil go Cathair na Mart*) PdeB 1553:53–5

Carrying turf (*Ag rith móna*) PdeB 1552:278–82

Cromwell (*Cromail*) LMacC 1008:117–20

Drink (*Scéal faoin ól*) LMacC 1009:160–1

Famine, The (*An drochshaol*) 1073:6, 14–50; Disc 1125/1126a; PdeB 1552:365–8, 371–3, Disc M1129c/e; RTÉ 79/68a, 157/72

Father Peadar Conway LMacC 1009:143–50

Fishing (*Iascach*) PdeB 1552:297–303 [see '*A Good Catch of Pollock: Marú Mór Mangach*' in Chapter 3]

Fishing and making boats (*Iascach agus déanamh bád*) Tape CB 0125.2

Fishing boats (*Báid iascaireachta*) PdeB 1553:228–32

Fishing in Roundstone (*Ag iascach i gCloch na Rón*), PdeB 1552:282–7, 304–7

Great load of fish, A (*Lucht mór éisc*) PdeB 1553:232–5

Great storm, A (*Stoirm mhór*) PdeB 1553:40–4

Inis Ní without anyone of the surname Mongáin (*Inis Ní gan aon Mhongáin*) 1281:307

Hallowe'en (*Oíche Shamhna*) Disc M 1130; RTÉ 100/68

Kelp (*Ceilp*) PdeB 1553:216–22

Landlord and tenants in Aran (*Tiarna agus tionóntaí in Árainn*) LMacC 1009:161–4

Light at the quay in An Spidéal (*Solas ag céibh An Spidéil*) LMacC 1009:88–92; PdeB 1509:258–62; 1281:428–31 [see 'Help from the Virgin Mary' in Chapter 1]

Lobster fishing (*Iascach gliomach*) PdeB 1509:262–6

Mackerel fishing (*Iascach ronnach*) PdeB 1552:257–60

Máire Joe, The (*An Máire Joe*) PdeB 1552:293–6

Maitias Ó Guairim, a boatwright (*saor báid*) Tape CB 0125.2

Making *poitín* and the good people (*Seanchas faoi dhéanamh poitín agus na daoine maithe*) 1281:134

Micheál Mhac Suibhne (poet) (*file*) 1281:309–10

Micheál Mharcais Ó Cualáin and his two sons (*Micheál Mharcais Ó Cualáin agus a bheirt mhac*) 1281:151; RTÉ 1247

Old Seán of the grassy upland (*Sean-tSeán na dTamhnac*h) 1281:418

Pádraig Labhráis Ó Flathartaigh PdeB 1553:5–9

Pádraig Ó Griallais and 'Bolg' (*Pádraig Mac Griallais agus Bolg*) PdeB 1553:3–5

Pádraig Ó Maoildhia PdeB 1552:288–90

Páidín Mac Clochartaigh and Seán na Báine (*Páidín Mac Clochartaigh agus Seán na Báine*) PdeB 1553:58–60

Páidín the tailor's son (*Páidín an Táilliúra*) PdeB 1553:9–12

Peter Stiofáin PdeB 1553:60–1

Seal in a net, A (*Rón in eangach*) PdeB 1553:235–7

Seaweed (*Feamainneacha*) Tape CB 0130.2

Shoes (*Bróga*) 1281:154

Strong winds at sea (*Gaoth mhór ar farraige*) LMacC 1009:92–6

Survival of Griallais after a sea adventure (*Griallais a tháinig slán tar éis eachtra farraige*) PdeB 1553:207–8

Tobacco (*Tobac*) 1281:208

Tobacco after food (*Tobac thléis bídh*) 1281:114

Tomás Máirtín LMacC 1009:156–7

Tomás Máirtín and the family of Seán Cearbáin (*Tomás Máirtín agus clann Sheáin Cearbáin*) LmacC 1009:158

Young seal – Colm and his father at sea, A (*Rón óg – Colm agus a athair ar an bhfarraige*) PdeB 1553:237–9

Waves – names and locations (*Maidhmeannaí – ainmneachaí agus áiteachaí*) PdeB 1553:48–53

Religious tales, lore and prayers

Baptism of children born out of wedlock (*Baiste páistí neamhdhlisteanacha*) LMacC 1009:167–8

Beetle, The (Devil's coach horse) (*An Deargadaol*) 1281:459–60

Catholic and a Protestant, A (*Caitliceach agus Pratastún*) 1281:263

Child who dies after baptism and without sin (*Páiste a fhaigheann bás tar éis baiste agus gan peaca*) 1281:132

Cock in the Pot, The (*Seanchas an Choiligh*) 1281:285–7

Colm Cille and Éinne (*Colm Cille agus Éinne*) LMacC 1008:97–100

Direct way to heaven, The (*An bóthar díreach go na flaithis*) LMacC 1008:91–3

Disrespect (*An dí-mheas*) LMacC 1009:172–4

Four posters at my bed (*Ceithre phosta faoi mo leaba*) 1281:301

God as guarantor (*Dia i mbannaí*) LMacC 1009:154–5

Grace before meals (*Altú roimh bia*) 1281:134

I save this fire (*Coiglímse an tine seo*) 1281:301

Mac Duach LMacC 1008:76–9

Man who sold himself to the devil, A (*Fear a dhíol é féin leis an diabhal*) LMacC 1009:139–43

May you have the sleep of the little calf at the rock (*Codladh an tsoicín sa gcarraig chugat*) LMacC 1008:88–9

Moses and the Ten Commandments (*Maois agus na Deich nAitheanta*) 1281:300–1

Priest who was curing people, The (*An sagart a bhí ag leigheas daoine*) LMacC 1009:165–7

Rowan thole pins (*Cnoga Caorthainn*) PdeB 1553:1–3

Saint Cáilín's well (*Tobar Cáilín*) LMacC 1008:73

Saint MacDara's Island (*Oileán Mhic Dara*) BBC 5297-SE

Saint Patrick (*Naomh Pádraig*) LMacC 1008:94–5

Saint Patrick and the hag of Beara (*Naomh Pádraig agus an chailleach Bhéarthach*) LMacC 1008:79–80

Saint Patrick curses in his sleep (*Eascainí Naomh Pádraig trína chodladh*) 1281:420

Saint Peter (*Naomh Peadar*) LMacC 1008:84–5

Salty sweat (*Allas goirt*) 1281:133

Short religious tales, Colm's mother liked them (*Thaitnigh scéalta beaga cráifeacha le máthair Choilm*) LMacC 1008:79

Son of God and the Virgin Mary, The (*Mac Dé agus an Mhaighdean Mhuire*) 1281:299

Son of God, Mac Dara, Mac Duach and Colm Cille, The (*Mac Dé, Mac Dara, Mac Duach agus Colm Cille*) 1281:284

Throwing and Hardness (*Caitheamh agus Cruas*) 1281:311–13

Woman who carried the Son of God, The (*An Bhean a D'iompar Mac Dé*) 1281:131–2; LMacC 1008:83–4

Rhymes

Riddles, sayings, proverbs and beliefs

For children

Are You Within, John Smith? 1281:330–1

Bull, The [?] (*An tarbh conra* [?]) 1281:314

Churlish fellow in a loft, A (*Bod ar lochta*) 1281:388

Did the piglets arrive? (*A dtáinig na bainbh?*) 1281:384; MM 19.122

Grandad had a pig (*Bhí muc ag deaideo*) 1281:173

Gugannaí Gú (nonsense rhyme) 1281:187

Hup, hup little pony (*Hup, hup a chapaillín*) 1281:176; MM 19.070

It is my discomfort and my distress (*Is é mo léan géar is mo chrá*) 1281:404; MM 19.099

I turned a little sod (*Bhain mise spreaibín*) 1281:129

Long ago there was a man (*Bhí fear fadó ann*) 1281:303

Lúrabóg, Lárabóg (nonsense vocables in game) 1281:203

'Meig Geig' says the goat (*'Meig, geig' deir an gabhar*) 1281:394

Pecker, hardy little one (*Cnogaire, cnagaire*) 1281:152

Sleep, sleep, blindfold (*Codladh, codladh, púicín*) 1281:213

Where did you get this little chin? (*Cé bhfuair tú an smigín seo?*) 1281:202

'Where were you last night?' says the dog (*'Cé raibh tú aréir?' 's an madra*) 1281:170

Who is that above my house? (*Cé hé siúd thuas os cionn mo thí-sa*?) 1281:170–1

Tales and anecdotes

Amusing anecdote, An (*Scéilín grinn*) 1281:350

Apparition of the small sailing boat, The (*Tais na gleoiteoige*) LMacC 1008:433–6

Basket seller, The (*Fear díolta na gciseán*) LMacC 1008:13–20

Bundle of rods, The (*An beart slat*) 1281:140–1

Cathaoir Mac Cába 1281:207

Conchúr of the two sheep (*Conchúr an dá chaorach*) Tape LC 1844b / 1846 / 1847

Cowherd in Sliabh Luachra, The (*Buachaill bó Shliabh Luachra*) LMacC 1008:74–5

Crows and the cobbler's head, The (*Na carrógaí agus cloigeann an ghréasaí*) LMacC 1008:296–7

Curses and the drowning of a boat (*Eascainí agus báthadh báid*) 1281:407–8

Day of the great squall, The (*Lá an scútháil mhóir*) PdeB 1552:254–6

Dead woman's family, The (*Clann na mná mairbhe*) LMacC 1008: 100–3

Death and youth (*An Bás agus an óige*) LMacC 1008:124–7

Dog, put out the lamb (*A mhada, cuir an t-uan amach*) 1281:163–5

Donncha Mór Ó Dálaigh 1281:280–2

Fairhaired merchant and the autumn night, The (*An Ceannaí Fionn agus an Oíche Fhómhair*) LMacC 1008:107

Four-leafed shamrock, The (*An tSeamair Mhuire*) PdeB 1552:260–4

Fox and the sea-gull, The (*An sionnach agus an faoileán*) LMacC 1008:298–9; 1281:288–9

Hag of Beara, additional lore, The (*Tuilleadh faoin gCailligh Bhéarthaigh*) LMacC 1008:80–1

Herb woman, The (*Cailleach na luibheanna*) Tape CB 0130.2

If you were in the west (*Dá mbeifeá thiar*) LMacC 1008:304–5

It was as difficult as music was for Anraí (*Chuaigh sé chomh crua is chuaigh ceol le hAnraí*) 1280:717–20

Man who brought hay to cattle, A (*Fear a chuaigh le féar chuig beithígh*) PdeB 1553:209–10

Man who sent his son to school, A (*Fear a chuir a mhac ar scoil*) Tape LC 1848

Man who took a skull from a graveyard, The (*An fear a thug blaosc as an teampall*) LMacC 1008:115–17

Man who was gathering seaweed, A (*Fear a bhí ag baint feamainne*) PdeB 1509:283–4

Micil Eoin Uí Chadhain LMacC 1008:109–14; RTÉ 124/72

Minister and the ants, The (*An ministéara agus na seangáin*) 1281:59

Ministers, The (*Scéal na Ministéaraí*) LMacC 1008:85–8

Mionachair and Meanachair (*Mionachar is Meanachair*) 1281:136–40

Poet and a priest going to Galway, A RTÉ M1129a

Rich man and wise beggar (told in English) BBC 22370

Story of the cliffclimbers, The (*Scéal na n-ailleadóirí*) 1281:306–7

Summary of tale about a bird's prophecy (*Cnámhaí scéil faoi fháistine éin*) 1281:346

Three districts of the Ciarbhánach, The (*Trí dhúthaigh an Chiarabhánaigh*) LMacC 1009:150–3

Three women asking the weaver for respite (*Triúr ban ag iarraidh uain ar fhíodóir*) 1281:387–8

Truth and falsehood (*An fhírinne agus an bhréag*) 1281:290–6

Woman I would prefer, The (*An bhean ba mheasa liom beo*) LMacC 1008:297–8, 1281:406

You are wet yourself now! (*Tá tú féin fliuch anois*) LMacC 1008:130–1

Fairylore and otherworld narratives

Advice from the fairy man to the girl (*Comhairle an fhir sí don chailín*) LMacC 1008:308–10; BBC 23101/23102

Being must have come to you, A (*Caithfidh sé go dtáinig neach chugatsa*) 1281:356

Draining a well (*Tobar a thaoscadh*) 1281:357

Fairy boat, The (*An Bád Sí*) LMacC 1008:427–30

Finnbheara LMacC 1008:105–7; PdeB 1552:291–3; Tape LC T67h; M1129e; RTÉ 157/72

Ghost, A (*Taibhse*) RTÉ 124/72a

Ghost moors a boat, A RTÉ 124/72

Killing seals near Sceirdí (*Ag marú róinte ar na Sceirdí*) LMacC 1008:104

Lakeside waste (*Brá thír locha*) 1281:214; BBC-5287-SE

Man who was fishing on a lake, A (*Fear a bhí ag iascach ar loch*) PdeB 1509:284–6

Man who was taken by the fairies, A (*Fear a tugadh as*) LMacC 1008:430–3

Mermaid, The (*An mhaighdean mhara*) 1281:385–6

Otherworld tales (*Scéalta sídhiúla*) PdeB 1509:278–82; Tape LC T67i

Seals in small lakes (*Róinte i lochāin*) PdeB 1553:45–7

Seán Mac Séamuis Tape CB 0130.2

Stray sod, The (*Fóidín mearbhaill*) 1281:356

Strong man, A (*Fear láidir*) PdeB 1553:213–15

Two-shilling piece, A (*Airgead chrois*) 1281:408–10

Woman who died in childbirth and returned to life, A (*Bean a fuair bás tar éis páiste agus a tháinig ar ais*) PdeB 1553:211–13

International tales

ATU 38/650/852/930 cf. The Cill Ghliosáin fool (*Amadán Chille Ghliosáin*) LMacC 1008:63–72; PdeB 1509:267–74

ATU 47B The fox and the wolf (*An sionnach agus an madra alla*) LMacC 1008:89–90, 1281:289–90

ATU 62 The cat and the fox (*An cat agus an sionnach*) LMacC 1008:114–15

ATU 72** The fox builds a house (*An sionnach ag déanamh tí*) LMacC 1008:90–1

ATU 155 The young judge (*An giúistís óg*) LMacC 1008:133–5

ATU 302/303 Donnmhac and Díonmhac the miserable person (*Donnmhac agus Díonmhac an díthriú*) LMacC 1008:259–79

ATU 302/550 Thady McGrath (*Tadhg Mac Craith*) Mairéad Ní Chathasaigh 326:5–26; LMacC 1008:28–58; Tape LC T68d

ATU 326/563 The heir and the widow (*An t-oighre dúthaigh agus an bhaintreach*) LMacC 1008:21–7

ATU 461 A man whose mother and father died (*Fear ar cailleadh a athair agus a mháthair*) PdeB 1552:249–54

ATU 500 Hughie Houster, the fairy weaver (*Hiúí Houster, an fíodóir sí*) LMacC 1009:168–72

ATU 671 cf. A boy who spent twenty-one years at school (*Buachaill a bhí ar scoil bliain is fiche*) PdeB 1509:251–5

ATU 756A A thief (*Gadaí*) PdeB 1552:265–7

ATU 759 The priest who cast his clothes (*An sagart a chaith an t-éadach dhe*) LMacC 1008:305–8

ATU 875 cf. 931 Dáithí the king (*Dáithí an rí*) LMacC 1008:279–88

ATU 938B A man who was working (*Fear a bhí ag obair*) PdeB 1509:245–50

ATU 1006/1210/1384/1540/1653 Tadhg in heaven (*Tadhg ins na flaithis*) LMacC 1008:289–96

ATU 1455 A cobbler, a tailor and a tiller (*Gréasaí, táilliúr agus talmhaí*) LMacC 1008:299–303

ATU 1535, 1539 A small merchant and a big merchant (*Ceannaí beag agus ceannaí mór*) PdeB 1552:267–72

ATU 1585 The price of advice (*Luach na comhairle*) LMacC 1008: 132–3

ATU 1641 The man who pretended he had secret knowledge (*An fear a lig air féin go raibh fios aige*) LMacC 1008:58–62. A man who was made poor (*Fear a bhí á bhochtú*) PdeB 1509:274–7; Tape LC 1844a

ATU 1940 Sodar got up and ate Sochar-bhoinn (*D'éirigh Sodar agus d'ith sé Sochar-bhoinn*) 1281:350

ATU 1950 The three lazy men (*An triúr fear leisciúil*) LMacC 1008:128

Curses

Curse of the bell on the clergy on you (*Eascainí an chloig ar an gcléir ort*) 1281:135

Curse of the father on the son (*Eascainí an athar ar an mac*) 1281:246

Curse of the old man, The (*Eascainí an tseanfhir*) LMacC 1008:130

Married for a month (*Pósadh míosa*) 1281:332

Collectors to whom Colm gave material[7]

Ciarán Bairéad (1905–76) was from Claregalway in County Galway. Ciarán worked as an archivist with the Irish Folklore Commission from 1949 to 1951, then became a full-time field collector from 1951 until 1975. His fieldwork covered a broad geographical area. For the most part he collected in County Galway, around his home district, but he also collected a large body of material in west Galway, and also in counties Clare, Limerick, Carlow and Kilkenny. His manuscript legacy from field collecting amounts to some 25,000 pages and around 155 reel-to-reel tapes. Most of his collection is in Irish. He had a significant input into material culture and the National Museum of Ireland. Some of his work with Colm Ó Caodháin resulted from a request for further information on songs and poets of Iorras Aintheach by Ríonach Ní Fhlathartaigh (uí Ógáin) in the early 1970s.[8]

Proinnsias de Búrca (1904–96) was a collector with the Irish Folklore Commission from 1935 to 1944 and again from 1953 to 1964. He was from Corr na Móna in County Galway and collected for the most part in that district. He undertook fieldwork with storytellers from An Spidéal to Maíros and also in the Irish-speaking districts in County Mayo. His fieldwork in the National Folklore Collection amounts to some 30,000 manuscript pages. He recorded 1,423 cylinders and 183 reel-to-reel magnetic tapes. The bulk of his collection is in Irish. A keen fisherman, he recorded many narratives relating to fishing and the lore of rocks, lakes and the sea. He and Séamus Ó Duilearga engaged in many discussions and expeditions associated with this shared interest.

***Séamus Ennis* (Séamus Mac Aonghusa)** (1919–82) was from north County Dublin and is best remembered as a piper. His piping style has influenced numerous *uilleann* pipers. His appointment as full-time collector of music and song with the Irish Folklore Commission (1942–7) was to have a significant influence on the rest of his career. He collected over 2,000 items of music and song in his travels for the commission, working for the most part in counties Galway, Donegal, Mayo, Cavan, Clare, Cork, Kerry and Limerick, and on some of the islands of Scotland. He recorded 276 12-inch acetate discs. Following his time with the commission, Ennis worked with Radio Éireann from 1947 to 1951 and then moved to the BBC, where he worked until 1957. His friendship with Colm Ó Caodháin is legendary and his field diary paints the life of a young collector in 1940s Ireland as he met and recorded musicians, singers and storytellers.

Liam Mac Coisdeala (1906–96) was from Kiltimagh, County Mayo, and was appointed a collector with the Irish Folklore Commission shortly after its foundation in 1935. He recorded around 1,560 cylinders and transcribed around 20,000 pages of material including *Eochair Mac Rí in Éirinn*, the longest folktale ever recorded from oral tradition in Ireland. Although Liam returned to his teaching career in 1946, he continued his work of collecting and submitting folklore material. Most of his collecting work is in Irish and relates to the Carna district, where he was a teacher. In the 1940s he and Séamus Ennis stayed in the same lodging house at An Coillín, Carna, County Galway, the house of storyteller Pádraicín Mhacaí Mac Con Iomaire.

***Mairéad Ní Chathasaigh* (Maggie)** (*c.* 1920– ?) was from An Aird Thoir, Carna, County Galway. In 1936 and '37 she contributed around 650 pages of material to the Irish Folklore Commission. She seems to have been the first person to have collected material from Colm Ó Caodháin. Her sisters Sorcha and Bairbre were also in contact with the commission, as they were interested in the tales and folklore of their district and wished to become collectors. Very little is known of Mairéad but a brother, Seán Ó Cathasaigh, was chief translator at the Houses of the Oireachtas in Dublin for a number of years.

***Caoimhín Ó Danachair* (Kevin Danaher)** (1913–2002) was from Athea, County Limerick. He began working for the Irish Folklore Commission in 1940. His particular area of interest was material folk culture and vernacular architecture. He made numerous sound recordings: 903 large acetate discs and 603 small acetate discs. He was a pioneer in the creation of the sound archive of the commission and also in the creation of the photographic archive. When the commission was transferred to University College Dublin (UCD) in 1970, Caoimhín became a lecturer in Irish folklore and ethnology at the university.

NOTES

Introduction

1. P. Woulfe, *Sloinnte Gaedheal is Gall* (Dublin, 1923), p. 450, lists the surname 'Ó Caodháin' followed by: 'Kane, Kean, Keane; a corruption in the spoken language of County Mayo of Mac Aodháin q.v.'. Both spellings 'Ó Caodháin' and 'Ó Caoidheáin' have been used in relation to Colm's surname. Colm's daughter Máire Uí Chonaire, An Coillín, Carna, explained that the Ó Caodháins were also called 'Ó Catháin'.

2. The Irish Folklore Commission (1935–70) is now the National Folklore Collection (NFC), at University College Dublin (UCD).

3. *Lady Dudley's Scheme for the Establishment of District Nurses in the Poorest Parts of Ireland, First Annual Report, 23 April 1903 – 23 April 1904*, p. 18.

4. C. Browne, 'Ethnography of Carna and Mweenish, Conamara', *Proceedings of the Royal Irish Academy*, vol. VI, 1901, p. 516.

5. Ibid., vol. VI, 1900–2, p. 520.

6. Ibid., p. 516.

7. Séamus Mac Aonghusa (Séamus Ennis) was a full-time collector of music and song for the Irish Folklore Commission from 1942 to 1947. His field diaries of 1942–6 are contained in Ríonach uí Ógáin, *Mise an Fear Ceoil: Séamus Ennis – Dialann Taistil 1942–1946* (Indreabhán: Cló Iar-Chonnachta, 2007), and in translation *Going to the Well for Water: The Séamus Ennis Field Diary 1942–1946* (Cork: Cork University Press, 2009), edited by Ríonach uí Ógáin.

8. From a recording made by the late Éamon de Buitléar, 27 July 1974, who gave permission to quote it.

9. National Folklore Collection (NFC) 1509:261–2.

10. NFC 1280:710. Seemingly the nickname stemmed from Colm's grandmother, who saw her husband at a distance and, because of the hat he was wearing, likened him to a landlord called 'Blácach' (Blake), who lived near Na Forbacha, County Galway. Colm's niece explained (November 2019) that Blake owned the wood on his land in An Cnoc Buí, near the village of Carna. When Blake visited, Colm's grandfather drove the sidecar for him. He collected Blake from the train in Sraith Salach (Recess). Colm's grandfather had to wear a jacket and tails and carry a whip. He dressed at home and walked to An Cnoc Buí to collect the sidecar and the mare.

11. NFC 1281:425. See 'Colm's Account of His Life' in Chapter 1.

12. NFC 1281:455.

13. Ibid., 235.

14. Ibid., 455.

15. Ibid., 127. Séamus Ennis learned much of his piping from his own father. He was about thirteen when he became interested in piping and, when he started, his father would correct him now and then. This was told to the late Liam Mac Con Iomaire by Séamus Ennis in an interview in 1979 (LMacCI 1979).

16. Ibid., 147.

17. Ibid., 82.

18. A note by the collector Séamus Ennis in NFC Music Manuscript (MM) 18.

19. LmacCI 1979.

20. NFC 1281:452. See 'Colm's Account of His Life' in Chapter 1.

21. NFC 326:5. Although the storyteller's surname is given as 'Catháin', because of the age, first name and address and also the tale title 'Tadhg Mac Craith', the storyteller is surely Colm. See also note 1 above.

22. The Irish Folklore Commission (1935–70) was established for the collection, preservation and dissemination of the folklore of Ireland. NFC correspondence file Bairbre and Máiréad Ní Chathasaigh. See, for example, letters from Ó Súilleabháin dated 5 November 1936, 1 October 1937. The correspondence indicates that Seán Ó Súilleabháin, archivist to the Irish Folklore Commission, thought highly of Mairéad's work.

23. NFC 1280:701. Colm told the collector Ciarán Bairéad that he had built forty-six houses, for people around Carna and An Caiseal. NFC CB 0125.2.

24. NFC 1281:445. See 'Colm's Account of His Life' in Chapter 1.

25. Iorras Aithneach (Iorras Aintheach) is a district in the barony of Baile na hInse (Ballynahinch). It approximates the Carna peninsula and includes the villages of Carna and Cill Chiaráin. The name probably means the peninsula of gorse (if the second word derives from *aiteann*) or it may mean the stormy peninsula, deriving from *ainbhtheach* (*anfach*), meaning stormy. See Tim Robinson, *Connemara: A little Gaelic kingdom* (London: Penguin, 2011), p. 110.

26. NFC 1281:452.

27. Conversation with Máire Uí Chonaire, Coillín, Carna, County Galway, 29 May 2018, and conversation with Margaret Cloherty (a niece of Colm's), An Caiseal, County Galway, November 2019. There is also an account of this in his own words in NFC 1281:425–57. See 'Colm's Account of His Life' in Chapter 1.

28. Ibid.

29. Conversation with Margaret Cloherty, An Caiseal, County Galway, November 2019.

30. uí Ógáin, *Going to the Well for Water*, p. 45.

31. NFC 1295:121.

32. NFC 1295:136.

33. NFC 1295:208.

34. NFC Ennis correspondence. Letter to Séamus Ó Duilearga, 24 November 1943.

35. NFC 1008:3–11. Mac Coisdeala wrote an account of this week-long collecting trip to Colm Ó Caodháin, which took place in September 1944.

36. The Ediphone was a mechanically driven recording device. Recordings were made on wax cylinders. See Chapter 1 for further details.

37. NFC 1008:3–11, p. 5.

38. Ibid., pp. 6–7.

39. Ibid., p. 8.

40. Seán Ó Súilleabháin, *A Handbook of Irish Folklore* (Dublin: The Folklore of Ireland Society, 1942).

41. In all, Liam wrote around 233 pages of material from Colm.

42. The 'Feis' was a celebration of arts and culture and included storytelling, singing, music and dance competitions.

43. NFC 1296:46.

44. NFC Letter to Seán Ó Súilleabháin, November 1944.

45. NFC 1281:419.

46. LMaCI 1979.

47. Ennis received an Ediphone machine in June 1944. The machine was sent by bus and the box of cylinders by post. See uí Ógáin, *Going to the Well for Water*, pp. 158–9.

48. NFC 1281:233.

49. This was probably the microphone.

50. From a recording made by Séamus Ennis and Caoimhín Ó Danachair in 1947. NFC SA Disc 358 CT087.

51. NFC 1281:217.

52. NFC Letter to Seán Ó Súilleabháin, November 1944.

53. See uí Ógáin, *Going to the Well for Water*, p. 350.

54. NFC 1296:238

55. NFC 1280:701.

56. LMACI 1979.

57. NFC Ennis correspondence, 10 June 1943.

58. Conversation with Margaret Cloherty, An Caiseal, County Galway, November 2019.

59. NFC 1295:208–9.

60. See, for example, NFC 1281:228.

61. NFC 1295:122.

62. See, for example, NFC 1297:39. On his trips to Iorras Aithneach, Ennis often stayed with the Ó hIarnáin family in Roisín na Mainiach.

63. *Poitín* is a home-distilled, illicit form of whiskey generally made in remote rural areas. It was made from grain or potatoes. In Conamara the many small islands and inlets were ideally placed for setting up the still and there was less chance of the distilling process and associated smoke being detected. In 2015 the government of Ireland outlined legal production methods for the making of *poitín*.

64. Conversation with Margaret Cloherty, An Caiseal, County Galway, November 2019.

65. NFC 1295:188.

66. Cognate of *creatán* meaning 'shortness of breath'; see Brian Ó Curnáin, *The Irish of Iorras Aithneach, County Galway*, vols 1–4 (Dublin: Dublin Institute for Advanced Studies, 2007), vol. 4.

67. NFC 1281:405.

68. LMACI 1979.

69. NFC 1296:27, 33.

70. NFC Ennis correspondence. Letter to Seán Ó Súilleabháin, November 1944. A similar account is also included in NFC 1281:323.

71. NFC 1296:140–3.

72. NFC 1296:197.

73. NFC radio script 11 (n.d.). Colm gave Ennis a version of this song; see '*Hóbhá, mo Leana*' ['Hobhá, my Child'] NFC 1281:304–5, MM 19.

74. Conversation with Máire Uí Chonaire, Coillín, Carna, County Galway, 29 May 2018.

75. Ibid.

76. NFC 1281:235.

77. NFC 1281:159.

78. NFC 1296:188.

79. NFC Ennis correspondence. Letter to Seán Ó Súilleabháin, 19 May 1944.

80. NFC 1295:141.

81. Ibid. See NFC Ennis correspondence. Letter to Seán Ó Súilleabháin, 19 May 1944.

82. NFC 1281:394–5. See track 7 in this publication with accompanying notes.

83. NFC 1281:166–7.

84. See track 30 in this publication and the accompanying notes. See also Francis James Child, *The English and Scottish Popular Ballads*, 5 vols (Boston and New York: Houghton, Mifflin & Co., 1882–98).

85. See track 4 in this publication and the accompanying notes.

86. NFC 1281:87.

87. See tracks 14–16 in this publication and accompanying notes.

88. NFC Ennis correspondence. Letter to Seán Ó Súilleabháin, 19 May 1944.

89. See, for example, tracks 16 and 30 in this publication and the accompanying notes.

90. NFC Ríonach uí Ógáin, T25c 14 September 1986.

91. NFC 1296:36–7. See also NFC 1281:198–201, where the words and background of the songs are given.

92. NFC 1281:381–3.

93. NFC 1281:411–12.

94. NFC 1281:158–9. Ennis entitled the song '*Amhrán a Chum Colm fúm Féin*' ['A Song Colm Composed about Me']. The first line is '*Muise a Shéamuis, tá tú tíocht chugamsa ó tháinig an samhradh*' ['Well, Séamus, you have been coming to visit me since the arrival of summer'].

95. NFC 1281:160–2. Ennis included this song in a letter, entirely in verse, to folklore collector Seán Ó hEochaidh, with whom he had collaborated closely during his work in County Donegal.

96. NFC 1281:187, 109.

97. NFC MM 19.128.

98. NFC 1281:187.

99. NFC 1073:1–55.

100. NFC 1008:11.

101. uí Ógáin, *Going to the Well for Water*, p. 277: 'Wednesday 1.8.45. My last visit to Ó Caodháin today. I wrote more little items from him. I read the account of the Famine I had written from him for correction, and I filled in little gaps in my manuscripts. I recorded an account of his life from him on the Ediphone and then I had finished. Although I can say that I have finished working with him, I could never pay him a visit that he would not have thought of something new for me to write.'

102. NFC. See Proinnsias de Búrca file in Ó Duilearga correspondence, letter dated 10 November 1958. There seems to be relatively little overlap between the items collected by different collectors.

103. For comments on the Radio Éireann disc recordings of 1947, see Bo Almqvist and Pádraig Ó Héalaí (eds), *Labharfad le Cách: I will speak to you all, Peig Sayers* (Dublin: New Island, 2009), pp. 192–3.

104. For comments on the BBC visit to Ireland in August 1947, see ibid., pp. 186–7.

105. See the documentary film *Miles and Miles of Music* made by Éamon de Buitléar in 1975.

106. Columbia Masterworks SL-204, USA.

107. The Department of External Affairs (1924–71) is now the Department of Foreign Affairs.

108. *Amhráin ar an Sean-Nós*, RTÉ CD 185, 1994.

109. UNESCO, *Ireland: Musics of the world* (CD) UNES08271, 1997.

110. Veteran Records CD, VT162CD, recorded by Terry Yarnell.

111. See Ríonach uí Ógáin, '"Cailín Deas Crúite na mBó" and the Impact of the Folklore Collector', *Béaloideas*, vol. 83, 2015, pp. 96–110.

112. Conversation with John Barrett, Inis Ní, 27 February 2019.

Chapter 1

1. See track 14. NFC 1281:425–57. In 1973, Colm also gave the folklore collector Ciarán Bairéad a brief account of his life (NFC CB 0130.1).

2. Letter from Carl von Sydow to Séamus Ó Duilearga, 24 March 1936, cited in Ríonach uí Ógáin, 'Some Comments on Context, Text and Subtext in Irish Folklore', in Lauri Honko (ed.), *Thick Corpus, Organic Variation and Textuality in Oral Tradition* (Helsinki: Finnish Literature Society, 2000), p. 161.

3. See, for example, Timothy Rice, James Porter and Chris Goertzen (eds), *The Garland Encyclopaedia of World Music. Vol. 8: Europe* (New York and London: Garland Publishing, 2000), pp 16–29 and pp. 378–97, especially pp. 385–6 and p. 393.

4. uí Ógáin, *Going to the Well for Water*, p. 277.

5. The Irish text is presented in normalised orthography while retaining forms and structures. Word forms are as found in Niall Ó Dónaill, *Foclóír Gaeilge-Béarla* (Baile Átha Cliath: Oifig an tSoláthair, 1977), Tomás de Bhaldraithe, *Foirisiún Focal as Gaillimh* (Dublin: Acadamh Ríoga na hÉireann, 1985), and Ó Curnáin, *The Irish of Iorras Aithneach* (Dublin: Dublin Institute for Advanced Studies, 2007).

6. i.e. '*pébí*'.

7. Question mark inserted by Séamus Ennis in his transcription.

8. 'Leitir a hArd' is a local form of the placename 'Leitreach Ard' as defined in www.logainm.ie (see https://www.logainm.ie/ga/18272?s=Leitreach+Ard, accessed 11 September 2019).

9. Question mark inserted by Séamus Ennis in his transcription.

10. 'Ceatharnaigh' may refer to the surname 'Kearney' and Colm is referring to 'the Kearneys'.

11. Ennis wrote 'Cylinder Two Continued' at this point.

12. Here Colm said that the Irish word *fíogaí* is 'dogfish' in English. Ennis wrote that the Ediphone cylinder was scratched at this point, indicating that some words may have been indecipherable or lost.

13. The word means a kind of noise and implies a kind of echoing sound.

14. The First World War, known as 'the Great War', dated from 1914 to 1918, and 'this war' refers to the Second World War, from 1939 to 1945.

15. An island near Inis Mór, the largest of the three Aran Islands off the coast of County Galway.

16. This refers to the dowry or woman's wealth that she brought to a marriage.

17. This may be a description of a place, *cloigeann doghrainne*, which would translate literally as 'the headland of difficulty'.

18. Séamus Ennis wrote 'Cylinder Three' at this point.

19. Ciara Breathnach, *The Congested Districts Board of Ireland, 1891–1923* (Dublin: Four Courts Press, 2005). The Congested Districts Board was established in 1891 in an attempt to find long-term solutions to endemic rural poverty in parts of counties along the western seaboard. It developed schemes around industries and fishing and one of its main policies was to raise living conditions by increasing the size of small farms, encouraging new agricultural methods and improving housing. For this purpose additional land was acquired and used to enlarge or rearrange existing farms. In some cases families were moved to new farms and houses within the district. In 1923 its functions were moved to the Land Commission.

20. Most likely, this refers to rundale, a system whereby land was leased to tenants and jointly worked. The system was commonplace in Ireland and was based on joint holdings and partnership tenure. See Sean J. Connolly (ed.), *The Oxford Companion to Irish History* (Oxford: Oxford University Press, 2002); Muiris O'Sullivan and Liam Downey, 'Post-Medieval Fieldscapes. Part 2: Rundale', *Archaeology Ireland*, vol. 22, no. 3, autumn 2008, pp. 22–5; Eoin Flaherty, 'Rundale and 19th Century Irish Settlement: System, space and genealogy', *Irish Geography*, vol. 48, no. 2, 2015, pp. 3–38, DOI: 10.2014/igj.v48i2.623.

21. Séamus Ennis wrote 'Cylinder Four' at this point.

22. Séamus Ennis added that Colm laughed as he said this.

23. *cora* (gen. *corann*) is a rounded hill that the tide would encircle.

24. Séamus Ennis wrote that this was said by Colm in response to a question.

25. Colm called the Ediphone machine an 'old man'.

26. Séamus Ennis wrote that Colm told his young son to 'Leave that alone!' as the child was disrupting him.

27. The gathering and burning of kelp is a distinctive seasonal activity and was commonly practised in the eighteenth and nineteenth centuries in Ireland. Kelp

– a term covering different seaweeds as well as the ash produced from them – yielded carbonate of soda and was first used in the manufacture of soap, bleach and glass; later the kelp industry concentrated on the production of iodine. Up to thirty tons of seaweed was required to produce one ton of kelp. The gathering of the seaweed harvest commenced in March, following the winter storms and high tides of spring. The seaweed was brought from the foreshore for stacking and drying. The dried seaweed was burnt in specially constructed low rectangular stone kilns during the month of June. The kilns, which had to be tended and fed (often throughout the night), produced dense plumes of smoke, once a typical feature of the Irish coastline at this time of year.

Chapter 2

1. See track 15.

2. Recorded by Radio Éireann in 1948 and transferred to the Irish Folklore Commission. NFC T0067p (0:46).

3. This recording was made by the British Broadasting Corporation (BBC) on 20 August 1947. Ennis had collected and transcribed a version of the song from Colm on 18 May 1944 at the beginning of a two-and-a-half-month period of fieldwork in the Carna district (1:44).

4. Note that song translations are not intended to be regarded as songs to be sung in English: they are an aid to understanding the lyrics in Irish. The songs were inherited largely through oral tradition and live performance. In the course of this transmission song lyrics were at times modified. In some instances modified phrases lose contextual meaning and are impossible to translate. The translations of Colm's songs therefore communicate the overall sense of the song.

5. All the images of transcriptions, music and lyrics are by Séamus Ennis as he wrote them from Colm Ó Caodháin. The collector generally wrote the lyrics of the first verse with the staff notation.

6. Recorded for the BBC in July 1954, 5297-BBC-SE (3:04). See also NFC 1281: 85–6; MMS 19, Disc 0363B.

7. Recorded for the BBC in July 1954, 5129-BBC-SE (1:41). See also NFC 1281: 142–4; MMS 19.082; Disc 0353–0366.

8. The song is classified as Roud 489: 'Soldier Will You Marry Me?' See https://www.vwml.org/vwml-help-2/ [accessed 20 October 2020].

9. Recorded by the BBC in July 1954, 5297-BBC-SE (1:44).

10. *cruach* means 'heap' or 'stack' and *cara* (al. *cora*) is 'of the stepping stones' or 'of the weir'.

11. *na Caoile* (nom. *An Chaoile*) means 'of the narrow stretch of water'.

12. i.e. on the nearby island of Cruach na Caoile.

13. Recorded by Radio Éireann in 1948 and transferred to the Irish Folklore Commission. NFC T0068c (1:00).

14. Francis O'Neill, *Waifs and Strays of Gaelic Melody* (Chicago: Lyon & Healy, 1922), no. 267.

15. James Kerr, *Kerr's First Collection of Merry Melodies for the Violin* (Glasgow: James Kerr, *c.* 1870), p. 19.

16. First part recorded by the Irish Folklore Commission in 1945, NFC Disc 120, T0066c; second part recorded by the BBC on 20 August 1947, BBC-5297-SE (4:18). See also NFC 1280:702–3; 1281:394–8; MMS 18.

17. Patrick S. Dinneen, *Foclóir Gaedhilge agus Béarla* (Dublin: The Educational Company of Ireland, 1927), gives for *giobóg*: amount of thing plucked, a rag, a fringe; a handful; the handful of flax taken at a time by clovers or flax-teasers (U.); an untidy woman; a gipsy, a sorceress; *cf. giofóg*; Ó Dónaill, *Foclóir Gaeilge-Béarla*, gives 'tiny bit; pick, scrap; snippert, rag; untidy woman, idle, worthless woman, and also refers to *giofóg*. The local interpretation in Iorras Aithneach is that of 'wretched woman'.

18. Nonsense vocables are sung as syllables or sounds and do not have a lexical or referential meaning. Colm sings these in place of a chorus and they carry the melody between the verses.

19. *pluid is leaba, agus pis bhreá phlacach* – 'a blanket and a bed and a fine protruding vulva' is the phrase in the manuscript transcription by Séamus Ennis, where he notes that Colm substituted the more earthy phrase with that on the sound recording.

20. Séamus Ennis noted that this was a cloth people kept at the hearth in order to hold a hot pot or anything they had on the fire. Long ago, houses had two of these, tied together with a piece of rope, for each side of the pot and they would hang it on a nail when it wasn't in use.

21. NFC 1281:394–5. Material in square brackets [...] indicates additional relevant material collected from Colm but not on the edited CD.

22. In his field diary, Séamus Ennis described his visit to Colm to make this recording. He brought with him a single wax cylinder given to him by the folklore collector Liam Mac Coisdeala. In the diary entry for 27 July 1945, Séamus Ennis wrote: 'I had brought one cylinder from Liam for Colm, because it is a wonderful piece and I would like to have it in the office to listen to it, even if it is only on cylinder, until we get the gramophone records again. Colm was fishing in the bay, but as he was tacking close to home, mackerel fishing up and down, I did not know when he would return home. I waited until he landed at eight o'clock. As I left him, I had "*Port na Giobóige*" ['The Unfortunate Widow's Tune] on wax cylinder, and other songs that the Ediphone did not record that well, and I had a supply of mackerel as a result of the visit, for myself and for the Ó hIarnáin family.' See NFC 1297:38–9 and see also uí Ógáin, *Going to the Well for Water*, p. 274.

23. Recorded by the Irish Folklore Commission in 1947. NFC Disc 361, T0066c (3:20). See also NFC 1281:120–1; MMS 19, Disc 363a.

24. Séamus Ennis wrote that this is the word *bruidheanach* meaning 'having many mansions', as found in Dinneen's dictionary.

25. Séamus Ennis gave an alternative version to the last line of this stanza: *Gur cailín óg a chloígh mé is níor éirigh liom í fháil* – 'That a young girl has destroyed me and I have failed to win her'.

26. For the phrase *ar bhruach na trá,* Séamus Ennis gave as an alternative *i mBaile an Chláir,* meaning 'in Baile an Chláir', which probably refers to the town of Claregalway. This image is in keeping with a feature of lyrical song in Irish where it is said that until the impossible happens the composer of the song will not betray his beloved. In this case the composer will not return until the cuckoo sings in winter or Renvyle Castle is being built in Claregalway.

27. NFC 1281:121.

28. Recorded by the Irish Folklore Commission in 1947, NFC Disc 363, T0066c (2:08). See also NFC 1281:179–81; MMS 19.

29. For instances of the word *síofróg* see Ó Dónaill, *Foclóir Gaeilge-Béarla*: 'elf-woman', 'fairy' or 'enchantress'; Tomás S. Ó Máille, *Liosta Focal as Ros Muc* (Dublin: Irish University Press, 1974), p. 198: *sióg* or 'fairy'; *Béaloideas,* vol. 22, 1953, p. 148: *sífreoir – síofróir;* Ó Curnáin, *The Irish of Iorras Aithneach,* vol. iv, p. 2593: *síofráil,* **síofróireacht*, 'jabbering'.

30. Séamus Ennis wrote a note to the effect that Colm did not know if he ever knew the first couplet of this verse. The note was dated 19 November 1944 and the collector subsequently drew a line through the note. He thought perhaps the first half of the fourth verse was sung before this: *Dá ba min í an raithneach agus araile,* 'If the fern were powder', etc. The collector then wrote a note that Colm heard the song from his grandmother who was *curtha caillte i dtalamh le deich mbliana fichead,* 'dead and buried for thirty years'.

31. These additional verses from Colm [ ] are in a different sequence in his version in NFC 1281:179–81.

32. See NFC 1280:385–6; 1280:567–8.

33. See NFC 1280:218–19.

34. Ibid., 490.

35. See NFC 1282:146.

36. See NFC 1282:315–16.

37. Recorded by the Irish Folklore Commission in 1947, NFC Disc 366, T0066c (2:16). See also NFC 1281:103–4; MMS 18.

38. NFC 1281:103.

39. Séamus Ennis wrote that Colm Ó Caodháin did not understand the Irish phrase *mailí bána,* and Colm thought it might be *cineál bréagáin* – 'a kind of toy', perhaps. It may well be *ealaí bána* meaning 'white swans'.

40. Séamus Ennis wrote '*Sin é a raibh ann ariamh*' ('That's all there ever was of it') at the end of the transcription. The comment may have been written following discussion with Colm (NFC 1281:104).

41. Recorded in 1947 for the Irish Folklore Commission, NFC Disc 359, T0066c (3:14). See also NFC 1281:91–2; MMS 19.

42. Séamus Ennis notes a date, 6 July 1944, in relation to this verse in the song transcription (NFC 1281:91). In his diary entry, 21 June 1944, Ennis wrote that Colm sang another verse of '*Neainsín Bhán*' – '*má théann tú chun an aonaigh bíodh an chaora leat*' ['If you go to the fair bring the sheep'], and so on. See NFC 1296:44; see also uí Ógáin, *Going to the Well for Water*, p. 160.

43. Recorded by the Irish Folklore Commission in 1947, NFC Disc 362, T0066c (2:40). See also NFC 1281:118–19; MMS 19.

44. The Irish name *Saile* is related to the English name 'Sally'. *Saile Óg* or *Sail Óg* is also written *Saileog*, the word *óg* meaning 'young'.

45. Séamus Ennis wrote '(2nd half of tune)' at this point.

46. Séamus Ennis included a note in pencil which consisted of the following verse which he collected from Máire Mulgrew (73), Mulrany, on 17 August 1944. He made a note to remind himself to ask Colm if this was the missing piece (NFC 1281:119):

In aois a sé déag is ea fuair mé féin í,
Ba deas an féirín í le fear ar láimh,
Ba deas a béilín agus ba cúrsa a héadain,
Agus a súile mar a' réalta thig roimh lá.
Mo ghrá do bhéilín 7rl

It was at age sixteen that I myself found her,
She was a nice little present for a man,
Her little mouth was sweet and her forehead was pleasant.
And her eyes like the star that comes before dawn.
I love your little mouth, etc.

47. NFC 1281:118.

48. Ciarán Ó Con Cheanainn in Micheál Ó Conghaile, Lochlann Ó Tuairisg and Peadar Ó Ceannabháin, *Leabhar Mór na nAmhrán* (Indreabhán: Cló Iar-Chonnacht, 2012), p. 822.

49. Recorded by the BBC in July 1954, BBC-5434-SE (1:17). See also NFC MMS 019.

50. A short-stemmed, clay pipe.

51. Tom Munnelly, *The Mount Callan Garland: Songs from the repertoire of Tom Lenihan* (Dublin: Comhairle Bhéaloideas Éireann, 1994), pp. 16–17.

52. See https://www.vwml.org/search [accessed 20 October 2020].

53. Recorded by the BBC in July 1954, BBC-5127-SE (0:22).

54. Recorded by the BBC in July 1954, BBC-5127-SE (0:23).

55. Recorded by the BBC in July 1954, BBC-5434-SE (0:41).

56. This is probably Colm's translation of the phrase *dá n-abraínn é* or *dá ndéarfainn é*, which literally translates as 'If I were to say it' and means 'I suppose' or 'If I were to go into it in detail'.

57. Recorded by the BBC in July 1954, BBC-5127-SE (1:03).

58. Recorded by Radio Éireann in 1948 and transferred to the Irish Folklore Commission. NFC T067j (3:30). See also NFC 1281:116–17; MMS 19.025. The song is also called '*Peigí Ní Fhlathartaigh*'.

59. NFC 1281:116.

60. Séamus Ennis wrote that Colm said his father had no additional lines at this point and had three couplets as appear here.

61. One might well expect two surnames here 'from ?? and from Ó Ceallaigh' but in this recording the song says 'from *céirseach* ('female blackbird') and O'Kelly'.

62. Recorded by the BBC in December 1953, BBC-5287-SE (1:26). See also NFC 1281:174–5; MMS 19. Tape CB 0125.2.

63. NFC 1281:174.

64. Ennis noted that Colm said *go gcaithfidh tú a rá gur cnámhannaí géill na bó báine a fuair sé in áit eicínt* ('you have to say that it was the white cow's jawbones he found somewhere'), NFC 1281:175.

65. This is an alternative for the final couplet of the fourth stanza and is given in NFC 1281:174. See also NFC 1281:219 for a stanza collected from Máire Ní Éanaí (74), Maíros, at the end of a day Colm and Ennis spent in search of song, 9 June 1944. Colm asked Máire about the song and she spoke the final verse of it. Colm questioned her about the song and she had the last verse just as Colm sang it in track 19 above.

66. NFC 1281:174–5.

67. See P. Ó Ceannabháin, 'An Samhradh sa bhFuacht idir Nollaig is Cáisc: Spléachadh ar fhilithe in Iorras Aithneach san 19ú céad', *Bliainiris*, vol. 10, 2012, p. 148, pp. 154–5.

68. Recorded by the BBC in December 1953, BBC-5287-SE (0:30). See also NFC 1281:203.

69. Recorded by Radio Éireann in 1948 and transferred to the Irish Folklore Commission, NFC M1123C (1:24). See also NFC 1281:309–10.

70. See Tim Robinson, *Connemara. Part 1: Introduction and Gazetteer* (Roundstone: Folding Landscapes, 1990), p. 49; Tomás Ó Máille (ed.), *Micheál Mhac Suibhne agus Filidh an tSléibhe* (Dublin: Foilseacháin Rialtais, 1934), pp. 1–5. See also Nancy Stenson (ed.), *An Haicléara Mánas: A nineteenth-century text from Clifden, Co. Galway* (Dublin: Dublin Institute for Advanced Studies, 2003), for information on a hackler associated with this district.

71. Recorded by Radio Éireann in 1948 and transferred by the Irish Folklore Commission. NFC Disc M1129-30 T0067 (4:04). See also NFC 1281:59–61, 420; MMS 19.

72. This is more generally pronounced *meidhreach* meaning 'full of fun'.

73. NFC 1281:61.

74. Recorded by Radio Éireann in 1948 and transferred by the Irish Folklore Commission. NFC T0067 (2:33). See also NFC 1073:52–3; 1281:182–3, 391.

75. See Cormac Ó Gráda in Ó Conghaile et al., *Leabhar Mór na nAmhrán*, pp. 63–4.

76. See NFC 1281:183.

77. See NFC 74:248.

78. Recorded by the BBC in July 1954, BBC-5433-SE (2:09).

79. See https://www.vwml.org/search [accessed 20 October 2020].

80. Recorded by the BBC in July 1954, BBC-5433-SE (1:47). See also NFC 1281:467.

81. https://www.vwml.org/search?q=wild%20rover&is=1 [accessed 20 October 2020].

82. Recorded by Radio Éireann in 1948 and transferred by the Irish Folklore Commission, NFC M1129–30, T0068c (2:12).

83. The words *spéir ghealaí* literally translate as 'moon night', meaning a very bright night but with no moon.

84. See, for example, Ó Súilleabháin, *A Handbook of Irish Folklore*, pp. 495–6; Máire MacNeill, *The Festival of Lughnasa* (Dublin: Comhairle Bhéaloideas Éireann, 1982 [1962]), p. 593.

85. Recorded by the BBC in December 1953, BBC-5287-SE (0:50). See also NFC 1281:214. More common in current parlance is *bruth fá thír*, which indicates waste from the sea or detritus, including organic particles. It may be that Colm is speaking so quickly that we hear *bráth thír locha*. Colm is referring to *fiogaí locha* (lake rushes), which come about from the heavy rain following a strong wind or gale. In the manuscript, NFC 1281:214, this is called a *seanfhocal*, meaning a proverb or old saying.

86. NFC 1281:214.

87. Recorded by the BBC in December 1953, BBC-5287-SE (2:16). See Andreas Vogel, *Leabhar Inis Bearachain* (Leitir Móir: Muintearas, 2010), pp. 48–50. See also NFC 1281:324–7; Learaí Ó Finneadha (M.F. Ó Conchúir (ed.)), *Ó Bhaile go Baile* (Indreabhán: Cló Iar-Chonnachta, 1993), pp. 68–71; Éamonn Ó Confhaola, *Tobar na 7 Scáil. The Well of the 7 Shadows*, Tír an Fhia (no date or place of publication/publisher), pp, 48–9.

88. This line reads as follows: *Claittir lib fert fiail-Eithne isin chill os Boinn Braenglais*, as presented by Kuno Meyer in 'Mitteilungen aus Irischen Handschriften'. It is taken from a text in the Book of Fermoy from the fifteenth century. See Kuno Meyer, 'Mitteilungen aus Irischen Handschriften', *Zeitschrift für Celtische Philologie*, vol. XIII, 1921, p. 17.

89. According to local oral tradition, Surlaí was a Protestant boy and Anna a Roman Catholic. Although they were in love, Patrick was not willing to marry them as Surlaí refused to change his religion.

90. NFC 1281:327.

91. Vogel, *Leabhar Inis Bearachain.*

92. See Máire MacNeill, 'The Legends of the False God's Daughter', *The Journal of the Royal Society of Antiquaries of Ireland,* vol. 79, nos. 1/2, 1949 (centenary volume), p. 100. The text of this version is published in An Seabhac and Séamus Ó Duilearga, 'Mairbhne Eithne Nó Mairbhne Phádraig', *Béaloideas,* vol. 4, no. 3, 1934, pp. 267–9.

93. Recorded by Radio Éireann in 1948 and transferred by the Irish Folklore Commission, NFC Disc M1129–30, T0068c (2:40). See also NFC 1281:73–4, SA 0353-66.

94. Micheál Ó Tiománaidhe, *Amhráin Ghaeilge an Iarthair* (Indreabhán: Cló Iar-Chonnachta, 1992 [1906]), lch. 15.

95. Recorded by the BBC in July 1954, BBC-5398-SE (4:02).

96. This is a literal translation of the Irish phrase *Bhíodar ag tarraingt le chéile,* meaning 'getting along with each other'.

97. See www.vwml.org 'Captain Wedderburn's Courtship' [accessed 20 October 2020].

98. Recorded by Radio Éireann in 1948 and transferred by the Irish Folklore Commission. NFC Disc M1129-30, T0068c (3:52).

99. See Kevin Danaher, *The Year in Ireland* (Cork: Mercier Press, 1972), pp. 200–27.

100. Recorded by the BBC in 1954, BBC-5434-SE (4:19). See also NFC 1281:250–3; Disc 0353-366; MM 19.017 (two versions).

101. The Queen of Sardinia is reputed to have been Siobhán, the wife of the poet Colm de Bhailís.

102. In mythology, Paris was the son of Priamus, the king of Troy.

103. Séamus Ennis wrote that this refers to a headland called Ceann Gólaim (Golam Head) in County Galway near Lettermullan (Leitir Mealláin) at L 82 22.

104. Tuirgéis is the Viking Thorgestr or Thorgils, who established a kingdom in Ireland from 822 until 845. See Gearóid Denvir, *Amhráin Choilm de Bhailis* (Indreabhán: Cló Iar-Chonnachta 1996), p. 137.

105. Many songs in Irish allude to figures from mythology and history which at times become altered in the process of oral transmission. See Ríonach uí Ógáin, *Faoi Rothaí na Gréine* (Baile Átha Cliath: Coiscéim, 1999), p. 94.

106. Recorded by Radio Éireann in 1948 and transferred by the Irish Folklore Commission. NFC T0068c (1:36).

Chapter 3

1. NFC 1281:233–4. Collected by Séamus Ennis between winter 1943 and summer 1944.

2. Séamus Ennis wrote at this point that the recording cylinder was full.

3. NFC 1281:229. Collected by Séamus Ennis in summer 1943.

4. NFC 1281:253. Collected by Séamus Ennis between June and November 1944.

5. NFC 1281:235. Collected by Séamus Ennis in summer 1944.

6. NFC 1281:236. Collected by Séamus Ennis in summer 1944.

7. Séamus Ennis noted in English here: 'There was no equalling them.'

8. NFC 1281:237–9.

9. Greatman's Bay.

10. NFC 1281:127. Collected by Séamus Ennis in the summer of 1943.

11. NFC 1281:297. Collected by Séamus Ennis between June and November 1944. The collector noted that this piece, 'The Music Tooth', is an example of the kind of fun Colm had with jolly people he met on his travels. He wrote that he heard many a buzz of merriment like this from Colm on the roads of the parish of Carna during the previous year. See NFC 1281:296.

12. NFC 1281:357. Collected by Séamus Ennis between November 1944 and summer 1945.

13. NFC 1281:134. Collected by Séamus Ennis in the summer of 1943.

14. Ibid. Séamus Ennis wrote that he told Colm about '*Tiúin Thaibhse Chonaill*' ['The Tune of Conall's Ghost'], which he had collected along with its associated lore in Teileann, Donegal. The story goes that two men were making *poitín*. One left to fetch a tool and the man remaining became lonely. He heard pipe music approaching. He had some holy water. The piping came closer and an apparition appeared. The *poitín* maker shook holy water and the apparition fled, burning the ground (NFC 1282:102–3). The place is known as *Tóin Dóite* (Burned End), as no grass grew there since. The piper played the tune known as '*Tiuín Thaibhse Chonaill*'. On hearing the story, Colm said to Ennis that it might not be the devil at all that came upon Conall making *poitín*.

15. NFC 1552:257–60. Collected on Ediphone by Proinnsias de Búrca in July 1959.

16. The collector Proinnsias de Búrca was also called Frank Bourke, the anglicised form of the Irish surname 'de Búrca'.

17. The Yellow Oyster-Bed.

18. The Grey Rock.

19. The Tip of the Arable Place.

20. The Tip of the Shoal.

21. A short line connecting the fishing line to a hook.

22. A sod of turf.

23. A small boring tool.

24. The silken fibre obtained from the intestines of the silkworm used in the making of fishing tackle.

25. One or other of several flies used in fishing.

26. This very large rock, *Carraig an Mhuirbhigh* (Murvey Rock), is out to the west of Roundstone. The name comes from *muirbheach*, 'sea-plain, referring to its area of closely-grazed sandy coastal pasture'. See Robinson, *Connemara. Part 1: Introduction and Gazetteer*, p. 83.

27. Caulty Rock.

28. 'The Wave of the Sea-bed'. 'The breaker of the floor (Floor Rock on the charts)'. See Robinson, *Connemara. Part 1: Introduction and Gazetteer*, p. 91.

29. This may be related to a spot in the sea that was called *Leathrach Labrú* (Labraí's Seaweed), whose meaning is unclear.

30. Mile Rock.

31. Toole's Shoal.

32. Mac Bán's Shoal is west of Cruach na Caoile, where large pollock were found.

33. Shoal Upper.

34. Skerd Rocks.

35. NFC 1552:297–303. Collected on Ediphone by Proinnsias de Búrca in July 1959.

36. In the 1830s, *Inis Leacan* (The Island of the Flagstones) had a population of around 200 but it declined over the years and the last family moved to Roundstone in 1985. See Robinson, *Connemara. Part 1: Introduction and Gazetteer*, pp. 77–8.

37. NFC 1552:297.

38. Mile Rock.

39. Possibly *Na Coirthíní, Na Cairthíní* (The Little Rocks) and *An Coirthín* (The Little Rock). See https://www.logainm.ie/en/28458?s=Coirth%c3%adn [accessed 20 October 2020].

40. Seán Mac Pádraig's Rock.

41. The Mound of the Turn.

42. The Large Rock.

43. The Split Rock.

44. See Dinneen, *Foclóir Gaedhilge agus Béarla*, p. 1129. '*stopóg* … a part of the sea with rocky bottom and the haunt of rock fish'.

45. A casting line.

46. Lit. The Fort of ?? The meaning here is unclear.

47. Lit. The Big Skerd.

48. The Goat's Rock is near *Inis Leacan*. See Robinson, *Connemara. Part 1: Introduction and Gazetteer*, pp. 77–8.

49. The Wave of the Seabed.

50. The Way by the Islands.

51. The Mound Hole. *Crúcha* is probably from *cruach* (mound). There are a few islands called *Na Cruacha* (The Mounds) close to *Cruach na Caoile*, and *Poll Chrúcha* (*Chruacha*) is probably located here.

52. The Red Flags are west of *Cruach na Caoile*.

53. Mac Bán's Shoal.

54. The Flags of Sea-Lace [?].

55. The Wood.

56. An iron hook for landing fish.

57. The Scorched Little Headland. This was very near the Ó Caodháin's house and was a natural harbour where they moored the boat.

58. A rope was loaded with hay in preparation for carrying and a rope was also put through the gills of the fish for ease of carrying.

Chapter 4

1. NFC 326:5–26.

2. This is a version of an international folktale, ATU 305 'The Dragon's Heart-Blood as Remedy', combined with ATU 550 'Bird, Horse and Princess'. 'Bird Horse and Princess' was previously entitled 'Search for the Golden Bird'. See Hans-Jorg Uther, *The Types of International Folktales: A classification and bibliography* (Helsinki: Academia Scientiarum Fennica, 2004), pp. 318–20. Seán Ó Súilleabháin and Reidar Th. Christiansen, *The Types of the Irish Folktale* (Helsinki: Suomalainen Tiedeakatemia, 1968 [1963]), does not include a version of ATU 305 on its own.

3. NFC 1008:28–58. Liam Mac Coisdeala recorded the tale on Ediphone in September 1944. In his transcription it is titled '*Scéal Tady McGrath* (*An fear a d'fhulaing trí bhás ar son na mná*)' ('The Story of Tady McGrath (The man who suffered death three times for the woman)'). Ó Súilleabháin and Christiansen, *The Types of the Irish Folktale*, includes this version in conjunction with ATU 302. See also NFC T68d.

4. The tales of the mythical hero Fionn mac Cumhaill, and his followers Na Fianna, make up the Fenian Cycle. Tales of Fionn and his band of warriors featured prominently in Irish oral tradition.

5. This phrase *an dtabharfá deoch an uisce dhomsa?* ('would you give me a drink of the water?') is in the version collected by Liam Mac Coisdeala (NFC 1008:28–58), although it is not in the transcription of the earlier version collected from Colm in NFC 326:5–26.

6. NFC 1008:58–62. Collected on Ediphone by Liam Mac Coisdeala in September 1944.

7. This is an international tale, best known as 'Doctor Know-All'. See Uther, *The Types of International Folktales*, ATU 1641; Ó Súilleabháin and Christiansen, *The Types of the Irish Folktale*, p. 289.

8. This is in English in the Irish text.

9. The collector noted that these words, in Irish, *gur diabhal corportha atá linn* ('that it was a supernatural being'), were not clear on the recording. He wrote that the words implied that the boy understood that the person was unusual and had special knowledge.

10. This is in English in the Irish text.

11. There is some confusion in the text at this point, as one might expect the girl to comment on what she saw or heard in the room.

12. This is in English in the Irish text.

13. NFC 1008:83–4. Collected by Liam Mac Coisdeala on Ediphone in September 1944.

14. This seems to mean that the woman who helped the Virgin Mary would have family waiting for her in Heaven.

15. NFC 1008:115–17. Recorded by Liam Mac Coisdeala on Ediphone in September 1944 and transcribed in March 1945.

16. *An Cheathrú* meaning 'quarter' or 'quarterland' occurs frequently in the placenames of Ireland, particularly in townland names. It is found in the placenames of County Clare on its own and in compounds, https://www.logainm.ie/en/gls/c/ [accessed 20 October 2020]. *Ceathrú* in this instance refers to a quarter of a townland.

17. NFC 1008:305–8. Collected by Liam Mac Coisdeala on Ediphone in November 1944.

18. This is a version of the international tale ATU 759 'Angel and Hermit' (previously 'God's Justice Vindicated'); Uther, *The Types of International Folktales*, Part 1, p. 416: 'Saint (Moses, Rabbi Joshua Ben Levi, St Peter, hermit) doubts God's justice and blames him for sending suffering to virtuous people and well-being to bad ones.' Mac Coisdeala's version appears in Ó Súilleabháin and Christiansen, 'God's Justice Vindicated', and the authors note that 'in Irish tradition the theme is considerably varied': *The Types of the Irish Folktale*, p. 153.

19. The collector noted that *lig sé fear marbh leis* in the Irish text meant that he uncovered a dead man.

20. NFC 1008:308–10. Collected by Liam Mac Coisdeala on Ediphone in November 1944. Another version collected by Proinsias de Búrca on Ediphone is in NFC 1509:278–9.

21. The collector noted that Colm said the word *ábhars* means *spraoi*, which translates as 'fun'.

22. NFC 1009:167–8. Collected by Liam Mac Coisdeala on Ediphone in January 1946.

23. NFC 1281:170–1. Séamus Ennis collected this in May 1944.

24. Séamus Ennis wrote that *luimpín* means 'a small round lump'.

25. *broc* may also mean 'burrow' in this context.

26. NFC 1281:350. Collected by Séamus Ennis between November 1944 and the summer of 1945.

27. This is a version of the international folktale ATU 1940 'The Extraordinary Names', a miscellaneous type which comprises various tales in which animals, people or things are called by unusual names, leading to confusion or disaster. The basis for the misunderstanding is either that the usual names have been switched (in humorous anecdotes) or that different names are adopted because of their symbolic, acoustic, or nonsense value (in cumulative tales, sayings, songs, and rhymes). Uther, *The Types of International Folktales*, Part 11, p. 496. See also Ó Súilleabháin and Christiansen, 'The Extraordinary Names', in *The Types of the Irish Folktale*, p. 330.

28. NFC 1281:385–6. Collected by Séamus Ennis in April 1945.

29. Lit. The Beach of the Little Field, a beach close to the village of Roundstone.

30. NFC 1281:203. Collected by Séamus Ennis in summer 1944.

31. This is a children's counting-out rhyme documented in many Irish-speaking districts in the first half of the twentieth century. The players sit around in a circle and the leader does the counting out on the participants' feet. See N.J.A. Williams, *Cniogaide Cnagaide: Rainn traidisiúnta do pháistí* (Baile Átha Cliath: An Clóchomhar, 1988), pp. 126–32, which contains a number of versions. As with many children's games, it features many nonsense vocables, and lends itself more to the rhythm and music of the words rather than to sense or meaning.

32. The meaning here is unclear. Instead of *péacóg* ('peacock' or 'sprout'), other versions have *fídeog* ('rush', 'taper', 'candle') or *míoltóg* ('midge'), for example. See Williams, *Cniogaide Cnagaide*, pp. 126–32.

33. NFC 1281:306–7. Collected by Séamus Ennis between June and July 1944 and November 1944.

34. NFC 1509:280–2. Collected by Proinnsias de Búrca from Colm on Ediphone in October 1958. Another version of this narrative was collected by Liam Mac Coisdeala in March 1945 entitled '*Eachtra a Tharla don Scéalaí*' ('An Adventure that the Storyteller Had'), NFC 1008:121–3.

35. This is probably a reference to the Congested Districts Board, as it supplied a variety of boats for trading and fishing to Conamara and other districts. See Breathnach, *The Congested Districts Board of Ireland*, Chapter 3, pp. 73–108, especially p. 108.

36. Ibid.

37. NFC 1553:1–3. Collected by Proinnsias de Búrca on Ediphone in September 1959.

38. In Irish folk tradition it is believed that the rowan (mountain ash) has protective powers and is used, for example, to prevent butter and milk profit being taken. It is hung up in houses and is used to keep the dead from rising. It is also used as a collar on a hound for greater speed. See Ó Súilleabháin, *A Handbook of Irish Folklore*, p. 282.

Appendix 2

1. Maurice Gorham, *Forty Years of Irish Broadcasting* (Dublin: Talbot Press, 1967), p. 164.

2. Anne O'Connor, 'Deconstructing the Archive? A reflection on collection-centred ethnology in the Irish context', *Béaloideas*, vol. 78, 2010, pp. 80–98, at p. 89.

3. Gorham, *Forty Years of Irish Broadcasting*, p. 204.

4. Ibid., p. 227.

5. RTÉ, *Hand Me Down*, 1981. Episode 1: Séamus Ennis (22.46–23.15).

6. Conversation of Ríonach uí Ógáin with Máire Uí Chonaire, Coillín, Carna, County Galway, 29 May 2018.

7. Devotion to the Sacred Heart of Jesus is primarily associated with the Roman Catholic Church, reflecting Christ's love for the human race. People display statues and images in their houses. Often a light is placed in front of the statue or image.

8. The Rosary is a form of prayer practised by Roman Catholics consisting of decades of prayers. The Rosary beads serve to count the constituent prayers.

9. In a report by Caoimhín Ó Danachair relating to sound recordings he made during a field trip to Kerry with Séamus Ennis from 13 to 25 June 1947, it is stated that thirty-nine double-sided 12" discs were recorded. In his comments, Ó Danachair wrote that at least eighty-eight acetate discs were recorded in County Galway, between 1940 and 1948. The NFC accessions register states that the discs recorded from Colm were made in 1947. Caoimhín Ó Danachair and Séamus Ennis probably made these recordings together in Glinsce, perhaps prior to, or following, their fieldwork in June 1947 in Kerry (NFC Reports: Sound recording 1947–1949).

10. Colm uses the term *an drochshaol* to refer to the Great Famine in Ireland, 1845–9.

Appendix 3

1. Séamus Ennis wrote that this piece never had a clearly identifiable air, but rather a kind of nonsense half-music and half-humming, resembling the air '*Rachaidh Mé Chun An Chaisil*' ('I Will Go to An Caiseal'), 1281:187.

2. These are contained in manuscript volumes 1280:616–17, 621–7, 701–54; 1281:55–147 *Amhráin Ghlinsce samhradh 1943* (Songs from Glinsce summer 1943), 148–67; *Amhráin ó Ghlinsce geimhreadh 1943* (Songs from Glinsce winter 1943); 168–240 *Bealtaine-Meitheamh* (May-June) 1944; 241a *Meitheamh-Iúil* (June-July) 1944; *Samhain* (November) 1944; 319 '*Seo deireadh ar bhailíos ó Cholm sa samhradh 1944*); 320 – *ag tosaí aríst Samhain 1944* (Here ends the material I collected from Colm in summer 1944); 320 – starting again November 1944); 433–458 [received by the IFC January 1946. No date of collecting given but probably 1945]; *Meitheamh-Iúil* June-July 459–460 1946.

3. In some instances it is said that a song is sung to the air of a different song.

4. The word structure communicates a jig or 'port', as Ennis noted.

5. This appears to be the first half of the slip jig 'Rocky Road', which is written beside the title, possibly in Ennis' hand.

6. The word *seanchas* or 'lore' is frequently used as a title for narratives of this kind. In this listing, key words have been selected indicating the thrust of the narrative.

7. For further details on the collectors, see Micheál Briody, *The Irish Folklore Commission, 1935–1970: History, ideology, methodology* (Helsinki: Finnish Literature Society SKS, 2007), particularly Chapter IV, pp. 227–77 and passim.

8. Ríonach Ní Fhlathartaigh, *Clár Amhrán Bhaile na hInse* (Baile Átha Cliath: An Clóchomhar, 1976).

BIBLIOGRAPHY

Almqvist, Bo and Pádraig Ó Héalaí (eds), *Labharfad le Cách: I will speak to you all, Peig Sayers* (Dublin: New Island, 2009)

Amhráin ar an Sean-Nós, RTÉ CD 185 (Dublin: RTÉ, 1999)

An Seabhac and Séamus Ó Duilearga, 'Mairbhne Eithne Nó Mairbhne Phádraig' *Béaloideas*, vol. 4, no. 3, 1934, pp. 264–76

Breathnach, Ciara, *The Congested Districts Board of Ireland, 1891–1923* (Dublin: Four Courts Press, 2005)

Briody, Micheál, *The Irish Folklore Commission, 1935–1970: History, ideology, methodology* (Helsinki: Finnish Literature Society SKS, 2007)

Browne, Charles, 'Ethnography of Carna and Mweenish, Conamara', *Proceedings of the Royal Irish Academy, VI* (Dublin: Royal Irish Academy, 1901)

Child, Francis James, *The English and Scottish Popular Ballads*, 5 vols (Boston: Houghton, Mifflin & Co., 1882–98)

Connolly, Sean J. (ed.), *The Oxford Companion to Irish History* (Oxford: Oxford University Press, 2002)

Danaher, Kevin, *The Year in Ireland* (Cork: Mercier Press, 1972)

de Bhaldraithe, Tomás, *Foirisiún Focal as Gaillimh* (Dublin: Acadamh Ríoga na hÉireann, 1985)

Denvir, Gearóid, *Amhráin Choilm de Bhailis* (Indreabhán: Cló Iar-Chonnachta, 1996)

Dinneen, Patrick S., *Foclóir Gaedhilge agus Béarla* (Dublin: The Educational Company of Ireland, 1927)

Duncan, Lilian, 'Altram Tige Dá Medar', *Ériu*, vol. 11, 1932, pp. 184–225

Flaherty, Eoin, 'Rundale and 19th Century Irish Settlement: System, space and genealogy', *Irish Geography*, vol. 48, no. 2, 2015, pp. 3–38, DOI: 10.2014/igj.v48i2.623

Gorham, Maurice, *Forty Years of Irish Broadcasting* (Dublin: Talbot Press, 1967)

Kerr, James, *Kerr's First Collection of Merry Melodies for the Violin* (Glasgow: James Kerr, *c.* 1870)

Lady Dudley's Scheme for the Establishment of District Nurses in the Poorest Parts of Ireland, First Annual Report, 23 April 1903 – 23 April 1904

Mac Con Iomaire, Liam, *Seosamh Ó hÉanaí: Nár fhágha mé bás choíche* (Indreabhán: Cló Iar-Chonnachta, 2007)

MacNeill, Máire, 'The Legends of the False God's Daughter', *The Journal of the Royal Society of Antiquaries of Ireland*, vol. 79, nos. 1/2, 1949 (centenary volume), pp. 100–9

MacNeill, Máire, *The Festival of Lughnasa* (Dublin: Comhairle Bhéaloideas Éireann, 1982)

Meyer, Kuno, 'Mitteilungen aus Irischen Handschriften', *Zeitschrift für Celtische Philologie*, vol. XIII, 1921, pp. 3–30

Munnelly, Tom, *The Mount Callan Garland: Songs from the repertoire of Tom Lenihan* (Dublin: Comhairle Bhéaloideas Éireann, 1994)

Ní Fhlathartaigh, Ríonach, *Clár Amhrán Bhaile na hInse* (Baile Átha Cliath: An Clóchomhar, 1976)

Ó Ceannabháin, Peadar, 'An Samhradh sa bhFuacht idir Nollaig is Cáisc: Spléachadh ar fhilithe in Iorras Aithneach san 19ú céad', *Bliainiris*, vol. 10, 2012, pp. 147–68

Ó Confhaola, Éamonn, *Tobar na 7 Scáil. The Well of the 7 Shadows* (Tír an Fhia; no date of publication or publisher)

Ó Conghaile, Micheál, Lochlann Ó Tuairisg and Peadar Ó Ceannabháin, *Leabhar Mór na nAmhrán* (Indreabhán: Cló Iar-Chonnacht, 2012)

O'Connor, Anne, 'Deconstructing the Archive? A reflection on collection-centred ethnology in the Irish context', *Béaloideas*, vol. 78, 2010, pp. 80–98

Ó Curnáin, Brian, *The Irish of Iorras Aithneach, County Galway*, vols 1–4 (Dublin: Dublin Institute for Advanced Studies, 2007)

Ó Dónaill, Niall, *Foclóir Gaeilge-Béarla* (Baile Átha Cliath: Oifig an tSoláthair, 1977)

Ó Finneadha (M.F. Ó Conchúir (ed.)), Ó Bhaile go Baile (Indreabhán: Cló Iar-Chonnachta, 1993)

Ó hÓgáin, Dáithí, *The Lore of Ireland: An encyclopaedia of myth, legend and romance* (Cork: The Collins Press, 2006)

Ó Máille, Tomás (ed.), *Micheál Mhac Suibhne agus Filidh an tSléibhe* (Dublin: Foilseacháin Rialtais, 1934)

Ó Máille, Tomás S., *Liosta Focal as Ros Muc* (Dublin: Irish University Press, 1974)

O'Neill, Francis, *Waifs and Strays of Gaelic Melody* (Chicago: Lyon & Healy, 1922)

O'Sullivan, Muiris, and Liam Downey, 'Post-Medieval Fieldscapes. Part 2: Rundale', *Archaeology Ireland*, vol. 22, no. 3, autumn 2008, pp. 22–5

Ó Súilleabháin, Seán, *A Handbook of Irish Folklore* (Dublin: The Folklore of Ireland Society, 1942)

Ó Súilleabháin, Seán and Reidar Th. Christiansen, *The Types of the Irish Folktale* (Helsinki: Suomalainen Tiedeakatemia, 1968 [1963])

Ó Tiománaidhe, Micheál, *Abhráin Ghaedhilge an Iarthair* (Dublin: Gill & Sons, 1906)

Ó Tuama, Seán, *An Grá in Amhráin na nDaoine* (Dublin: An Clóchomhar Teoranta, 1960)

Rice, Timothy, James Porter and Chris Goertzen (eds), *The Garland Encyclopaedia of World Music. Vol. 8: Europe* (New York and London: Garland Publishing, 2000)

Robinson, Tim, *Connemara. Part 1: Introduction and Gazetteer* (Roundstone: Folding Landscapes, 1990)

Robinson, Tim, *Connemara: A little Gaelic kingdom* (Dublin: Penguin Ireland, 2011)

Stenson, Nancy (ed.), *An Haicléara Mánas: A nineteenth-century text from Clifden, Co. Galway* (Dublin: Dublin Institute for Advanced Studies, 2003)

uí Ógáin, Ríonach, 'Cruach na Carra', *Sinsear: The folklore journal*, 1979, pp. 23–7

uí Ógáin, Ríonach, 'Fear Ceoil Ghlinsce: Colm Ó Caodháin', *Galway: History and society* (Dublin: Geography Publications, 1996), pp. 743–8

uí Ógáin, Ríonach, 'Colm Ó Caodháin and Séamus Ennis: A Conamara singer and his collector', *Béaloideas*, vol. 64/5, 1996–7, pp. 279–338

uí Ógáin, Ríonach, *Faoi Rothaí na Gréine: Amhráin as Conamara a bhailigh Máirtín Ó Cadhain* (Dublin: Coiscéim, 1999)

uí Ógáin, Ríonach, 'Some Comments on Context, Text and Subtext in Irish Folklore', in Lauri Honko (ed.), *Thick Corpus, Organic Variation and Textuality in Oral Tradition* (Helsinki: Finnish Literature Society, 2000), pp. 161–79

uí Ógáin, Ríonach (ed.), *Mise an Fear Ceoil: Séamus Ennis – dialann taistil 1942–1946* (Indreabhán: Cló Iar-Chonnachta, 2007)

uí Ógáin, Ríonach, *Going to the Well for Water: The Séamus Ennis field diary* (Cork: Cork University Press, 2009)

uí Ógáin, Ríonach, '"Cailín Deas Crúite na mBó" and the Impact of the Folklore Collector', *Béaloideas*, vol. 83, 2015, pp. 96–110

UNESCO, *Ireland: Musics of the world* (CD) UNES08271, 1997

Uther, Hans-Jorg, *The Types of International Folktales: A classification and bibliography* (Helsinki: Academia Scientiarum Fennica, 2004)

Vogel, Andreas, *Leabhar Inis Bearachain* (Leitir Móir: Muintearas, 2010)

Williams, N.J.A., *Cniogaide Cnagaide: Rainn traidisiúnta do pháistí* (Baile Átha Cliath: An Clóchomhar, 1988)

Williams, Seán, and Lillis Ó Laoire, *Bright Star of the West: Joe Heaney, Irish song-man* (Oxford: Oxford University Press, 2011)

Woulfe, Patrick, *Sloinnte Gaedheal is Gall* (Dublin: Gill, 1923)

INDEX